The Diary of a Breast

Elisa Segrave was born in 1949 and grew up in Madrid, Berkshire and Sussex. She went to school at the Convent of the Sacred Heart, dropped out of Edinburgh University and then travelled around the United States in a Greyhound bus collecting underground newspapers. She has lived in New York, Paris and Peru, worked in a hospital linen room and a London law centre, and is the author of several unpublished manuscripts. Between 1981 and 1990 she was married to the writer Andrew Barrow and had two children, now aged eleven and thirteen.

Elisa Segrave's articles and short stories have appeared in the *Observer*, the *Guardian*, the *Independent* and the *London Review of Books*, and in several anthologies published by Serpent's Tail. She recently compiled an anthology of stories called *The Junky's Christmas* (Serpent's Tail). She is now working on a new book.

The Diary of a Breast

Elisa Segrave

faber and faber
LONDON · BOSTON

Although some names and details have been changed to protect privacy, this diary is otherwise based on real events that occurred between September 1991 and May 1992.

First published in 1995
by Faber and Faber Limited
3 Queen Square London WC1N 3AU

Photoset by Parker Typesetting Service, Leicester
Printed in England by Clays Ltd, St Ives plc

A CIP record for this book is available
from the British Library

ISBN 0-571-17446-9

10 9 8 7 6 5 4 3 2 1

To Harriet and Louisa

September 1991

1 September

Extremely powerful dream. I am in my grandmother's woods, which are ice-bound. It is very difficult for me to get out of this ice-bound cavern. Eventually I manage to climb out. I am frightened because these woods, which I used to love, have changed out of all recognition.

2 September

My cousin Lulu and I are sitting in a square in Soho. A literary agent called Jay Cox has just rejected my latest manuscript. She did not seem to find it at all funny. In fact, throughout our interview, which Lulu insisted on attending, she kept a very grim look on her face.

Her expression changed as we were leaving, when Lulu said how much she liked *Hello!* magazine. At this the agent brightened up. Obviously we should have talked about *Hello!* much earlier. She then showed us the draft of a book whose author she *was* representing. It was a collection of profiles of famous people. She seemed very proud of having this author as a client.

I had bumped into the agent last week in my local underground station, having met her once at a dinner-party in Clapham. I had thought that meeting her by chance like that meant she was destined to be my agent, but clearly I was wrong.

3 September

I have a lump in my breast. I found it when I was fiddling with the top of my nightdress. I told Lucy, my ten-year-old daughter, as she was in the room with me. My first instinct was to pretend it wasn't there. I tried to forget about it.

The fact that I might have breast cancer did not hit me at once, since I am sick with worry about my mother. On 6 August, the night she had arranged for us all to go to the Russian circus, my mother fell and broke her hip for the third time. As before, she fell because she was drunk. Now the lady who looks after her keeps telephoning and asking if she should give my mother alcohol, even though the doctor said she shouldn't have any. Thinking about this is making me ill. Soon after my mother fell I began getting terrible pains in my chest.

For the first time in my life, perhaps, I am getting some emotional and physical reaction to the things that have happened in my family, where people are always dying.

On my seventh birthday my brother, aged five, drowned in my grandmother's swimming-pool. My father died of cirrhosis of the liver when I was twenty-four. My second brother, also alcoholic, died of an overdose of sleeping pills on his twenty-fourth birthday, three days before Christmas. My mother's father was killed when she was three, in 1917, on an afternoon's leave while fighting in France. My mother's baby brother, born the month her father was killed, lived only two years. My grandmother's second husband died of cancer. My grandmother's third sister, the one I was named after, drowned in her thirties, swimming in the Mediterranean.

I separated from my husband two years ago and am now about to get divorced.

The good things are: (a) I am not poor; (b) I have my children; (c) I have friends.

While my mother was still in the nursing home to which she was transferred after her hip operation, I escaped to Los Angeles with my son to do a house-swap I'd arranged in June. But even there I kept getting telephone calls about my mother. Some of the calls were about her dog. I had to give the vet the go-ahead to castrate it without her knowledge. Last year it bit a plumber and he had to have forty stitches in his arm. It was feared the dog might bite the nurse who was going to look after my mother when she came home. It is an outsize basset. Why can't I have a normal mother? Is there such a thing?

4 September

Last night I was in a state of nervous energy and depression. This was mainly due to worry about my mother. Once again I had pains all over my body.

In desperation I phoned a friend's brother, who's in Alcoholics Anonymous, and described the goings-on at my mother's. I told him how her friend Jane, whom she'd known all her life, kept ringing me about my mother's drinking.

He said I could draw boundaries if I wished. It was none of Jane's business what I did with my mother. I should say to Jane, 'I'm sorry you're in pain.' He added that if, after seventy years, Jane hadn't realized what my mother was like, it was her fault. I hadn't chosen to be my mother's daughter; she *had* chosen to be her friend.

Early this morning I had a very unpleasant dream in which my bathroom overflowed and became filled with dirty water. Two creatures climbed out and started running along the floor. They looked like creatures from outer space and were vile.

I told my friend's brother about the dream. He said these figures were invaders and I was being invaded. The bathroom was normally a place of privacy and relaxation. The dream reflected my mental state.

Later I realized that if I do have breast cancer, I am being invaded from within as well. I still have not been to the doctor.

I telephoned my friend Miranda and said that this summer I had tried to make a new life with my children in the country and that they liked it. Now my mother was dragging me back into the world of chaos I remembered from my childhood. Miranda told me to go to the doctor at once about the lump.

5 September

I went to my local GP's surgery yesterday evening. There was a new young doctor. The old one, Dr Rawlings, had just died of cancer and the two women doctors whom I normally see were both on holiday.

I was disappointed that Mrs H, the receptionist, had left. She provided entertainment in the waiting-room by yelling out people's personal details in front of the other patients and bullying the weaker ones, mainly old people and foreigners. She used the waiting-room as a theatre for her own solo performances, with everyone else unwittingly playing walk-on parts.

Instead of Mrs H there was a young person with wild blonde hair trying to deal with the files, and I had to spell out another patient's Polish surname to her three times.

The new doctor said the lump was probably nothing, but sent me to make an appointment at the breast clinic at St Charles' Hospital, off Ladbroke Grove. I drove straight there with his letter, but was told I wouldn't get an appointment for at least two weeks.

6 September
Hal arrived yesterday after a slightly drunken call from a phone box near Hyde Park. He is over from Paris. He then made love to me for over an hour. He told me twice that he loved me and said he didn't care that I didn't have 'the emotional structure' to respond. He said other men allowed me to dominate them but he didn't. Was this right? I sort of said Yes.

He complimented me on various parts of my body again and again and reminded me he had been making love to me for eighteen years, apart from a long break between when I got married in 1981 and when I separated in 1989. He said he would go on doing so.

'That's right, isn't it?'

I muttered a reply.

Later I felt sorry I had not responded in a more affectionate way.

Before he left, I said casually that I had a lump on my breast and made him feel it. He told me to go to a private doctor straight away and not to wait for the appointment at the breast clinic. When he'd gone, I thought about how he had said he loved me *before* I had told him about the lump. I carried his words around with me for the rest of the day, like a small present.

In the evening I went to the cinema with Cynthia, whose only brother has just died of cancer. She too told me to go privately for something as serious as this and gave me the name of a private doctor in my area.

7 September

I was bowled over by the waiting-room at the private doctor's. There was hot coffee in a percolator and the latest copies of the *Spectator* and the *New Yorker* as well as all the daily papers. Rather than a frightening receptionist like Mrs H there was a polite New Zealand girl behind a computer. The doctor, who seems very nice but looks about twenty, immediately sent me to the Princess Grace Hospital, near Harley Street, to have a mammogram and an ultrasound, which I paid for. It cost seventy pounds. The hushed atmosphere in the exclusive waiting-room of the X-ray department was also unlike the local surgery. Instead of making me feel more secure, this made me feel isolated.

9 September

Something dubious has shown up on the mammogram and I have to have the lump out. On finding out I wasn't insured, the private doctor rang a surgeon at Charing Cross Hospital and booked me in to see him as soon as possible – next week – on the National Health. He told me, 'Have a good cry if you want to.' However I don't feel like it.

10 September

Coffee with my friend Clare, a mother at my son's school. She has already had three lumps out, all benign. This morning she showed me the scars. She said the first time she had a lump she became very melodramatic and thought she would die. She started staring at the tulips and thinking, I'll never see those flowers again.

Now she is quite blasé about having a lump every so often.

We talked about novels we'd read recently, then about our childhoods. Clare's father was an alcoholic who encouraged her to drink heavily from the age of sixteen. When she later told him she'd cut down, he said, 'Oh good, I was afraid you were becoming an alcoholic.'

I said I had understood that with alcoholics you were supposed to throw the responsibility back at them.

Clare said her mother had been very cold and done very little for her and her brothers. She had compensated by giving them objects and gifts. Now, she said, after several years of being angry, she is indifferent to her mother.

I explained how my daughter, Lucy, had said she didn't want the kite my mother had bought her for her birthday in August. I admired this. I wouldn't have been able to say I didn't want it, or that Lucy didn't want it, out of guilt. Lucy knew instinctively that my mother had bought the kite because she liked it herself.

As we went up the street, Clare became even more animated on this subject. We stood outside the underground and talked about how badly we had been treated by our mothers. Clare thought it was a pity that if you suffered as a child you got off on the wrong foot and then had to suffer as an adult, whereas other people, who had 'normal' mothers, got off scot-free and sailed through life. Do they really?

This afternoon I typed out a comic account of the house-swap Joseph and I did this summer. I have sent it to the *Tatler* and the *Spectator* and *Woman's Journal*. If I am going to die of breast cancer I must get some more things published first.

12 September

My son, Joseph, arrived back in London yesterday. He has been with his father in Spain. The poor little thing was dressed like a ragamuffin – shirt too small for him and corduroy trousers with the zip open at the top.

After their father left, the children and I took our dog, Toby, to Holland Park, then walked up Kensington High Street and I bought Joseph a new pair of lace-ups. At Video City in Notting Hill Gate we rented the video of the cartoon *Robin Hood*. Joseph said that the American children had ruined his copy while they were in our house during the house-swap. This turned out not to be true. He now has two videos of the same film.

At five this morning Joseph woke me up and I was furious. He clung to my body and said, 'I haven't seen you. I must see your face.' I was angry about being woken, but liked having his warm little body near me.

He went off to see a child therapist today, as he cannot relate to other children. Afterwards he said, 'He talked to me about very frightening things. I told him about all the world being dark and he talked to me about that.'

13 September

I went to Charing Cross Hospital to be examined by a cancer specialist. After eating a prawn and celery sandwich from the hospital shop on the ground floor I sat in the waiting-room of Clinic 8.

I was a bit put off by the dialogue between the receptionist and a nurse.

Nurse: 'Old lady?'

Receptionist: 'Mrs Heepes . . .' Takes out a file. 'Gor 'er 'ere.'

Nurse: 'Chuck 'er in!'

Gradually I became aware that I was in a cancer clinic. On the noticeboard were three notices referring to cancer: The Charing Cross Cancer Association, Helping People Live with Cancer and Cancer Counselling Service.

Most of the people waiting didn't look particularly ill, until a very young woman arrived with a young man. This woman looked as if she was going to die in the next few weeks, if not days. Her face was very pinched and so sallow it was almost green. I hoped the man was her boyfriend, sticking by her till the last.

As I sat there reading yesterday's papers I realized that the young receptionist with her broad cockney accent, permed hair and face tanned from her holiday on a Greek island (I heard her tell one of the nurses this) was very efficient at dealing with the files and the people who came in.

The off-putting thing was that there was no attempt to make

any of us feel that we were anything other than cattle. One poor foreign man had been put in the middle of the passage in a wheelchair and left there. When I had arrived, a nurse had said something about his being moved to another clinic, but half an hour later he was still there. No one spoke to him. Eventually a woman with a veil appeared, probably his wife, and wheeled him off down the corridor.

My name was called and I went and sat in the passage outside the doctors' rooms. At last I was summoned in. A nurse covered with freckles asked me impertinently where I had been on holiday.

I replied, 'America.'

I then lay on a couch with bared breasts, listening to a doctor talk confidently on the telephone. I heard him say that they had 'lost an anaesthetist' and that a woman waiting to have her breast removed had signed a paper giving her consent three days ago, so even if she protested now, they should get on with it.

He came and examined my breasts. When I'd put my top on again, he showed me the mammogram pinned up beside the desk and ultrasound pictures. I didn't understand the mammogram, but in the ultrasound pictures I could make out a lump. He said I would have to have it out to establish what it was.

He telephoned another doctor to try to get me a day appointment to have it removed; none was available for two weeks. He rang a different extension and arranged for me to come in to a ward next week. For this I would have to stay in at least two nights.

The date he gave me was my son's birthday. He will be eight.

My cousin Lulu and my friend Emily, a performance artist, are both getting divorced, Lulu after nineteen years of marriage. She is a practising Catholic. When she told her priest, he said, 'Don't worry – mass murderers, dictators and psychopaths are here receiving Communion.' He is a radical and spends a lot of time visiting Gorbachev. I must go to his church and see if I can spot any of the people he mentioned. Maybe I will return to the Catholic Church. I am lapsed.

Emily's husband, Paolo, who's an Italian psychiatrist, wants a divorce because he is sick of Emily's old boyfriend, Ben, coming round all the time. Even on their wedding night Ben was with them till 3 a.m. drinking vodka and eating peas. Paolo is also tired of the flat being full of the objects that Emily uses for her acts. Last week she had two horse tails from an abattoir in the bathroom.

I told Paolo on the telephone today about my house-swap. He said he liked the way I 'banged at life's doors' and 'wanted another room to explore'. Paulo has thick black hair and a black beard. He looks like a combination of Pavarotti and Castro.

14 September
Weekend in Sussex. My mother bought this house in the late seventies, after she became a widow. She was supposed to sell her other house at once and move into it, but then my grandmother died, leaving her house (which we sold), some money and a lot of furniture. My mother, who is a hoarder, refused to leave her own house and her possessions and I moved into the new house, having filled it with my grandmother's furniture. I sold the stuff that was too big.

My daughter's now away with her father.

In the night Joseph clung to me like a limpet and I couldn't sleep. I became exasperated and even hit him twice. He said he was frightened by a dream I had recounted several months earlier, about a child in a wheelchair. Eventually he said, 'All right, I'll go and sleep downstairs if it makes you happy.'

I thought this was a grown-up thing to say.

In the morning I went out on my daughter's piebald pony, which I'd bought for her birthday in August. I took her through a farmyard, then in some fields behind a friend's house. As I rode across the stubble towards the Downs, I imagined I was riding a coloured pony across the plains of New Mexico, where I had been with Joseph for three days during the house-swap. I imagined that I was a teenager again. I loved the pony; she seemed to have a sweet temperament.

In the afternoon I set off in the car for the Downs with Joseph plus a kite my mother had given him for his birthday, like the one she had wanted to give Lucy. I parked in a valley and walked towards Nicholas Mosley's cottage. He is a novelist and a Booker judge this year with Edward, a friend of mine. I walked into the garden, where he was stooping over a stream, and asked him if he wanted to come to lunch next day. He accepted and we started having a conversation about the Booker.

He said how much he liked Edward, but that they completely disagreed on their choice of books. Edward liked one called *Alma Cogan*. Nicholas said he also liked another judge, Penelope Fitzgerald, but *her* favourite book, *The Van*, was about an Irish family who kept swearing and nothing happened.

Joseph and I then took the kite to the top of the Downs. When we tried to fly it, it didn't work. Maybe it needed a tail.

I drove on to visit my mother, who had come out of the nursing home a week before. Two friends of hers, Jane and Mrs Mortimer, were there having tea. My mother was dressed in blue and a Zimmer was beside her. They were talking about Florida, which my mother said she hated; she couldn't think why anybody would go there. I said the reason so many English people went in the winter was because there were cheap flights and package holidays. My mother retorted, 'When I was there, there was a storm and fire danced on the water.' She then went into a garbled account of how she had talked Spanish to a taxi-driver in Miami.

Jane said, 'You're so clever, Anne, with your languages.'

Mrs Mortimer seemed irritated that my mother wasn't keeping to the point and said, 'Where have we got to now?'

I was sure my mother's attack on Florida sprang partly out of jealousy that I had been there two years running to stay with our American cousins. She had known them all her life, and Tiggy, the one she knew best, had begged her to come and stay again, but my mother had decided that Florida was boring, possibly because I had started going there. An only child, my mother does not like to share, even with her own children.

Later she became more pleasant and said she wanted to take some photographs of Lucy's pony soon. As we were leaving, a local minicab turned up with Val, a temporary New Zealand cook, and Delphine, a temporary nurse from Zimbabwe. They had come to look after my mother.

This encounter with my mother caused a terrible pain of grief in my heart. Is this why I have a lump in my breast? I did not say anything to her about it – the lump, I mean.

Monday 16 September
London. My cousin William arrived promptly for lunch yesterday in Sussex, which was unlike him. His new half-Swedish girlfriend was dressed in rather an old-fashioned way, in beige and white, with a thick necklace round her neck. I liked her.

I told William that Nicholas Mosley was coming, and he said he knew his son.

Nicholas then arrived and we drank some wine. Nicholas told us about going off to fight during the Second World War when he was twenty. In the officers' training sessions it had been implied that the men would obey them, but when it came to it, they often didn't. On his first day of action he had told the men under him to fire, but they had just said, 'Fuck you!'

He had then met his first wife at Oxford. They married and went to live on a Caribbean island owned by a woman called Mrs Snowball. There he had written his first novel.

He said that another novel, *Accident*, which was made into a film starring Dirk Bogarde, had been turned down by Barley Allison at Secker. She had also thought of turning down his last novel, *Hopeful Monsters*, the one that won the Whitbread Prize. The day she wrote him a despairing letter about it she dropped dead of a heart attack. I took comfort from this anecedote, with regard to my own unpublished writing.

I did not mention the lump on my breast to anyone at the lunch. I am trying to forget about it.

Last night Lucy arrived back with her father. She was excited that I had ridden her pony, but annoyed I had worn the wrong clothes – jeans instead of jodhpurs.

18 September
My son's birthday.

In hospital. I have brought a book on women mystics in with me in case I die under the anaesthetic. One of the essays, by Karen Armstrong, an ex-nun, is on Juliana of Norwich.

Last night my friend Nick, a solicitor in Paddington, came to the hospital on his motor bike after work and took me to a local restaurant. When Nick was in his twenties he had Hodgkin's disease – cancer of the lymph glands – twice. His mother had a related lymph cancer and died when he was a child. (She was one of the first, in 1957, to get large-scale radiation therapy. They overdid the dose and she died of leukaemia, which she developed as a result.) Nick was in Charing Cross Hospital three times in the seventies, each time for several weeks. He had had Hodgkin's disease for eighteen months before it was diagnosed. Once he managed to look at his own medical notes. They said he had a 50 per cent chance of recovery. He is now forty.

Over supper in a Thai restaurant in Fulham Palace Road, near the hospital, Nick talked calmly about his experiences. He said at one stage of his illness he had joined the Oncology Club. The two founding members were Janet, who had cancer of the cervix, which had spread to the liver, and Michael, who had cancer of the brain. Janet was beautiful and sexy and worked as a croupier. Nick said all her 'fast car' boyfriends dropped her when she became ill, but she still looked very striking even when bald. Membership of the club was confined to those who had a connection with Charing Cross Hospital. The pitch was 'Join the shortest-lived club in town!' They used to go on cheap outings to the opera and to meals at the Dumpling Inn in Chinatown – usually six people per outing, all bald or partially haired.

Despite being so full of life, Janet died soon afterwards. Does taking a positive attitude make any difference to recovery? My friend Liz Whipp, a cancer doctor at the Bristol Oncology Centre, isn't sure. It could be arbitrary. In her experience women who are very 'down' all the time sometimes live longer than those who take a gutsy approach to the illness. The only thing she has noticed is

that, in the terminal stages, the people who have accepted calmly
that they're going to die often outlive the ones who are terrified.

During most of Nick's illness, except when he was in hospital,
he determinedly went on working as a solicitor. I admire this. He
says the great thing about continuing to work was that it meant he
had other things to think about, rather than just the disease. He
did not become 'solely a patient, someone who is operated on and
does nothing'. The worst part of being a patient – worse even than
the pain and tiredness – is the 'sense of the loss of power'. It was
wonderful to be earning money when he was ill. The men who ran
the firm, by continuing to employ him, helped him retain his
dignity, which, he thinks, ultimately 'saved his bacon'.

After breakfast in the ward I chat to Ivy, the old lady in the bed
next to me. She had one breast off ten years ago. Now she has a
lump in the other.

We are both having our operations mid-morning.

3.30 p.m. Ivy's lump was taken out an hour after mine.

The anaesthetic did not agree with her and when I offered her
some of my orange barley water, even though it was several hours
later, she was sick. I find her gentle voice and pink cheeks very
soothing. For many years she worked in the LEB showrooms in
Hammersmith. She is terrified of the doctors and has begged me to
ask them questions on her behalf when they come on their rounds
this evening.

My own operation would appear to have gone well. The
wound, where I had the lump cut out, does not seem to be too
severe. Not long afterwards I was reading Colin Thubron's latest
novel, about some people in an unnamed place who get a weird
skin disease.

19 September
A nurse brought round a form and invited me to fill it in. She said
she thought I would prefer to do it myself instead of her sitting
there posing questions. The form asked about my personal
situation.

I wrote: 'I live alone with two young children. I am about to get divorced. My son is at a school for children with difficulties. I think my mother is an alcoholic. I am a freelance writer and I am probably suffering from stress due to not getting my work published.'

After I had filled in the form and given it back to the nurse I did not hear anything more. Surely they should be worried? I might commit suicide.

Lulu, who came to visit me this evening, thinks it is just as well. I could be surrounded by concerned social workers and psychiatrists. My children could be taken into care.

20 September

I went with Duncan Fallowell to the launch of the new Everyman series in a house in St James's recently redecorated by one of the Rothschilds. As people went admiringly from room to room, wondering whether to get more excited about the gilt mirrors or seeing the famous guests, Darryl Pinckney, a black American writer who has recently finished his first novel, *High Cotton*, said, 'I've just seen Jerry Hall getting ideas for her interior décor.' This made me laugh delightedly.

I was on a high and told a couple of people I had had an operation, but I did not say what for. I stayed at the party rather late as I was enjoying myself.

Two days later

I am in limbo this week waiting for the result.

I have registered for a local-authority Spanish class at the primary school five minutes from my house. I am trying to keep things normal. I want to be able to speak Spanish when I go on holiday to Majorca next summer. I might even go to Cuba next spring if I can get my ex-husband – as I must now call him in preparation for my divorce – to look after the children for two weeks.

24 September

Edward rings up in a state of excitement. Nicholas Mosley has resigned as a Booker judge. He was annoyed that not one of his choices is on the short list and he doesn't think any of the other books chosen are any good. Nicholas claimed at the judges' meeting this afternoon that the modern novel was going nowhere and that most of them were 'full of mad people buggering one another'. Edward tried to stop him resigning, saying that if he did, the philistine press would gang up and write a lot of articles about pinkos. Edward then offered to give up one of his votes, so that Nicholas could have it. But this resulted in *Time's Arrow* by Martin Amis being put on the short list instead of Edward's own preference, a novel by Peter Carey.

A dog walker whom I met at a party this summer came round today to meet Toby, as I must get someone to exercise him if I'm ill. He is a Cavalier King Charles spaniel. The dog walker is a tall young man with floppy blond hair and pink cheeks. When he spoke to Toby, Toby slunk under a chair and looked very nervous. I think he thought he was going to be given to the dog walker for ever. The dog walker's car number-plate is WUF.

I went to my Spanish class this afternoon. I took an immediate dislike to one of the other pupils, a Frenchwoman called Marie-Ange. She had long red hair and flirted a lot with the young teacher, a Chilean called Pedro. I could see she did not like me either. Marie-Ange and I may come to blows before our course is finished.

During the coffee-break we all filled in the forms for the course. In one section they asked us to give our ethnic group. White, Asian, European Asian and White European were among the categories. The last box was 'Prefer not to say'. I found this enigmatic and wished I had ticked it, but I had already marked 'White European'.

26 September

Emily and Paolo asked me to supper last night. Paolo has not moved out yet. Edward was there as well. He has invited me to

the Booker Prize dinner in October. I am very excited about this.
We ate frozen brains, which Paulo had brought in a bag from
Rome, and argued about religion. Edward is very anti-Catholic.

Paolo complimented me on my clothes – I was wearing a
multicoloured jacket I'd bought in Los Angeles – and said how
well and young I looked. The imminent break-up of Paolo and
Emily's marriage was not mentioned.

Emily looks far iller than I do. She is much too thin as a result of
anorexia and her exhausting lifestyle – drinking in clubs till 2 a.m.
with her lover, Ben, then getting up early to work on her weird
sculptures, besides teaching dyslexic children and illiterate adults.
Tonight she downed three glasses of neat vodka, refused the
brains and went off to Harrow Road on a bicycle to teach a West
Indian lady to read.

30 September

I worry about whether the lump is cancerous. This morning
Joseph, who's been away for the weekend with his father, gets into
my bed soon after six. He's very affectionate. During the time he
lies beside me I am half asleep and have a few minutes of total
recall of my childhood, before my brother was drowned. We lived
for four years in a rented house on a common in Berkshire. We
were a happy family, I think, and my mother was always smiling. I
started telling Joseph a bit about this. I then went back to sleep.

Yesterday – Sunday – I went up to Kentish Town for lunch with
Peter Ayrton, a friend who runs Serpent's Tail publishing
company, and who's had one of my manuscripts for several
weeks. It was just Pete, his wife, Sarah, and their two children. We
had cold meat, tasty food out of pots, such as aubergine salad, a
selection of delicious cheeses and half a bottle of *rosé* from the
fridge.

Pete's wife didn't drink any wine, She was friendlier than she's
ever been; previously she has always seemed shy and reserved.

Before that I went to my local Catholic church. An incident

occurred that prompted me to write a letter to Mary Killen's
problem page in the back of the *Spectator*. Perhaps I will get into
print this way if no other.

Dear Mary

I was in my local Catholic church on Sunday when a white-
haired woman in the bench in front of me fainted or had a
stroke. Luckily an Irishwoman and an aristocratic-looking
Frenchman dealt with her. (The two Filipinos beside the
woman did nothing, and I am hopeless with sick people.)
However, the Frenchman turned to me and asked me to get a
priest to fetch a doctor.

My first instinct was to rush up to the side of the altar and
interrupt the Mass, but I got there to find only two nine-year-
old choirboys, who did not understand my excited gesticu-
lations. I became embarrassed about making a fool of myself
in front of a famous writer's wife who was among the
parishioners as I know one of her sisters, so I walked back
wondering what to do.

Suddenly I remembered that a very disturbed man of my
acquaintance was also along the congregation. I had seen him
earlier, handing out pamphlets at the back and going in a
secret side-door to help with parish matters. I rushed down
the aisle, tapped this man on the shoulder and whispered that
a woman was dying near my pew. He acted promptly and
went to the porter's lodge to call an ambulance.

My question is: what is the normal procedure if this
happens again? If I had not known this disturbed man (who,
by the way, is a convert) would I have had to yell out and
interrupt the Mass by shouting loudly for a doctor?

My cousin, who, like me, is from a very old Catholic family
which, unlike that of the Duke of Norfolk, never gave up its
faith, says that priests are used to mad bag ladies shouting in
Catholic churches and he would have taken no notice.

My aunt, who is also from a very old Catholic family but
has gone ecumenical, says it wouldn't have mattered if the

woman had died in church. What better place is there for her
to die?

Signed
Troubled Catholic

I sent a copy of this letter to my mother via Molly (the young
woman who's just started working as my mother's secretary for
two days a week) as I thought it would appeal to her sense of
humour. My mother is not Catholic, but was married to my father,
who was.

October

1 October

Today I get the results of the test on the lump on my breast. Last
night I had the following dream. I'm in a house with Patrick, a
painter, and some other people. Someone tells me to go down the
road and get petrol. I don't go. Patrick and I are left behind in the
house. He's painting and I'm writing.

I think I then *do* go out on some errand. I have to buy some food
for a woman on the sixth floor of the house. When I get back how
will I recognize this woman?

The end of the dream is that I return and look up at the house.
The woman leans out of the window. How do I recognize her? The
woman, who has dark-brown hair, is 'the picture of health'.
What's more, she's me.

Afternoon. I'm in Clinic 8, waiting for my result.

Again I cannot ignore the fact that I am in a room with people
with cancer, and that I may have cancer myself. This is very
frightening. When I was a child, the lady operating the puppet
Muffin the Mule, whom my brother, Raymond, and I watched
every week on Children's Hour, died of cancer; so did my step-
grandfather in 1955, and also the aunt of some children with
whom we went on holiday in Devon. I remember that the word
'cancer' was always spoken in a low voice by the adults.

As I sit there reading the *Independent*, Ivy, wearing a lovely red
cardigan, comes out of one of the rooms looking shocked but
dignified. She says her lump was malignant and she has to go on
Tamoxifen to prevent a recurrence. She wishes me good luck.

I have to go and wait in the passage outside the doctors' rooms.
Beside me is a black woman reading a Bible. A woman wearing

Middle Eastern robes comes out of one of the rooms, sobbing. Her husband is with her. My husband and I are separated. Is this why I got the lump, through worry and guilt? I do not know if my husband would be much good in these circumstances. When I was in St Stephen's Hospital three years ago, he seemed terrified and when I got home, he immediately left me alone in the house while he went out with our son. I told a friend, who said it was normal; most men hate illness, or they hate their wives to be ill. Yet when we were about to get married, I got mumps, and my husband nursed me throughout this. He brought me a white azalea. We got married soon afterwards. It was January.

I go into the room to find a doctor I haven't seen before, with glasses. He looks at me directly and tells me that the lump was cancerous. He draws a diagram and tries to explain what it means, what kind of lump it is and what the next stage will be. I pretend to concentrate, but I don't. I am shocked. I'm grateful, however, for the straightforward way he has broken the news to me. Now I have to have the lymph glands under my right arm out to see if the cancer has spread. He flicks through a calendar and asks when I can come in for this operation. I want to go in as soon as possible so I can go to the Booker Prize dinner with Edward on 22 October. Also, I would like to have the operation done before my children's half-term so I can spend it with them.

After fixing a provisional date with the doctor – if there's no bed vacant, the operation will be postponed – I go down to the lobby. I must have a bar of chocolate. I am desperate for a bar of chocolate. I buy a half-pound bar of Cadbury's Dairy Milk from the hospital shop and wolf it down. Then I wait for a bus.

At the last minute, instead of going straight home, I go round to Miranda's flat, which is just up the road, and collapse into an armchair. She fetches me a cup of tea.

I have to break the news to my children. My son is already obsessed with death. He is morbid, fanciful and doesn't find life easy.

My daughter is sensible, but is at the age when the word 'breast' is embarrassing. How could her mother get 'breast' cancer? She doesn't want anyone at school to know. I promise I won't tell any of the mothers of her friends.

2 October

I have had several more telephone calls about my mother. I went round to see Miranda again this morning. I told her I was consumed with worry about my mother's drinking. She advised me to write a letter saying I'm not to be bothered by the people who are looking after my mother while all this is going on. It's possible that cancer is made worse by stress.

She helped me compose a letter in rather formal language. She used the phrase 'occasioned me': 'I cannot overestimate the worry your last fall has occasioned me.'

She told me to send the letter care of Molly. Thank God I asked Molly to work for my mother a few weeks ago, before I knew I might have cancer. I am hoping she will take the burden of responsibility off me.

When we had sealed up the letters, I sat back, feeling exhausted. I said aloud for the first time, 'I'm ill.' It seemed odd to me. I am not in any pain and I am still very brown from my holiday in America. I don't look ill, though I am thinner than I sometimes am.

I have received a letter from Pete of Serpent's Tail about my book on childhood, 'The Merry Meadow'.

Dear Elisa

It was good seeing you on Sunday. I hope your news from the hospital is OK.

I spent part of yesterday reading your manuscript – it was enjoyable. I definitely can see the autobiography being published, but not by Serpent's Tail. It is well within the belles-lettres tradition. You could send it to Constable.

All the best,
Pete

Even if my manuscript was good enough – and I'm not sure of that – my childhood was too privileged for Serpent's Tail. If I'd been a disadvantaged Finnish punk, Pete might have published it. I think he deliberately made an effort to finish reading it this weekend because of my situation. I've already sent another copy to Anthony Blond, who's starting a new company in the village of Blond in France. He liked a story I'd had in the *London Magazine* in 1981 called 'The Raw Food Eater'.

3 October

Lulu wants me to go and see an expert on breast cancer in Harley Street. His name is Henry Whittaker and he has been examining her and her mother's breasts for years. He is a world authority and a few years ago was booked to lecture on a cruise that Lulu's mother, Nancy, was going on. Lulu said that he cancelled because he was obviously terrified that her mother, who talks non-stop, was going to accost him all the time with questions about her breasts. Lulu gave me the name of his charming secretary and told me to ring immediately.

4 October

Henry Whittaker is a handsome man with the manner of an absent-minded professor. On learning that my grandmother was the great-aunt of one of his best friends, he talked for some time about the family and showed me photographs of his holiday cottage, which is near the home of this friend. At first I thought we weren't going to get to my breast at all, he seemed so keen to discuss his best friend's family. He then began reminiscing about some other cousin of my grandmother's who had died early of breast cancer. He did not seem to realize that, although this woman was not actually my blood relation, it was rather tactless, in the circumstances, to mention her early death.

He took notes about my situation and said that it was correct to go ahead with the arrangements that had been made with Charing Cross. I would have exactly the same treatment if I were treated privately.

He eventually examined my breasts with great skill and sensitivity. I felt that he knew exactly what to look for, almost as if his hands had some power of their own.

As I left he said he wasn't going to charge me as I was the cousin of his best friend. When I told Lulu, she said she was rather jealous.

Later Molly rang and said my mother had found the letter about the incident in the Catholic church hilarious. Mary Killen also phoned and said she wanted to publish it in the *Spectator*, but must think up a suitable reply first.

5 October
I have had a letter from *Woman's Journal* rejecting my house-swap article. 'I enjoyed it and think it's a great idea for a feature . . . but in these recessionary times our features quota has been reduced . . .'

I went out and posted it to the *Independent on Sunday* travel section.

I also posted a copy of 'The Merry Meadow' to Constable as Pete had suggested.

8 October
Letter from the *Spectator* about the house-swap article: 'I enjoyed reading it, but am afraid it is far, far too long for publication, and anyway it's not really quite suitable for us.'

Also a letter from my mother's friend Jane (to whom I had written to explain that I had cut off communication with my mother at the moment because of the breast cancer): 'My thoughts and prayers are with you and lots of love. There will be no communication from your mother. God bless you.'

9 October
I went to the Earls Court Poetry Society last night to hear M read from her latest book of poems. An old friend, James L, came with me. He is a doctor who writes a medical column in the *Sunday Telegraph*. I knew from my Indian friend Vaneeta that he knew I

might have breast cancer, but we didn't mention it. After the reading the four of us – me, James, M and her husband – went to the Chelsea Arts Club.

M said she is writing a short story for an anthology called *God*. I want to write one as well, so this morning I rang one of the editors. She said it was a bit late, but to send a story anyway.

Joseph, early this morning: 'Mummy, it took a bloody long time for me to get potty trained, didn't it?'

Last night, when I got back from the Chelsea Arts Club, he was in my bed wearing the new pyjamas I'd recently bought him in Marks & Spencer.

He asked what the hospital was like. I described the ward and the old lady, Ivy. I then began having flashbacks to my childhood again. I told him how my brother, Raymond, and I were often given barley sugars on long car journeys.

Once more he clung to me and said, 'I want to see your face.'

I said, 'I love you. I really love you.'

10 October

A ward in Charing Cross Hospital. Tomorrow I am having a further part of my lump taken out. I am also having my lymph nodes removed. I am then having a six-week course of radio-therapy. If the lymph nodes are affected, I will have to have chemotherapy as well.

The only other person in the ward is a woman called Betty, who lives near Heathrow Airport. She had her lymph glands removed a few days ago. Tubes are dangling from her left arm into a bottle covered with a flowery material. She has to carry this bottle with her everywhere. When the lymphatic area has drained properly, she can go home.

This afternoon a young woman in silk pyjamas from Marks & Spencer came in from another ward and talked to me and Betty. She also has breast cancer, but doesn't seem worried about it. Later Betty, said she was a 'bit full of herself' and 'liked showing off her body'.

At 6 p.m. my ex-husband came in, bringing an article written by a friend of his about having a breast off. This article is supposed to help me. The writer, who recently had a mastectomy, explains how she had to wait for her results to see if the cancer had gone into the lymph nodes. 'If it hadn't, I knew I stood a much better chance of not developing secondary cancers.' Later in the article she rejoices that the cancer has not spread into the lymph nodes.

How crazy to give this to me just before my operation when I will not know for at least two weeks whether my lymph nodes have been affected or not! My husband had not read the article and probably does not understand the implications, but surely his friend should have had the sense not to send it before I know my results?

I went into a panic. Luckily a sweet young nurse called Jackie came and talked to me for some time, sitting on my bed. She said it didn't matter if it *had* affected the lymph glands.

11 October

Day of operation. Emily turned up at eleven. She was wearing an odd *décolleté* strapless bodice and said she hadn't been allowed into Harrods in it the day before. I wasn't due to have the operation till one. My pre-med was supposed to be at twelve. At 11.40 the young ward doctor told me I must go down for a chest X-ray.

Emily and I went down to the X-ray Department on the third floor and waited. There were a lot of other people waiting, mostly with blank expressions on their faces. One old man's face lit up when he saw Emily's bodice. Then he started wheezing very badly. We told the woman behind the glass three times that I was having a pre-med in twenty minutes. At last I was allowed to jump the queue.

We waited ages for a lift back up to my floor. Finally we got into one, but it didn't leave the ground. We got out; another lift arrived. I leaped in and Emily was left behind. I then got stranded on the fourth floor. A doctor helped me find another lift and at last I was back in my bed.

Vaneeta turned up and waited with me while I had the pre-med.

She brought me a bright-pink bag containing a strawberry
ointment from the Body Shop. It smelt delicious. I became drowsy.
I started thinking about my children and about being on top of the
Sussex Downs with them last summer.

Just as I was falling asleep, a nurse came in and handed me a
large brown envelope. In it was a drawing by my daughter of her
pony, saying, 'Good luck from Lucy and her lucky piebald pony.'

There was also a photograph of both children on their cousins'
pony, taken by my ex-husband. Later I found out that he had
brought it in very late last night.

After operation. When I came round in the recovery room, a nurse,
I think Australian, was talking in a very loud voice about her plans
for the evening. I was furious and wanted to shut her up, but I was
in such a vulnerable position I didn't dare, in case she got
annoyed.

Later I slept a great deal. I woke up in the ward to find there
was a drip in my arm. I was attached to a large stand. I felt
completely helpless.

At about six my friend Vivian arrived, bringing a bunch of
freesias. It seemed appropriate that Vivian, with her delicacy and
gentleness, should bring these flowers, whose scent and fragility I
love.

She stayed for half an hour or so and I talked a bit about my
mother. I said, 'My mother's never been there when I needed her.
She nearly didn't come to my wedding party because she had a
cold. Everyone was saying, 'Where's your mother?' The summer I
had my first baby, she went on holiday to Majorca for four weeks
instead of two.'

For the first time in my life I was admitting that I felt completely
abandoned. Vivian understood this. It was why she had come.

That night I dream that I am in a foreign country or a room with
three tall blond men. We go outside and it becomes very cold. It's
night-time. We start to shiver. At one end of the road are high
gates and brickwork; very beautiful, but remote. We're not
allowed in there.

It gets colder, and windy; we shiver and hold blankets around ourselves. Cold rain beats down. Will anyone help us?

A light goes on in one of the windows, a voice shouts out to us in Greek. It's still not clear if we'll be allowed in.

Martin, a kind man who used to work on my grandmother's farm, comes to drive me up the road in a van. (Martin is dead and so is my grandmother.) I drive on with Martin to my grand-mother's village. But when we get there, it's survived a terrible snowstorm and has been icebound for weeks.

We're in a house in the country. No one's there. Just as we leave, my grandmother appears outside the house as a young woman. A black and white dog, a spaniel a bit bigger than our dog, Toby, follows the car up the road, barking. I wonder whether to turn back and see my grandmother. But she'll wait for me.

Later in the dream I kiss Vivian on the cheek and thank her for coming the night of my operation, when I was so helpless.
Then she asks me, 'What was it like before your second brother was born?'

I answer with some surprise, 'My brother and I were constant companions.'

As I wake up, I realize I've spoken the truth about my brother, who was drowned on my seventh birthday, and what he meant to me.

12 *October*
10 a.m. Betty is talking to a woman with hennaed hair who was bitten by her corgi, or her daughter's corgi, I'm not sure which. The corgis are father and son. The son attacked the father and they fought viciously till the woman managed to force a Hoover down one dog's throat. She then shut one corgi in the garage, but the other bit her severely in the wrist. Her wrist is poisoned and she has to stay in hospital several extra days.

My movements are somewhat impeded by being on a drip attached to a stand. I have to walk with this to the telephone at the nurses' desk if anyone rings, and to the lavatory. I am slowly getting the hang of it.

My friend Duncan arrived at teatime, bringing a copy of *Viz* magazine to cheer me up. He also brought me a miniature rose in a flower-pot. It was orange. I associate Duncan with life and energy. I was very pleased with the rose.

A few weeks ago Duncan was commissioned by the *Evening Standard* to write an article called 'Keep Puritanism off the Streets'. It has now been rejected for being too liberal. He has thus been censored by the very thing he was asked to oppose. In the early seventies Duncan had a pop column in the *Spectator* and could say whatever he liked. Is this new puritanism a symptom of the nineties?

He is interviewing Nadine Gordimer tomorrow.

At about seven my children came to see me with my ex-husband. My son tried to get into my bed, but this was impossible because of the drip. It must be frightening for them to see me like this. They brought me a small box of Quality Street. I am rather exhausted.

Sunday

Ben, the newspaper boy, comes in even earlier than usual. He wakes me and Betty by waving the *News of the World* and shouting about the 'Long Dong Silver' and Anita Hill case, which he's longing to discuss. He describes two videos he's seen – *Misery*, in which a man's legs get tied to a plank and chopped off, and another film, in which psychopaths dressed as clowns stab children. When he's gone, Betty says, without irony, 'Happy little soul.'

At four Peter, a journalist on the *Observer*, arrives with his wife, Susan (she brings home-made truffles) and a copy of the *Sunday Sport*.

He looks at my get-well cards, including one from a woman I don't like and who, I thought, didn't like me. Peter, who knows this woman, jokes that the card really means 'Get well slowly.'

Three friends then come to see me all at the same time, which is annoying, because they don't know each other and have nothing in common.

Emily brings a book on the Bristol Programme. This is a holistic centre in Bristol for people with cancer, which encourages them to eat more healthy food and do meditation and relaxation techniques. It stresses the relationship between the mind and the body.

My cousin Lulu, who never went to school and now works in a hospice, has never seen the *Sunday Sport*. She says all she ever reads is *Hello!*. Last Sunday she was propositioned by a dying man who asked her what positions she liked. She had been advised to humour the patients so she told him.

Cynthia is absolutely furious at Peter for bringing the *Sunday Sport*. She says it is degenerate and has the wrong view of women. She brings me Shusha Guppy's latest book of memoirs and a copy of the *Observer*. She says seriously, 'If you feel mutilated, my brother's ex-girlfriend knows a surgeon in California who can change everything to look the same.'

Until that moment I had not felt mutilated. After all, my breast has not been cut off.

When my friends have gone, I read the *Observer*. There is a two-page spread on breast cancer. 'If three or more lymph glands are affected, 30 per cent of women survive for ten years.' I do not know how many lymph glands have been affected. I am extremely worried.

I flip through the book on the Bristol Programme. Is my only hope of survival to live on pulses and bean sprouts for the rest of my short life?

14 October

I asked the breast nurse about the article in the *Observer*. Are these statistics correct? She says yes and asks if she can borrow the article to have it photocopied for her files. She rushes off to do this at once.

My initial dislike of this woman is confirmed. She is obviously on an ego trip and likes following the doctors around instead of consoling the patients, which is what she's meant to do. I wish that Dr Isaacs, a young doctor I find very attractive, had come. I am sure he'd have been more sympathetic.

After lunch Terence, a young Irish male nurse with big blue eyes, arrives to remove me from the drip. He grabs my copy of the *Sunday Sport* and becomes engrossed in an article about blonde naked women 'brickies'. He takes my first drain out in an incompetent way, talking to himself. He gets the two bottles muddled up, then says to the nurse who's come to help him, 'You're supposed to wear rubber gloves for this.' He isn't.

I am now attached to a bottle, like Betty. Tubes are dangling out of our arms, draining the lymphatic area. They lead into bottles that we have to carry with us everywhere.

In the late afternoon Betty and I go downstairs to have an ultrasound.

After the ultrasound I am given a folder whose cover states: 'NOT TO BE HANDLED BY PATIENT'. I immediately open it up and read as much as possible without Betty noticing. There is a letter from Henry Whittaker, the Harley Street specialist, to the surgeon about me: 'Her domestic situation is somewhat fluid.' I also read: '*In situ* carcinoma. Some spread to lymphatic area.'

I thought they didn't yet know if cancer had spread to the lymph glands. I thought they had taken the lymph glands out to see if it *had* spread. I am absolutely terrified. At the same time my instinct is to look around for a photocopying machine. I can't find one.

A Chinese woman, whom I hardly know, arrives from north London at my bedside. I am touched and impressed by this. A mutual friend of ours, James T, put her in touch with me. She had a breast off two years go; when he told her about me, she said she would love to talk to me. According to James, she's normally shy and retiring, but had explained to him that when she had her mastectomy, an older woman, who'd had one previously, helped her.

She tries to reassure me by saying that her operation, having her whole breast removed, was worse. This gives me the slightly uncomfortable feeling that I have nothing to complain about. She gives me a bottle of Floris bath essence – jasmine. I love the scent of this. She thinks it's very important to talk openly about having cancer. If you remain tense and keep it all inside you, 'the spirit is broken' and it's more difficult to recover.

When she's gone, James himself turns up and sits by the side of the bed, looking at me intently, like a fox or a wolf. He is a mixture of warmth and egocentricity. When I first told him the news a few weeks ago, he said tenderly, 'Elisa, your poor breast!'

Tonight he subtly makes it clear that he's sacrificed his time in coming from north London to see me. Nevertheless I'm touched.

Tuesday, 15 October
Two other women have arrived for operations: Carmen, who's Spanish, and Rosemary, a vegan from Ascot.

Rosemary has a strange health-food drink with her made from acorns. Just before her pre-med she lies on her bed with headphones on, listening to soothing music, a blissful expression on her face. Ten years ago she found a lump in her breast. The doctor in the hospital she went to told her that she must have her breast cut off. She refused and walked straight out. The new lump, which was removed last week, was her first recurrence for ten years. Now, like me, she has to have her lymph glands taken out to see if the cancer's spread.

While Rosemary and Carmen are having their operations, a physiotherapist comes into the ward and teaches me and Betty a few exercises, so that the arm and shoulder where the lymph glands were cut out don't get frozen. She gives us the exercises on a sheet of paper. We are supposed to do them every day. My right arm hurts like hell. I daren't even look properly at the stitches under the armpit. My arm will never feel the same.

The young doctor I like, Dr Isaacs (who has black hair and glasses), came to see us. He told Betty her drain will be taken out tomorrow. Then she can go home. Dr Isaacs seemed to find me amusing. There were several other doctors with him. One, an uncouth and red-faced Scotsman built like a rugger-player, I did not like. I thought he was uncomfortable with women. Will I ever be able to talk to Dr Isaacs on my own?

*

Later Rosemary and Carmen return from their operations. Carmen's husband, in a chef's hat (he works in the hospital canteen), and her sister, in a dark-blue uniform and a little white hat (she also works in the canteen), and Carmen's son, who is a medical student in the hospital, all lean over her bed, expressions of concern and patience on their faces.

She doesn't wake up.

6 p.m. A man in a striped T-shirt rushes into our ward and shouts, 'Have you ever tried to jump off a high building?'

Luckily a male nurse from Mauritius is there with a trolley-full of pills.

Betty asks, 'Who's he?'

The nurse explains that the man's escaped from the psychiatric unit on the third floor.

'They've probably mislaid him,' he says.

During this disturbance Carmen comes to. She is then sick several times very loudly.

Wednesday, 16 October
Something very exciting has happened. The person being wheeled up and down on a bed with a big bag of urine in front of her has changed sex.

The woman who was bitten by the corgi told Betty this. Apparently they are in the same ward. She came in as a man and is now a woman called Caroline.

There is no water in the hospital. After breakfast Carmen, who is very lively, sent her son downstairs for bottles of water for all of us. This morning her sister came up early from the canteen with rounds of toast and offered it to everyone. Carmen also offered me a cup of espresso from her sister's thermos. This seemed incredibly luxurious and I accepted – as a one-off treat. I have decided to do without coffee for the next few months because I have cancer. This is very depressing. There is something ghastly and dead-end about a determinedly healthy diet, particularly when one's ill.

Rosemary, the vegan, refused the toast. Later she said, 'Carmen,

I hope your sister wasn't offended, but I only eat brown bread.'

Just before lunch the person who'd had the sex change was at the nurses' desk in a flimsy blue nightdress, asking if she could wash her hair. But there's still no water. Caroline looked very excited about her new life. I am longing to talk to her, but can't think of the right approach.

Carmen says she was once called up from the canteen to interpret for a man who had come especially from Spain for a sex change. But the doctors told him he couldn't have one; his tests weren't adequate. He threatened to complain to the Spanish consulate.

Duncan, who visits later, says this hospital is famous for sex changes. (He wrote a book on April Ashley and knows a lot about it.) I ask if he will come with me and talk to Caroline about her experiences. We can buy some cigarettes and pretend we're smokers and approach her outside the lifts, where she sits smoking most of the day in her blue nightdress.

Duncan thinks this is terribly vulgar, however, and refuses to do it. Also, he says, according to research at Johns Hopkins University, it's been discovered that people who change sex commit suicide at the same rate as they would have done if they had stayed as they were. One reason may be that when they find they're not completely accepted in their new gender they're extremely disappointed. I feel worried for Caroline, who at the moment looks so happy.

This afternoon Edward rang asking if I can still come to the Booker next week. I hope my drain will be out by then. If not, Sandra, one of the nurses, says I might be able to go carrying the drain, heavily disguised by a shawl. I may be on television.

Evening. I am sick of being in hospital. My lymph glands aren't draining quickly enough and I may be in here for longer than I expected. I am very worried about missing my children's half-term next week. Rosemary, who seems very calm, tries to pacify me by saying I should use the period in hospital to rest; I won't be much good to my children if I'm exhausted. I suppose she's right.

Her daughter, a student at Durham University, came down today on a bus from the north to see her.

Tonight I got three calls from Los Angeles, one from Lauren, another from my old friend Liza, whom I met on a skiing trip to Poland in 1971, and one from Paul, who's in the record business and whom I saw this summer when I was doing the house-swap. Being summoned to the nurses' desk three times to receive these long-distance phone calls made me feel like a film star. Even Liza, who hardly ever makes long-distance calls – she's too poor – talked to me for several minutes.

Paul, who telephoned first, said he had just come across Liza at an AA meeting in Santa Monica. (He met her originally through me, when we all lived in London in our twenties.) I am stunned by this. Surely Liza is not an alcoholic?

A few minutes later Liza herself rang and I asked what was going on. She said, 'I didn't want to tell you because of your mom, but I've been going to AA meetings for a whole year.' Liza then spoke very good sense to me about my mother. 'Your mother has not spent her life as a maid or in a shack in South America. She has travelled everywhere and met very interesting people. If she chooses to drink herself to death, it is not your responsibility.'

This made me feel better. But, although she is materially well off, my mother has had a sad life. Her father was killed when she was three; her only brother died aged two, and her two sons died.

Thursday, 17 October
I missed my Spanish class on Tuesday, and am too inhibited to practise speaking Spanish to Carmen in the ward. This morning an Irish priest came to see me and Carmen. I had put 'Catholic' on one of the hospital forms I had to fill in. He blessed me.

Emily telephoned and said she'd been up all night worrying about *her* mother. She's going to ring her and tell her to stop drinking. Do I support this? I said I didn't have a clue. After I put the phone down I felt a sense of outrage that she had asked me something so complicated so soon after my operation. It's not up to me to make decisions about her mother. Anyway, I think Emily herself is alcoholic.

Midday. Miranda comes to see me with some flowers and a copy of *Vogue*. She offers to ring Emily, whom she hardly knows, and tell her to stop bothering me about her mother while I'm in hospital. My own mother is bad enough. I agree to this, though I realize Emily won't like it. Miranda can be very strong-minded.

Betty is now wearing a pink velvet track suit and is all ready to leave the hospital. She had her stitches removed and her drain taken out this morning.

At lunchtime I am given the vegetarian meal by mistake. It is much better than anything I have previously eaten here. After lunch Betty's husband arrives to take her home. As they exit from the ward, he winks at me as usual. Goodbye Betty!

The rest of us then talked about having breast cancer. When Carmen first heard that she had it she cried and cried. A few days later she said to her husband and two sons; 'We all have to die one day.' Her eldest son told her, 'That's why you're going to hospital, because you're mad.'

Rosemary, who teaches music, said she knew in her heart that she had cancer before she was told the result. She has a heavy crucifix on a ribbon lying on the bed. She seems to be getting annoyed with Carmen, who keeps offering her fruit when she already has some.

This afternoon two other women arrived for operations, one for a lumpectomy, the other to have the lymph glands out.

I particularly like these new patients. Pam, who's about fifty, looks as if she's spent all her life working in a garden; she has pink cheeks, bright, grey eyes and a friendly, energetic manner. When she was nineteen, Pam told me, she became pregnant, her boyfriend deserted her and her parents made her leave home. She went to live with her baby in a single mothers' hostel. Luckily the place where she worked had a crèche, so she could take her baby

in to work. Now her daughter's in her twenties and works on the
floor of the Stock Exchange.

The other new patient, Jenny, is my age, forty-one. (Everyone
else in the ward is older.) Jenny is single and has a job in an
accountant's office. She has just been in hospital to have eye
surgery. Because of this, for the lumpectomy tomorrow she has to
wear eye-pads. No pressure must be put on her eyes which have
just had micro-surgery. Jenny has a soft voice, very fine, straight
hair and a gentle manner. She doesn't look as though she can
stand up for herself. I notice she uses the word 'albeit' a great deal.
Is there really any reason why we five women have breast cancer?
Do we have anything in common? Have we all repressed our
emotions, or suffered from some terrible grief or loss?

I asked Pam if she felt angry with her parents for throwing her
out when she was pregnant. She said no, but surely she must have
felt very angry when it happened? Jenny seems too gentle and
passive for her own good. But what about Carmen, who doesn't
seem to have difficulty in expressing emotion? What secrets does
Rosemary have, Rosemary who appears to have everything
worked out? It may be a complete fluke that we have breast cancer
and other women haven't.

Teatime. Emily comes in with tomatoes, mozzarella and two little
cakes from an expensive bakery. She went to the preview of Derek
Jarman's *Edward II* last night. She said she found the film so
disgusting that she didn't go to the party for it at Heaven
afterwards.

Paolo did, however. Is Emily homophobic, I wonder?

Later, when she'd gone, Paolo arrived with some smoked
salmon. I found his hairy masculine body sitting on my bed
comforting. I told him about my dream, the one that ended with
Vivian asking me about my dead brother. He said he had recently
had a similar dream, about his mother. The dream ended with
forgiveness, with his mother absolving him of some childhood
transgression.

Paolo said he was tired of being a psychiatrist. His patients all tell him the same stories. He even found his last patient, who thought he was a horse, 'a terrible bore'. 'A terrible bore' is one of Paolo's favourite expressions.

Friday, 18 October
The newspaper boy wakes us up very early by shouting, 'Who's seen *Predator 22*?'

I pretend I'm still asleep. I can hear Pam and Rosemary discussing which newspaper to buy for me. Rosemary favours the *Telegraph*, but Pam says I normally have the *Independent*. When the boy starts telling the women the plot of yet another film, involving descriptions of spurting blood, Rosemary asks, 'Isn't it time for you to go to school?'

In the afternoon my ex-husband brings the children in to see me. My daughter's very excited about half-term, which starts today. It looks as though I won't be out of hospital in time as the lymphatic area under my arm has still not drained enough. Maureen, the girl who looks after them, is taking them to the house in Sussex in two hours and my ex-husband will join them there tomorrow morning. When they've gone, I open the letters they brought from my house. There is an enigmatic card from Anthony Blond. 'I was puzzled and intrigued by your MS.' I fear this means he doesn't want to publish it.

There's also a note from Peter O'Connor, a mutual friend of my ex-husband and myself, written from my ex-husband's flat yesterday.

> All will be well – you have a great deal to do with your mind and your mind's eye.

I like the quiet conviction of this note. I believe what it says – or, at any rate, I want so strongly to believe in it that I do.

Merrill, my friend from New York, is arriving at Heathrow tomorrow. She is over here to promote her new novel. I had no idea I'd be in hospital when I invited her to stay with me. I don't know her that well. I met her two summers ago at a party in a garden in north London when she was over to promote another book.

That evening I was crippled with back pain, which I think was psychosomatic. (I had just started having an affair with a man with an enormous penis to whom I wasn't emotionally committed.) I was drinking neat whisky as a painkiller. Merrill stepped forward and offered a suggestion to ease the pain. A week later she herself was inexplicably crippled with a bad back and at one of her readings had to read lying down.

Later Emily came in and tidied my locker and the whole area surrounding my bed. This was so thoughtful I was quite stunned. I had forgotten how practical Emily can be. Sometimes she seems so fey.

Miranda then arrived with some flowers. She said Merrill could collect my house key from her; Merrill is being met at the airport by a woman who's writing a novel about a female vampire.

Just as she was leaving the young ward doctor came in and asked me some questions. One was 'Are you at all worried?'

Miranda said, 'Of course she is, you wally!' and laughed. When he'd gone, she said, 'He's terribly young. He reminds me of my sixteen-year-old nephew.'

The window in our ward hasn't been open for six days. This evening Carmen's husband tried to open it by brute force, but couldn't. There is only one handle to open it and all the other windows on this floor. The handle is lost.

Edward arrives after supper, carrying a new bicycle helmet in psychedelic colours. I ask him to put it on. He looks extraordinary in it. While he's talking to me he stares at Carmen's son, the one who is a medical student. He's sitting on Carmen's bed. Edward is sure he's seen him recently in a sauna in Shepherd's Bush.

Edward and the other judges must decide next Tuesday on who has won the Booker Prize. They are already arguing about their favourites for the short list. Edward likes a novel by an Indian writer, Rohinton Mistry. But Roddy Doyle's *The Van* is more popular. This is the one that Nicholas Mosley said he couldn't read as it was full of incomprehensible dialogue and four-letter words.

8 p.m. Terence, the male nurse, finally opened the window. He had to go downstairs and fetch a handle from another floor. Soon after this, however, Carmen asked him to close it again as she was cold.

Saturday
I rang the house in Sussex with my phonecard and my son told me he had been locked in a shed in the garden for two hours. No one came to find him. Although he often exaggerates, I am now consumed with anxiety. Maureen is rather lazy. She really only likes watching TV and driving the children about in a car. They love her, though, because she's so placid, buys them sweets and watches videos with them; my son thinks her blonde hair is pretty.

Teatime. Jacob, my friend who's an actor and usually out of work, arrived without a present, not even a newspaper. Vaneeta came in shortly afterwards, with a large bunch of flowers. Jacob then felt guilty and went down to the hospital shop. He returned with a packet of chewing-gum, which he sheepishly handed to me.

Miranda phoned to say that Merrill had arrived safely from New York. She thought my house was freezing, so Miranda went in to turn up the heating. Miranda has never been to America and tried to be superior about Merrill, implying that she was some sort of Californian hippy. I put her right; Merrill is a New York urban intellectual who couldn't be less like a Californian. She has probably never done any physical exercise in her life.

Sunday
Merrill visited, bringing me a bunch of purple chrysanthemums. As I saw her approaching my bed I thought she looked frighteningly out of place. She is a short woman with a worried, kind, extremely intelligent expression and a large heart-shaped face. She looks like a mixture of an animal out of Beatrix Potter – a hedgehog perhaps – and a decadent figure from Andy Warhol's Factory. As usual, she was all in black – black trousers, black

jumper, black boots and extremely long wiry black hair. I think it is a wig. So far I have not seen Merrill in a domestic setting, only at book launchings and arty venues like the ICA, where I once came across her in the Ladies crying about a bad review of her latest book.

She had quickly mastered my answerphone and brought several confusing messages written on a piece of paper, some of them out of date.

1 The dog walker called to take the dog out, but there was no dog.
2 Your mother's butler called. (Mr Mainwaring, who works for my mother, is not a butler.)
3 Your sister called. (I have no sister.)
4 Liza called from Los Angeles, saying *anybody* at my house call back. (Merrill did this, but of course Liza had already got the hospital's number from my ex-husband.)

Merrill seemed worried about how to get back to my house. In New York she hardly ever leaves her area, which is full of crack dealers.

At teatime Athena arrived. Athena, who is a powerful, dark woman with a face like a sheep, was brought up in a village on a Greek island surrounded by shepherds, then went to university in the States. She suggested that I go in for a rebirthing experience. She has just been rebirthed herself and said it was marvellous. I told her I did not feel it was appropriate for me at the present time. I asked Athena to help me wash my hair since I couldn't raise my right arm where the lymph glands had been taken out. We went into one of the bathrooms in the corridor and ran some water. She started acting rather roughly and ordered me to take my clothes off. It wasn't necessary to undress as I was only washing my hair, so I refused. I realized that Athena, who for years I had seen as an earth mother, might be brutal and sadistic. My new situation of vulnerability must have awakened these feelings in her, or am I imagining this?

Monday, 21 October

8.40 a.m. Suddenly I have been told I can go home. I had only just finished my breakfast of Weetabix and hot milk when the doctors came, five of them together, including the attractive one with black hair and glasses, Dr Isaacs, who seems to find me amusing. They looked briefly at my drip – at least, the overweight Scotsman, the one I don't like, did. Then they said I could go home, as my arm had drained enough. (In fact I saw on the measurement that it had not.) I will have to have the stitches under my arm out this morning.

I had become resigned to staying in hospital till my appointment in Clinic 8 tomorrow, when I was supposed to be told the important result of my operation – whether or not my lymph glands have been infected. Now I have to wait till the clinic the Tuesday after. I have to wait eight more days for my result.

10.15 a.m. The ward doctor came in and I expressed my anxiety about not knowing the results. He gave me a bleep number, in case I was desperate to phone in for my results tomorrow, but he advised me that it was better to wait for the appointment in Clinic 8, in eight days' time, when everything would be explained to me by the surgeon and the professor of oncology. He then told me I must have a back X-ray sometime this morning.

A few days ago I wanted to leave the hospital, but now I'm being told I can I don't want to. I've quickly become used to being treated like a child and having everything done for me, to the regular meals, the safe atmosphere of the ward, the friendliness of the other women, my friends coming to see me. I suddenly don't want to go.

I rang Miranda and told her the news. She said she would come and collect me at two, during her office lunch-break, and bring me home.

I told Pam, Jenny, Rosemary and Carmen that I was leaving.

At about eleven, one of the student nurses arrived to take the drain out of my armpit. She did it very well, hardly hurting me at all. I asked at the nurses' desk three times, but no one came to take the stitches out from under my arm and I couldn't go till this was done.

Then the breast nurse, whom I thought I disliked, arrived and sat on my bed. This time she seemed a bit emotional. Previously I had found her unsympathetic and tactless. Today I thought maybe she *was* sympathetic, but simply did not know how to deal with people's problems. She has a white spot under her nose that I kept staring at.

She explained that if I had chemotherapy as well as radio-therapy I'd probably have it once a month. I said my American cousins had invited me to Florida sometime this winter. She seemed to want to fit in with my plans. She advised me to go and have the X-ray for my back before having the stitches taken out.

At that moment, however, Pam summoned us to the day-room, where Rosemary was playing Strauss waltzes on her flute. She played well and looked very pretty – she always has pink cheeks and was wearing a nightdress covered with roses. We all clapped. I said that I missed my typewriter.

Rosemary said: 'I play music, you write, Pam makes clothes. What do you do Carmen?'

I thought this was a bit patronizing. I went down to another floor for my X-ray. I waited nearly an hour. It was freezing. Then I had to wait again for the results of the X-ray. I stared at a photograph of Michelangelo's *Pietà*, which was in front of me. I remembered seeing the *Pietà* for the first time in St Peter's in Rome when I was travelling round Europe on a motor bike with Nick, before he had Hodgkin's disease. We were twenty-one. It was seven years before my brother committed suicide, but I remember staring at the statue for a long time. I thought it was terribly sad, a mother holding the body of her grown-up son, who shouldn't have died before she did.

When I returned to the ward I was in rather a bad temper. My lunch, fish pie, was on a tray on my bed. It was cold. After lunch I started packing. Pam helped me. Suddenly I saw that Carmen was crying by the sink and that Rosemary had rushed across the room to comfort her. I heard Rosemary murmur, 'I'm sure there's

Someone up there.' She asked Carmen if she had Faith.

I nearly shouted out, 'You're crying because I'm leaving, Carmen!'

Then Jenny, who'd had two operations in one – when they took her lump out they discovered it was cancerous, so they removed her lymph glands at the same time – advised me to ask again about having my stitches out. I went to the nurses' desk yet again. I said that my friend was collecting me at two and I'd already been waiting four hours to have the stitches removed. A nurse then came and took them out. Jenny congratulated me on being assertive.

Then darling Miranda arrived, and efficiently started piling up my flowers and belongings. I was worried that Duncan's miniature rose would get squashed. In the corridor we met Caroline, the person who'd changed sex, in a new outfit, a light-brown three-quarter-length skirt and top. I heard Caroline tell a nurse that she'd been 'a bit sore' in the night. She still looked very excited about her new life, and I regretted that during my stay in hospital I had been too cowardly to engage her in conversation.

Evening. I am now back at home. My bedroom, which is yellow, is full of flowers. I have put up my get-well cards again.

Miranda has gone out to get several frozen meals from Marks & Spencer so I don't have to cook. I allow her to do this. It is very unlike me to be so dependent on other people. I realize I have to allow my friends to do things for me. For the first time in my life I am helpless. I can't even drive a car because my arm hurts.

At five Anna, my godmother, came round to visit me, bringing a miniature rose like Duncan's except hers is pale pink. I have not seen her much since I grew up. She has six children and umpteen grandchildren. Her husband is the brother of a duke, and she knows several members of the royal family. Respectability was what she always wanted. In some ways I envy the stability of Anna's life – it's so far removed from mine – and her priorities. She puts family life before anything else. But in reality I would find living like that too restricting.

While Anna's there, Miranda returns with the frozen food. Anna seems relieved that I have friends to help me in my hour of need. Just as she's leaving Merrill arrives, again wearing nothing but black. She brings me a present of some dried rosebuds. She has spent most of the day taking part in a radio discussion about contemporary art.

Later, Merrill's on my phone all the time, promoting her book. No one can get through to ask how I am.

Then Hal telephones from Paris and is very affectionate. He says it would be awful if I died. He simply can't imagine it. I have known him eighteen years. The year I spent in Paris, much of the time with him, was one of the happiest of my life.

Tuesday, 22 October
Day of Booker Prize dinner. Merrill brings me a cup of her favourite decaffeinated tea in bed. (She brought the tea over from New York.) I am determined to go to the Booker dinner whatever happens. Miranda has offered to drive me to Guildhall, where I'm meeting Edward.

I have a rest. Merrill wakes me at 5.30. I am wearing the yellow, purple and turquoise jacket I bought in Los Angeles. I put a black shirt on, but Merrill suggests a turquoise one instead. I don't want her to see the wounds from my operations and I tell her to go out of the room while I change the shirt.

I am on three types of painkillers, all suggested by different women. Lulu, who telephones, suggests neat whisky, Merrill presses three Advil (American aspirin) into my hand and Miranda says Solpadeine is the thing. She rushes round with two packets of Solpadeine. I stuff them in my pocket with the Advil. Lulu says she's making enquiries about a cheap cook who will provide simple meals during convalescence. I don't really want a cook.

Miranda valiantly gets me into her car and we make our way to Guildhall. As we arrive, I take the Solpadeine, mixing it with a bottle of water I've brought with me.

The first person I see, in the Ladies, is the wife of Nicholas Mosley. Why are they at the ceremony if he resigned from being a judge? Upstairs I bump into Nicholas himself, waiting for his wife. I had forgotten how much I like him. He is an immensely tall man with a stick, a gentle manner and a charming stutter. He seems delighted to see me and says how grateful he is to the other judges, including Edward, for making sure that he was paid for all the novel-reading he did even though he resigned. The others invited him to the dinner, so he decided to come.

I go into the main hall with Nicholas and his wife and after a few minutes Nicholas spots Edward for me. Edward is over-excited. He whispers that he has just fallen in love with a Turk.

As we at last file into the dining-room for the sit-down dinner, Timothy Mo, whose novel *The Redundancy of Courage* is on the short list, whispers, 'Okri's got it.' He adds that at least the staff of *Boxing News*, which he writes for, will have won money, as he had a premonition and advised them all to bet on Okri.

Edward and I are seated at a table with Kingsley Amis and one of his wives and two couples who aren't in the literary world. The men work in the City. I am next to Kingsley Amis, who gruffly talks about his stint teaching at a university in the Deep South, where he was surprised and shocked by the force of ordinary white people's prejudices against blacks.

At the end of the dinner the six writers on the short list are called up one by one to receive a specially bound copy of their own book, in a small box like a coffin. When Martin Amis goes towards the platform to receive it, his mother – it must be his mother; doesn't Kingsley Amis live in a threesome with his wife and ex-wife? – starts weeping at our table. Her husband doesn't seem at all concerned about this, perhaps because she does it often. Is she weeping because she's afraid Martin hasn't won the Booker, or because she's so proud that he's got on to the short list? Is she a person who cries very easily or is she just drunk? I'm longing to know, but can't really ask her husband.

There's a long speech by a man who has a stutter. I think he's president of the Booker. Jeremy Treglown, chairman of the judges, then makes a speech. At the end he announces the winner, Ben Okri.

I am on the table behind Ben Okri. Our backs are almost touching. Photographers leap forward and start snapping him. I stop turning round. I don't want to look vulgar, as if I'm longing to get my face on TV.

Kingsley Amis and his wife leave our table and go to join more important literary friends. There's a lot more standing around. I'm exhausted and my arm hurts. I take two of Merrill's Advil with water.

I talk to a couple Duncan calls 'Mr and Mrs Publisher', whom I've met before. They both have high positions in London publishing. Edward and I are invited to a party for two of the runners-up, Rohinton Mistry and Roddy Doyle, at the Groucho Club, starting in half an hour. At first I don't think I can survive any more standing up, but suddenly I get a second wind and can't resist going. Everyone else is being collected in chauffeur-driven cars or ordered taxis, but we have to walk what seems like miles to a bus-stop. No bus comes, and no taxis either.

At last we see a taxi and in the end arrive before everyone else. The young Irish waitress standing at the drinks table is extremely interested in Roddy Doyle and has read *The Van*. On the floor below is what has turned out to be the most important party, the one for Ben Okri, given by his publishers, Cape.

Rohinton Mistry is sitting on a chair on his own looking rather shy. Edward goes over to him and says how much he liked his novel *Such a Long Journey*. Roddy Doyle and his wife are also standing awkwardly alone. His wife tells me they came over on the ferry from Ireland today. When the publishers arrive they talk to each other more than the authors. Edward and I stay half an hour longer then go home.

23 *October*
Constable, which Pete recommended, have already read my manuscript.

Dear Elisa

I think your (untitled) novel is very clever – I can admire it objectively for its skill and wit.

But our tastes here are rather conservative and we like novels with plots and a strong story line.

It seems ironic that Serpent's Tail should urge you in our direction.

Best wishes

When Merrill brought me tea this morning she said, 'You're a very brave woman.' I replied, 'Well, what else can I do?' She said if she were me she would cry all the time. She has been in therapy fifteen years.

She then handed me a newspaper. I opened the obituary page and saw that a woman I'd met last summer with Athena had died. That evening she'd been ebullient; in fact, her gaiety had seemed so 'over the top' it had been almost abnormal. Did she already know then she had cancer? She was my age.

I rang Athena and asked her what her friend had died of. Athena's voice sounded nervous. (Was it on my account or her own?) She then admitted that it was breast cancer, and added, 'But she refused to have any surgery. She was very into alternative medicine.'

When I put down the telephone I realized for the first time just how quickly breast cancer can kill you.

I am taking a sleeping pill every night. They started doling them out at the hospital. If I don't take one I can't sleep, or I wake abruptly after a very short time. I may be more worried than I want to acknowledge.

Also, I have started experiencing the same sensations as I used to have as a child – getting 'fixed' in bed, being unable to move, just as I'm falling asleep, and feeling as if I'm about to fly. Am I having an out-of-the-body experience brought on by my condition?

When I ask Emily, she says it is fear. She remembers having the same feeling after she was in hospital following a car accident. She thought she was going to die.

I am supposed to be going to a dinner-party in south London tonight given by James, my doctor friend, and his wife. He kindly rings and says he's arranged for a woman who lives near me to give me a lift. This good Samaritan turns out to be Jay Cox, the agent whom I went to see with Lulu at the beginning of September and who rejected me as an author.

When Jay Cox arrives she says she feels ill herself and was violently sick in her own dustbin just as she was leaving her house. But she is going to drive me to south London.

Jay Cox only stayed at the dinner for twenty minutes. Then she felt so ill that she had to go. A publisher who's just been made redundant after nine years in one company gave me a lift home.

24 October

Merrill is still on the phone all the time. The telephone is like a third arm to her. I am beginning to find her determined self-promotion undermining. She has published at least three books and made some avant-garde films; I have only published occasional articles and a couple of short stories. I gave up when I had my first baby. Lucy's now ten. I should be pursuing my own career with more tenacity. I have two books on the go. One is about the sixties and a publisher has had it for eight months; the other, 'The Merry Meadow', has been rejected by three publishers. I have also heard nothing from the *Tatler* and the *Independent on Sunday* about my house-swap article.

At last Merrill's off the phone and in the bath. I ring up the *Tatler* and the man there says he likes the article, but is dithering as he is about to leave the magazine and move to a newspaper. He'll let me know by midday if they'll take it.

At twelve Merrill is on the telephone again. I lose my temper and seize it from her. She is talking to a young man from the BBC. I am rather fierce with this man and say I have just been in hospital and must use my own telephone. He rings off politely. Merrill then says that my rudeness has ruined a radio interview she was setting up. (She later admits that the young man had called to say he had flu and couldn't do the interview anyway.)

When I get through to the *Tatler* again, my young man says he still can't decide whether they have space for my article and will ring me next week.

I flop back into bed exhausted. Merrill goes off to meet a person from Channel 4 for lunch.

Merrill's reading at Waterstone's, Hampstead, tonight. We're going up there with Jacob. He is a brilliant mimic, lives in Sidcup and has a social inferiority complex. Like me, he writes short stories, and so far has not had many published. He gives up too easily. In the cab, driven by an African student, Merrill lectures us about taking ourselves more seriously. She says if editors mess us around, we should 'pull the piece'. I say I don't feel I have the authority to do this; they're pulling *my* pieces, not the other way round. Merrill replies; 'Decisive action *gives* you authority.'
Jacob then says in a la-di-da accent, 'The bottom line is, I'll pull the piece. My good woman, if you're not careful, I'll pull the piece!'
We end up shrieking with laughter.

Among the audience are bald men with ear-rings in one ear, a hard-line gay woman (who once criticized an Irish writer for writing his novel from the point of view of a woman and not a gay man), one exiled writer from Somalia, three Brazilians, two young booksellers, several aspiring writers, several published writers, at least two former members of the Socialist Workers Party, Geraldine Cooke, my friend who's been in publishing for over ten years, and many others I don't recognize.

There's wine and beer afterwards. I ask the gay woman what kind of writing she likes. Her reply is 'Marginal.'

I'm tired. My friend Gina, who writes a *Guardian* column about her naughty teenage daughter, offers to drive me home, though she lives in the opposite direction. As we're walking down Hampstead High Street to her car, I suddenly see Emily sitting in the window of a restaurant opposite a dark-faced distinguished-looking man. This gives me rather a shock. They both seem very serious. Just as I'm passing, Emily sees me. She raises her hand in an uncharacteristically dignified manner. She is not wearing her *décolleté* bodice tonight, but a black shirt with a high white collar. Gina asks; 'Who's your friend dressed as a nun?'

Friday, 25 October
I rang Emily to find out what she was doing in a Hampstead restaurant last night dressed as a nun. The handsome dark stranger is her new psychiatrist. She went to consult him on her anorexia and he immediately asked her out to dinner. She is already married to one psychiatrist. Surely she should start going out with someone who has a different profession?

Cynthia rang and I asked her if it was normal for a psychiatrist to ask his patient out to dinner on the first consultation. She said she thought it was a breach of his code of practice. Cynthia, who put her back out in a group therapy session last year, beating a cushion meant to represent her mother, has been in several different kinds of therapy. She said she had been to a psychiatrist some years ago who made a habit of getting his female patients to fall in love with him. One of his lines with her was to tell them that they would collaborate on a book together. She said to tell Emily to be very careful. Her new psychiatrist could be irresponsible.

Cynthia has asked a woman called Paquita if she would teach me shiatsu to get me to relax. She urged me to contact her as soon as possible. When I rang and told Paquita I had breast cancer, however, she sounded terrified and said she would have to think about it.

Cynthia calls again at eleven and says she's sending round a woman with a black box. This woman cured her when she had a poisoned leg and all doctors had failed. Vivian then phones and tells me a simple relaxation technique and says she thinks I should do yoga. I hate yoga. The only time I did it everyone else seemed to be able to bend their bodies into contortions that I couldn't possibly do.

Later. The woman with the black box was absolutely charming. She simply held my shoulder and hand for a few minutes and I had to hold a little box in the other hand. She left me a meditation

tape (American), which I enjoyed and found soothing, though the
effect was rather ruined by the strenuous advertising at the end of
the tape. Later Cynthia rang to tell me the lady with the black box
said I was in good health, whatever that means. I was pleased, of
course.

Afternoon. There is an odd message on my answerphone from a
woman called Falina. She can recommend a French chef, but he
has a jealous wife and she would advise me to ring him in the
mornings when his wife goes out shopping.

I can't make head or tail of this, but I then realize it is something
to do with Lulu. I call Lulu and she says that Falina is a friend of
hers. She is a deb turned healer who met the French chef recently
at her fencing class. He is looking for work and is very handsome.
I do not think I can deal with a handsome French chef at the
moment. I couldn't cope with telling him what to cook, and surely
he must be very expensive? I am already paying Maureen to look
after my children while I'm ill.

At teatime Emily phones and says she has been told about a
marvellous woman in Notting Hill Gate who massages feet.
Apparently she massages the feet of a famous pop group. Would I
like her to arrange an appointment?

Jay Cox rings up to ask how I am. She drove the whole way
back from Clapham alone the other night feeling terribly ill and as
soon as she reached her house was sick in her dustbin again. She
seems to like me better than before, but has obviously not reversed
her decision about taking me on as one of her authors. I will have
to get a dynamic new agent.

A second copy of the Bristol Programme has been dropped
through my letter-box, by a neighbour. Although a friend of Emily
went there and liked the place, I don't want to go, partly because
I'm afraid of meeting terminally ill people. I don't want to see
what might happen to me in the end.

Miranda came round at five with some lavender bath oil and
eau-de-Cologne, which she said would help me relax. Everyone

seems desperate to get me to relax. One theory is that women who get breast cancer don't look after themselves properly. We should be treating ourselves to massages, lying in baths scented with aromatic oils, cooking ourselves delicious meals and having facials. This seems self-indulgent and rather a waste of time.

Saturday, 26 October
I have decided that I like having Merrill in the house during this stressful period. It is very cosy. She's generating life around me, promoting her book, meeting new people and getting on with the business of living; I don't have to organize my own social life. She now reminds me even more of a Beatrix Potter hedgehog, with her long wiry hair sticking out all over the upper part of her body and her stubby little legs. She makes her decaffeinated tea several times a day and unless she's going out, she wears the green tartan man's shirt that she also sleeps in. Her black hair is not a wig after all. Some long strands of it were in the bath. She's offered to cook me a stew that I can eat for lunch.

Later. She couldn't get the beef so she is going to cook a tiny corn-fed chicken instead. She doesn't seem to bother much about food. When I went to her flat in New York last Easter Sunday at lunchtime, all we had was black coffee.
    Someone's told Merrill that we are five houses away from a famous London writer whose work she admires. She is very excited about this.

Sunday
I have decided to go to church again as I might die. The Famous Writer's wife, who was there that day the woman fainted, is a Catholic and I have seen her in our local Catholic church several times in the last few years.
    I told Merrill that this is her chance of meeting the Famous Writer. She can take a note round to his wife asking if she can take me to Mass. But Merrill chickens out, saying she has to catch a train to Oxford, where she's visiting an old friend, so I go round

there myself with my note.

> Dear Mrs C
> I have just had breast cancer and wonder if I could
> accompany you to church as I can't drive. I am a friend of
> Janey and Gavin.
> (Janey and Gavin are her sister and brother.)

There is a cleaning-lady scrubbing the steps of Mrs C's white pillared house; rather odd for her to be working on a Sunday. I give her the note to take in and she tells me in broken English to wait.

She comes back after a few minutes and says importantly, 'Señora C is doing pee-pee, but please come in.'

I am led into a rectangular drawing-room with a view of the garden. On the coffee-table is an expensive illustrated book anti the motor car, by chance by the husband of the woman Merrill has gone to visit in Oxford.

As I'm sitting there I see the Famous Writer through the window. He is walking up the path towards the house, and yes, he is about to enter the drawing-room where I'm sitting. When he comes in, I say defensively, 'It's all right, I'm allowed to be here.'

'I know you're allowed to be here,' he repeats, in a friendly though formal manner, then leaves the room.

I realize that the exchange that has just taken place between me and the Great Man is exactly like the dialogue that peppers his works. His characters often repeat the sentence that someone before them has said. This has a threatening, sinister effect. Just those two simple lines of dialogue between us made me feel that I was enmeshed in a scene of enormous complexity.

After a few moments the beautiful Señora C comes in, smiling and gracious. We get into her car and I make some small talk about publishers. As we arrive at the church, she suggests we separate. She will wait for me outside the newsagent's when it's over.

Some of the characters involved in the dramatic scenario a month ago are here again. The lady who rescued the woman who fainted is in the same pew in front of me. The disturbed man is also in his usual place across the aisle. The Filipino family, who I fear did nothing, are absent.

The sermons in this church are very boring. I know it's difficult to preach a good sermon. My mother, a Protestant, once said that the best sermon she had ever heard was in a Methodist chapel, given by a local milkman. (On another occasion she went to a smart Catholic church in London with my father to hear a fashionable priest, and said she was disgusted because the priest was obviously in love with Our Lady.)

The part of the Mass I like best is the Creed, in this church sung in Latin. It reminds me of my father, who sang the Creed next to me every Sunday at our hideous local church in Sussex. He had a very good voice.

Afterwards Mrs C drives me back. She tells me disarmingly how much she loves the Famous Writer. She also says to ring her next Sunday if I want to go to Mass.

Evening. My ex-husband brings the children and the dog back. They have been visiting one of his brothers in the country. My son tells me that he was stuck up a tree the whole afternoon 'pop-eyed and quivering'. When I asked where he had found this odd phrase, he said it was from a Sherlock Holmes story.

Before he goes to bed he makes a model of a little bird out of paper. Then Lucy reads him a story in bed. He seems calmer and not so skinny.

Monday
Merrill's giving a lunchtime talk at the ICA. The children are at school. Tomorrow I'll know the results of my operation, whether or not my lymph glands are infected and whether or not I'll have to have chemotherapy. I can't concentrate on my writing, except my diary, which I write every few days, sometimes every day now, since I've been ill, in longhand. I've been doing this since I was eighteen.

At the ICA I recognize an old acquaintance of mine in the

audience, a woman comedian. When I tell her I have breast cancer, she bursts out laughing. This is disconcerting. Is it because she finds it embarrassing or shocking, or is it because she's now used to treating every aspect of life as comic?

Tuesday, 29 October
Today is the day that I will know how bad my cancer is. My appointment at the hospital is at three.

Duncan took me to the B.B. King concert at the Albert Hall last night. A friend of his called Bunny met us there. We were up in the gods. You either had to stand leaning over the balcony or sit on the floor where you couldn't see the stage. I was exhausted and had to sit against a pillar much of the time. I practised my arm exercises, to prevent my arm from getting stiff. Later Bunny said that when she realized what I was doing she was impressed.

I did not tell Duncan about my life or death appointment the next day. A few days ago he went privately to have an AIDS test. (He didn't want to have it on the National Health as it would take longer to get the result.) This morning he was told he is OK. He is jubilant. It is typical of Duncan to take the test. Other gay men I know have never taken the test, out of fear. They would rather not know.

After the concert I was extremely anxious. I went home, drank some whisky and went to sleep. I dreamed I was in a strange house in the country when suddenly a fire broke out in the night. My priority was to save my own manuscripts. But they were in more of a mess than I had thought. I knocked a door down into a small room. I grabbed a green file, the one on my life in Paris. That was intact. Then I grabbed some other papers.

Then I saw a whole crowd of people descending from upstairs, including Colin Thubron, whose book I'd read in hospital in September. They had come down the staircase and were going out of the house in a conventional way. I was one step ahead of them. I jumped out of a window on to the ground floor. This was easy.

Before I jumped I saw a whole collection of china ornaments, little horses I had had when I was a child, on the window-sill. I wondered whether to scoop them up, but then decided to abandon them.

In real life these ornaments are still at my mother's house in the country, a place I don't like going to.

5 p.m. I am just back from the hospital. Miranda came with me. This is what happened. I am absolutely furious.

Miranda and I arrived at Clinic 8 at about a quarter to three. Rosemary the Vegan was there already, and so was Jenny. The waiting-room was extremely crowded, and Miranda and I had to sit outside in the corridor. Rosemary joined us. I got the feeling that Miranda was ill at ease with Rosemary, who was very friendly and sweet. She showed us a get-well card that one of her music pupils had painted for her, a picture of pink roses in a vase. She was full of plans for her own future, concerts she would go to, a holiday with her husband and daughter, a new pressure cooker. Then she went in for her appointment.

Next Pam arrived with her sister. They'd come up to London specially and her sister had taken the day off work. I noticed that Pam, who's normally so cheerful, looked tense. Meanwhile I had spotted Carmen, round the corner in the waiting-room, sitting with her husband and one of her sons.

Rosemary was the first to get her results. They were good. Her cancer had not spread to the lymph glands, so she only had to have six weeks of radiotherapy, no chemotherapy, which is supposed to be so unpleasant. She wished me and the other women luck and set off home, saying she'd keep in touch. The next one to go in was Jenny. When she came out she told us her cancer had spread to the lymph glands. As soon as Jenny told me this, I had a feeling that the same thing would happen to me.

I was next. First I had to go and wait in the dark passage outside the doctors' rooms. Miranda stayed where she was. Suddenly I saw the head of the doctor I liked, Dr Isaacs, through a glass door. He was with the doctor who had originally told me, very tactfully and kindly, that I had cancer. I hoped that my appointment would be with those two in that room. But when I was called in, by pure bad luck I got the doctor I didn't like, the Scot who was built like a rugger-player and seemed awkward with women.

I sat at his desk waiting apprehensively. Beside me, also sitting down, was a nurse. She did not address a word to me and once she yawned. The doctor was embarrassed, defensive and tactless. After he had told me that three out of twenty-two of my lymph glands were infected and I would have to have chemotherapy as well as radiotherapy, I asked where the surgeon and the professor of oncology were. He went out of the room to find out and came back saying they were at a conference in Florence. Now I would have to wait another week before knowing what my schedule of treatment was. I felt utterly confused. The nurse still said nothing to me. When I said I was annoyed that I had been misled about the surgeon and the oncologist being there today especially to talk to us, and that I had been told not to telephone last week for my results because I would see them today, he said patronizingly, 'Calm down.' He then explained that there was no way I could find out any details about the times of course of treatment until a week later at this same clinic. To propitiate me, I think, he rang the Radiotherapy Department and said I could go down there and talk to a Dr K. This would be better than nothing, he implied. When I got back to the waiting-room, Pam and her sister were still there. I told them what had happened and said it was infuriating. Pam's sister agreed and said she had taken the day off work especially to talk to the two experts. Carmen, meanwhile, had already gone in with her husband and son for her appointment.

Miranda and I then went downstairs to the Radiotherapy Department. I told Miranda I was going to write a letter of complaint. As we went downstairs, I could feel adrenalin surging through my body; I felt my anger was a kind of energy. I was determined not to be passive and let myself be treated so casually about something so important. How would the specialists like it if they had cancer?

The young woman doctor in Radiotherapy, Dr K, was very friendly, but explained that she was not in a position to give me the actual date of when I would start the course. Nevertheless, I felt calmer after I had seen her.

Later I rang Pam at home and discovered that she, like me and Jenny, had infected lymph glands. Because she is menopausal, unlike us, she is going on to Tamoxifen instead of having chemotherapy. I also rang Carmen, and her lymph glands are clear. She offered to come and look after me the day I have my first chemotherapy treatment, which was kind of her.

Wednesday, 30 October
I have written a letter to the surgeon complaining about what happened yesterday.

Dear Mr X
As you know I had a lumpectomy on 18 September, and when it was found that I had an *'in situ* carcinoma' with some invasion, I had more of the area round the lump removed and the lymph glands under the right arm removed on 11 October also by you.

The number of lymph glands involved is thought to be a fair indication of the chance of recovery; according to statistics, only 30 per cent of patients with three or more lymph glands affected survive for ten years. I was consequently amazed and disoriented to find yesterday, the 29th, that neither you nor the professor was at the clinic when I was given the disturbing news that three out of twenty-two lymph glands were affected and that I would have to have chemotherapy as well as radiotherapy.

It seemed to me that the doctor I saw was not prepared either practically or emotionally to give this information and the nurse with him said nothing to me at all. The doctor had not even been told that the professor was in Florence. When I expressed some annoyance that I would have to wait yet another week to make arrangements for Christmas for my two young children (my husband and I are separated), he told me aggressively to calm down.

To be in this situation is distressing enough without any

added confusion. I know that the other women in my ward who have chemotherapy were also upset not to see the people they expected to see.

Why were were not told that you and the professor would be in Florence? Why wasn't the breast nurse in the room when I was told the news yesterday? Why wasn't it explained to me by the doctor who, when he first broke the news that I had cancer, did it extremely well, drawing diagrams and making sure I understood what I was being told and explaining the treatment?

I look forward to seeing you and/or the professor next Tuesday.

I rang up Miranda and read her the letter. I also rang Vaneeta's friend Shabu Karimjee, who used to work at the Royal Marsden. She said I was right to complain about having to wait ten days to see the experts, especially when I then did not see them.

I phoned Pam and Jenny, urging them to complain. Although Pam admitted that her sister was furious that the crucial appointment with the experts in Clinic 8 had not taken place, I did not think that either she or Jenny would actually write.

Thursday, 31 October
I forgot my appointment with the headmistress at my daughter's school earlier today. When I called to apologize, she was very understanding and offered me one next week.

People keep ringing up to ask about the result. I have to keep telling them my lymph glands are infected. I am tired of saying this, though of course it would be worse if no one rang to find out. While I was telling Emily, Patricia, the Colombian girl who sometimes comes to clean the house, was in the kitchen. I like her tremendously. She's beautiful and small-boned and delicate, with a face like a pansy – wide, with big dark eyes – but she's physically very strong. Patricia doesn't speak much English, but I realize that she understands what I'm saying to Emily. When I put the receiver down I see that she's crying.

November

1 November

Pete Ayrton gave a party for Merrill's book. I went up there alone in one of the Shepherd's Bush minicabs. It cost over eight pounds. I'm still not driving and I don't want to walk alone after dark or travel alone on the tube. In fact, I've never felt so vulnerable in my life.

Jacob was also at the party. The night before, after going to a meeting for disadvantaged gay men, he fell over a post at Waterloo Station on his way to catch the last train to Sidcup. He hurt his leg quite badly and is going to sue Lambeth Council for leaving the post exposed. A pregnant woman or an old lady could have fallen over it.

Well-meaning people keep coming to tell me that among the guests is a woman who also has cancer and is wearing a machine strapped to her body. This machine is administering regular doses of chemotherapy to her. Apparently she is tall and blonde. There are two very tall blonde women, one of whom, I think, is an ex-model.

I wish the woman with cancer wasn't here. I don't want to meet someone else with cancer at a party. I'd rather forget about the whole thing.

By ten I'm sitting on the staircase ready to leave. My arm hurts. Pete telephones for a minicab. Suddenly I see the journalist who wrote the alarming article my ex-husband brought into the hospital. She does not approach me, though I'm sure she knows who I am. Probably I remind her of her own operation, which she'd rather forget. I expect she's more frightened than she admitted.

Then the party gets better and I forget about going home. A playwright whom Jacob has nicknamed Mr Goat is here, and so's

Rose, the comedienne who burst out laughing at the ICA when I told her I had breast cancer. There's my friend Geraldine Cooke, who says she wants to teach me the Alexander technique to help me relax, and M, who told me about the short-story anthology.

It's an hour later and Pete is now telephoning for more cabs for other people. Why didn't mine arrive?

One of the tall blonde women is now also waiting to go. Merrill and Jacob have decided to leave too.

The doorbell rings and several of us rush to answer it. Two minicabs are waiting, one driven by a Sikh with a turban. Jacob and Merrill and I clamber into it, then someone shouts that the blonde woman also wants to come in our cab. (I'm still not sure if she is the woman with cancer.) A black cab pulls up; the driver gets out and demands, 'Which of you is Eliza?'

No one answers until the blonde woman points to our cab and denounces me.

The driver marches over and sticks his head through the back window. 'One of you is definitely Eliza. You ordered a cab. Now you get out and come with me.'

I say firmly, 'I am *not* Eliza!' I wind up the window and shout to the Sikh, 'Drive on!'

He reverses quickly out of Pete's cul-de-sac and we set off home laughing. Out of the back window I see the blonde woman get into his cab with some other guests.

2 November
I received in the post an appointment for the Breast Clinic at St Charles's Hospital. It is next week. This would have been seven weeks after I first saw the GP with the lump. I have written asking if this is the normal waiting time for women who can't afford to pay for a mammogram.

Every night I hear odd banging noises coming from the house next door. Can the woman who lives there be employing night builders at a cheaper rate? She once took a year to pay us fifty pounds for a party wall.

3 November

Ali Forbes has a long-winded letter in the *Spectator* about Diana
Cooper's nicknames. (He is a permanently tanned journalist and
writer who lives mainly in Switzerland. He once rented the cottage
Nicholas Mosley rents now and was seen hoovering it with no
clothes on.)

'Nancy's sister Diana (*ci-devant* Guinness, now the Widow
Mosley) had been "Honks" long before Waugh had even met the
other Diana . . . So that Baby became Honks Cooper to distinguish
her from the genuine article, the late Lord Head even going so far
at one time as to call Honks any woman who happened to have
been christened Diana . . .'

I have written a two-sentence letter in reply to this. I have
become like a retired colonel, firing off letters, hitting out to get rid
of my aggression. Now I understand why retired people so often
write letters to newspapers. They probably feel impotent and
ignored much of the time. If they get into print they're validated,
made real again.

4 November

I had lunch with Mary Killen, the *Spectator*'s agony aunt, at a club
in Soho to which we both belong. I joined it when I first separated
from my husband, two years ago. Edward and Jacob are also
members. On the form that I had to fill in to introduce Jacob to the
club, I wrote: 'He wants to meet more people in central London.'
Ever since I met Jacob ten years ago he has been apologizing for
living in Sidcup. I fear he will probably end up dying there.

When I arrived at the club Mary was already there. Her hair was
tied back; normally it hangs in a thick, loose mane, which makes
her look like an attractive Shetland pony.

Mary asked me some details about when I'd first discovered the
lump and what treatment I was having, then told me that six girls
in the offices of the *Tatler*, where she used to work, had had
cervical cancer in the last eighteen months. Having read the house-
swap article I'd sent her, she thinks I should write a diary covering
a year or a six-month period; my humour is 'cumulative' and

would best fit this form. If I started the diary with having breast cancer, other women who had it would be encouraged by seeing I had survived.

Let's hope I do.

She then said that there was some doubt about the woman journalist who'd written the article about her mastectomy that had terrified me in hospital. Mary's now heard through the grapevine that this woman's breast was so big that it wouldn't fit on to the mammograph. Apparently she'd had it removed just to be sure and may not have had cancer at all.

5 November

Bonfire Night, my ex-husband's birthday, and the appointment at Clinic 8.

At about 2.30 Miranda and I go off in her car to the appointment with the specialists we were all supposed to see this time last week. I love being driven. I always seem to end up with people who can't drive or have motor bikes. My ex-husband couldn't drive either when I met him. I suppose I associate too much with literary types. In my experience non-drivers often disrupt social occasions by making others drive them to stations to get the last bus or train. They even seem to manage to get lifts home to remote areas of London from good-natured people going out of their way.

Miranda's car is smooth and luxurious. She spontaneously puts a handful of one-pound coins from her own purse into the meter in the hospital car park. This generosity means a lot to me. I do not tell her this, however, as I am too inhibited.

Miranda and I wait ages in the clinic waiting-room. A healthy-looking young man arrives with a squash racket in a bag. Miranda wonders if he has breast cancer. Jenny and Pam are here again as well. Jenny is alone as usual; I don't know anything about her life, unlike Pam's.

When Jenny comes out from her appointment she says she has been asked to be part of a trial for a new chemotherapy drug. She seems bewildered by this yet she was asked to decide in a couple of minutes.

When Pam comes out she confirms that she has been put on Tamoxifen. She's going to ask her employers if she can take some time off work. Jenny, however, who's younger, wants to go on working as much as possible.

I am the very last in the whole clinic. Miranda whispers that this is because of my letter; I am probably going to get full attention. This time we are determined that she will come in with me, to ask questions I forget to ask myself.

In the room there is the surgeon, the professor of oncology, a smiling black nurse (not the one who yawned last week while I was being told my lymph glands were infected) and the breast nurse, looking rather nervous. (My letter, in which she is mentioned, is out on a table.)

Everyone is very apologetic. The motherly nurse takes me to get weighed and Miranda and I then sit down and have a discussion with the doctors. I make notes of the chemotherapy drugs I will be given, and the date of my first chemotherapy, which is tomorrow.

I will have two doses of chemotherapy this month, then six weeks of radiotherapy, then chemotherapy for five more months, twice a month, starting in January and ending in May. The drugs combination I will be on is CMF. I am not sure what this means, though the professor tells me the name of each drug and I meticulously write down the long, unknown words. I am dazed by all the things I have to remember; in the past couple of weeks I have scribbled words and phrases haphazardly all over the last two pages of the notebook that I also use as a diary. I write some more now: 'Two injections every month. Chemo. CMF standard. This Friday (crossed out) Wednesday. 3-week break from . . . 2 injections – one course. Radiotherapy 6 weeks. Therefore the next lot of chemo would be delayed. Medical Oncology near X-ray near lifts. 9.30. Say they start 20th. Chemo. A total of 5 months after radiotherapy.' On the same page I have written: 'Merrill's flight to Paris: BA 308 11.15 a.m. Pam 0402 458643. Jenny 995 4355. Priest. Book review.' At the top of one page are the words from Henry Whittaker's letter that I read in my hospital file last month: 'Her domestic situation is somewhat fluid.'

After the discussion is over Miranda leans forward and says to the doctors, 'Please tell her that her tumour is very small.' It turns out that no one thought to tell me that the tumour is only 1.2 centimetres. Is there hope for me, then?

As we go off down the corridor to the Radiotherapy Department, Miranda says very firmly, 'Elisa, this is not about death. The prognosis for breast cancer is very good. All this will be over in less than a year.'

The Radiotherapy Department is strangely silent. Occasionally you hear the low buzzing of a machine. There are frightening notices everywhere, warnings about not going into rooms where high doses of radiotherapy are given. I am interviewed by a very sweet young woman doctor with pale-red hair, Dr W. Now at last I am given some sort of timetable for the course of my radiotherapy treatment. My first dose (radiation applied to the breast and surrounding area, to kill any possible remaining cancerous cells) will be on 18 November. I will then have it every day except weekends for six weeks, finishing just before Christmas.

The fact that I now have a schedule of treatment is reassuring. Any rumours of radiation being harmful I push to the back of my mind. A friend of Emily, because she had MS or ME – I'm not sure which – wasn't allowed to have radiotherapy when she had breast cancer. She went on a radical diet of pulses and is now, two years later, all right. One of Emily's sisters, who's rather New Age, told Emily I shouldn't have chemotherapy because she didn't approve of chemicals being pumped into one's body. Emily retorted, 'She has young children. Of course she must do everything possible. I bet you would.'

Later the children and I attend our street's annual bonfire party in the communal garden near our house. I hear someone's husband announce that Robert Maxwell's body has been found at sea.

Mrs B, who lives next door where the banging comes from, is standing by the bonfire with her little girl. I ask Mrs B whether she has builders working at night. Without hesitation she replies, 'Oh, that's my daughter; she's a head-banger. It's supposed to be the sign of a disturbed child. I'm terribly sorry. But now that you know what it is, it won't worry you so much.'

But it does worry me. I'm very concerned about the child and wonder why it's banging its head.

Emily also comes to the fireworks party, at my invitation. My ex-husband arrives at the end to take the children out for a pizza. (It s his birthday and he hates Bonfire Night. All his life he's been upstaged by Guy Fawkes.) I thought Emily was supposed to be having supper alone with me, but suddenly I see her running down the hill shouting to my ex-husband that she wants a lift to Kensington High Street. Emily is another of my friends who doesn't drive; at least, she does, but normally she's off the road for driving while drunk, then for driving when she's banned. Also, her cars usually have a ridiculous impediment, such as a front safety-belt that jams when you try to undo it.

There's a message on my answerphone from Julian, who lives in the Far East and is married to a Japanese woman. I went out with him a few times last summer. Julian spends several months of the year alone in London as his wife doesn't like it here. Last summer he said he wouldn't be coming back to London until Christmas. He has invited me out to dinner tonight. I ring back and accept, telling him I have had breast cancer. He sounds shocked, as well he might be. Halfway through the meal I can't finish my pasta and suddenly can hardly speak. Julian, who's very sensitive, notices my exhaustion and drives me home.

I then play a new message, from my American cousin Dita, saying I must come to stay with her and her mother for Christmas in Florida. This seems so remote to me, and so desirable. I love the sun. But I won't be able to go. I can't leave my children, particularly at Christmas.

6 November

This morning Merrill left for Paris, where she will give another reading of her book and have a party at Jim Haynes's studio. She will fly from there straight back to New York. At the front door she hugged me and put a fifty-dollar bill into my hand, for her telephone calls. She explained 'It's in dollars, to make sure you come back to America.'

I would have liked to have gone with her – I've told Hal and his wife, P, to go to the reading and the party – but today I have my first injection of chemotherapy.

Chemotherapy. The oncology ward is like this: there are six beds in a line; the predominant colour in the room is grey. There is one window at one end, which doesn't give much light. There is a purple plant on a table, near two large tins of biscuits. (You are offered these as you're lying there, to stave off hunger and sickness; ex-patients bring them in as presents.) In a tiny room off this main room the medicines are prepared. There are two nurses, Bridie and Nurse Blair, and one assistant, Rosie, who, because of her voice and her name, reminds me of the maid in *Upstairs, Downstairs*. These women are all extremely kind. For Bridie, particularly, I already have enormous respect.

The most off-putting thing of all is seeing the other patients on drips; it makes me want to vomit. At least I don't have to be on a drip; my chemotherapy drugs are administered by injection. It isn't the idea of the needle that revolts me, but the idea of poison going into my body, and the association of this with cancer. When I see the other patients lying there, I don't want to talk to them. Like an animal with another animal who's sick, I shy away. I hate looking at their bald heads. Will I also go bald? (The professor of oncology said that with my drug combination I easily might not.)

My attitude to these patients is quite different from my attitude to the women I was in the ward with a few weeks ago when I had my lymph glands out. Normally I'm very friendly. But now it's as though by not talking to these other cancer patients I am telling myself I am not as ill as they are.

I arrived at the hospital at ten and was surprised to see Emily in the lobby. I assumed that she had come spontaneously to be with me for my first injection, but it turns out that her mother, who was a friend of Robert Maxwell – she met him during the war – collapsed with shock when she heard the news of his death and is lying upstairs in the ward I was in last month. She already had a bad heart and now something has gone wrong with her pacemaker. She is refusing to wear any clothes and has already drunk several bottles of wine that her new boyfriend, whom she met at an AA meeting, brought in for her last night. Emily is distraught, but is trying to appear calm. Ironically, for her to come and sit with me in the oncology ward for a few minutes is a welcome relief from trying to deal with her mother, who apparently has been insulting the nurses and demanding yet more alcohol. Emily says she'll go to the hospital shop and buy all the papers so we can read about Robert Maxwell.

The waiting-room, in an area with no windows, has a newspaper cutting on a board about Bernie going skiing. Bernie, a man with cancer, has tried to overcome it by leading an active life. To see this notice about Bernie going skiing in the middle of his chemotherapy treatment is absolutely infuriating. It is like Emily's sister, who, meaning to be kind, told me about a woman in Oxfordshire who went hunting every time she had chemotherapy. This kind of thing simply makes one feel inadequate. Beside the notice about Bernie is a huge container full of water with paper cups beside it.

Emily returns with several newspapers. Bridie, the Irish nurse, asks me to go into the ward and lie down on one of the beds. Emily sits on a chair beside me.

Knitted toys are dotted about the room – a golliwog, a doll with yellow hair and even a doll carrying its own drip, to simulate some of the patients. I suppose an ex-patient has made and contributed this macabre item. On the bed beside me a middle-aged Indian man, rather gaunt, lies motionless, a drip in his arm.

I would rather they didn't have toys in what seems like a crazy attempt to cheer us up. It's the same thing as calling the department oncology instead of cancer, and having it stuck behind the hospital lifts near Accident and Emergency, so that the first time you try to find the department you can't; you spend ages looking for the signs.

But what is the alternative? Should they have the word 'cancer' stuck up everywhere here, as they do in Clinic 8? Would this be more honest? Would all our secret fears of never recovering, despite the chemotherapy, be better out in the open? Should there be loud jazz playing in the ward, instead of this ghastly silence? Should the place be made like the cabin of an aeroplane, with videos on all the time, showing funny films? Should they bring in comics to do sketches about cancer, so we, the patients, could 'bite the bullet', 'grasp the nettle' and perhaps feel better?

I remember how before I had my first baby I asked a few women what childbirth was like. One person, Elizabeth, an ex-girlfriend of my husband, said, 'It hurts like hell.' As soon as she said that, I was immensely reassured, because I knew she must be speaking the truth.

Wouldn't it be better if someone said to us out loud, 'Yes, it's true that some cancer patients never recover. The reason for this silence and the fear that you see in the eyes of someone like Athena, who has not been in touch since she came to the hospital, is simply the fear of death. Everybody is afraid to die.'

Now Emily and I spread the newspapers out on the beds. In the *Daily Mail* is a short piece on Maxwell entitled 'He was always one for the grand gesture'. A. Alvarez, 'who has devoted his life to studying suicide', is quoted: 'Suicide is extremely rare for business tycoons and even rarer at sea. It is their nature that they are just not that type. Not if they have made the money themselves. If the person inherits money, it is different. Some crazed sprig of the aristocracy is much more vulnerable. The tycoon is so set on making money he doesn't have time for regret.' Emily points out that in the Depression in America hundreds of self-made tycoons flung themselves off skyscrapers.

It seems that I will have to wait ages for my injection since the consent form wasn't given me to sign the day before as it should have been. These new forms of consent are part of the Patients' Rights Charter, which came into effect only a couple of weeks ago. The charter is meant to make patients' lives easier.

Hours pass and I have still not had my injection. Emily has gone back upstairs to see her mother. I am fed up. I am in a novel by

Solzhenitsyn. I am in a psychiatric prison waiting to be tortured. They are making me wait as long as possible. Despite the sweetness of the three nurses, this small grey room is intolerably grim. Bridie's already rung upstairs several times to try to get the consent form sent down. This is in between making up the doses for other patients and giving them injections. She seems to have far more combined responsibilities than a doctor, yet she remains incredibly calm.

At 1.30 a young woman with blonde curls and a cockney accent bounds into the room, as perky as if she's about to go dancing. I can't understand why she's so lively. She lies down on the bed next to me to have her injection. She overhears Bridie apologizing to me for the long wait, and, realizing I must be hungry, she kindly offers me her second pork pie out of a Marks & Spencer pack. I accept it gratefully, though normally I loathe pork pies.

At two o'clock Emily returns after battling with her mother, who is now trying to bribe the nurses to bring her the ward telephone so she can call Maxwell's widow. She cut her hand on one of her empty wine bottles when she got up to try to find a phone – Emily says she's paralytically drunk – and will have to have several stitches. She is refusing to have a general anaesthetic. The nurses have told Emily that she won't be able to have the operation until the evening; by that time maybe she will be in such pain that she will agree to the anaesthetic.

The consent form finally arrives. I have been here four hours. By this time I have read all the papers on Maxwell and feel I know so much about him he could be my chosen subject on *Mastermind.* I've read about him being brought up as a boy in a village in Czechoslovakia, being captured by the Germans, escaping to fight with the Allies, winning a Military Cross in 1945 and so on. No one knows, however, whether he committed suicide or was pushed off the yacht.

Emily stays with me while I have the injection. The combination of drugs I am on is CMF – Cyclophosphamide, Methotrexate and Fluorouracil. I have to take the Cyclophosphamide (small white pills) by mouth. Bridie gives it to me with a glass of water. She

then gives me the injection, having first shot a saline solution into
my arm. I'm not sure why – to test the veins, I think. Bridie has
pale-blue eyes and a saintly manner, The volunteer who's
normally here is ill herself, so Bridie has to let the ward telephone
ring unanswered while she's giving me my injection. Emily sits
and watches from her chair. She says I'm terribly brave as I didn't
flinch when the needle went in, but Rosie, who's attending to a
patient on another bed, says, 'You looked very worried.'

So far I feel physically normal, but mentally unreal. Bridie tells
me to relax for a few minutes until I get off the bed. In the bed two
away from mine the curtains are closed and I can hear the woman
in there informing her male companion that she comes from
Rotherhithe. She tells him proudly that she comes from six
generations of a seafaring family. I love the sea – my father was a
sailor – but in boats I often get seasick. I have been given anti-
sickness pills now, called Dexamethasone. I have to take them
every four hours.

The first time you have chemotherapy you have to stay
overnight in hospital, to see how you react. Emily, carrying my
overnight bag, escorts me along several passages and into the lift
to Ward 6 North. I don't like this ward nearly as much as 8 South,
the one I was in a few weeks earlier, but unfortunately there are no
free beds there today.

In 6 North the patients seem much iller than the women I was
with in 8 South. I hate the word 'north'. It reminds me of all the
things I most dislike: extreme cold, grey streets in Scottish towns,
winter and even death.

Emily leaves, after rushing downstairs to get me a bunch of
flowers from the hospital shop.

I am on my own. In the bed opposite me is a gaunt pretty
woman of about forty-five, wearing a lilac dressing-gown and a
brown towel on her head. I assume she's very ill, she looks so thin
and pale, and that the towel is part of her treatment. Does she
perhaps have cancer of the head? But no. In a soft, slightly
southern American accent she explains that she's been wearing
this towel for twelve days as there's a permanent draught from the

window next to her and the handle to close the windows is lost. She is in here because she had a pregnancy that went wrong and left a cancerous residue in the womb. There are all sorts of pills beside her bed.

In the bed next to me is an old lady called Maggie with very little hair. She is reading the *Sun* and does not respond to my overtures.

In the fourth and last bed is an emaciated woman with green hair, cut very short, in a scarlet dressing-gown. She is being visited by an emaciated man, tall with a shaggy beard. I assume, because of their extreme thinness, that they are junkies, but I could be completely wrong.

After a while the oncology nurse, Di, arrives. A friendly girl, Di has a lisp and red hair neatly tied in a pony-tail with a dark-green velvet ribbon. She is the sort of girl I would normally expect to be efficiently cooking meals for twenty people in a shooting lodge or ski chalet. I like her because she is genuinely cheerful and, as my grandmother would have said, 'means well'. Today Di uses a long word I haven't heard before – 'prophylactically'. By this she means that my chemotherapy is a preventative (to stop further cancer cells developing) rather than a cure. When I ask her to explain the differences between my own treatment and Jenny's, Di replies that there is very little difference, and that the trial drug Jenny is on will probably be accepted everywhere in a few months. Then she says, 'Your chances of survival are greater if you take this course.'

The word 'survival' gives me a terrible shock. I feel as if I am in one of those rockets that used to be at Battersea Fun Fair, strapped in by just a belt; while it is turning upside down, I very nearly fall out.

After a few minutes, though, I am indignant. Survive, me? For Heaven's sake! Yes, I damned well am going to survive. I'm not going to be one of those women who die after five years despite the treatment. I'm certainly not going to die. (I hope.)

I decide to take a break and visit Emily's mother, Joan, in the ward upstairs. I do not feel sick, but rather manic instead.

Joan is not in the six-bed ward I was in last month, but in a tiny room on her own up the corridor. She appears to have no clothes on under her sheet and is smoking. Her shock of grey hair is unbrushed; she is wearing no make-up, her eyes are sparkling unnaturally and she looks overwrought. In her high, girlish, over-precise voice – she pronounces 'handbag' as 'hendbeg' – she asks me to see if she has any more cigarettes. She has obviously been smoking very heavily – there are three full ashtrays by her bed – and the room is suffocating. When I offer to open the window, however, she says the nurses have lost the handle that opens every window in that wing. (Has this happened on every floor of the hospital?) Suddenly Emily's mother grasps my hand and a few tears fall from her eyes. She says, she's very worried she has cut her hand so badly she won't be able to play the piano. (She used to be a concert pianist.) She then admits she hasn't played for eight years.

Still grasping my hand, Joan asks, 'How long do you think it would take to fly to Jerusalem?'. She is planning to attend Maxwell's funeral, which is in three days. I say I think it takes about four hours. I have only ever flown to Greece, never to Israel.

While we're discussing this, one of my favourite nurses, Jackie, a slim girl with a blonde plait, comes in. She was very kind to me when I was worried about whether my lymph glands were infected.

Jackie tries to argue gently with Emily's mother, saying she should have the general anaesthetic as it is nearly time for her operation. Joan starts yelling hysterically that she can't have a general anaesthetic as she might never wake up. 'I have a lot more concerts to perform and I don't want to die before my time!'

I hope Jackie doesn't think I'm a close friend of Emily's mother. Her behaviour is a bit embarrassing.

I offer to make some telephone calls for Joan with my phonecard; to Emily, who has now gone home for some sleep, no doubt, to Joan's son, David, or to her GP, Dr Toms, who was supposed to be coming between four and five. It is now 5.30.

'Where the hell is the bloody little man?' shouts Emily's mother.

'He's probably stuck in traffic,' says Jackie calmly. She goes out and returns a few minutes later, saying that it's all right, Joan has now been given permission by the doctor in charge to have just a local anaesthetic. The operation will take place in about an hour.

Joan's reply to this is 'Good. Will it be a talkative and witty surgeon?'

At this moment David, who works in the City, walks in, a red carnation in his buttonhole. 'Goodness, Mother, what have you been doing?'

Then another man arrives in Joan's room, an unshaven middle-aged man in a tattered coat with a strong Scottish accent. Joan introduces him to us as Fergie. I realize that this is the man Emily referred to as her mother's latest boyfriend.

'Have you brought me any booze?' Joan asks him.

Leaving the three of them together, I tell Joan I'll visit her again the following morning and go back to my own ward.

The American woman in the bed opposite is being visited by an elderly man and a small boy. She is still wearing a towel on her head. The woman in the scarlet dressing-gown is asleep.

Still unable to relax, I decide to switch on the television news to see if there's anything more about Robert Maxwell. I ask Maggie, the old lady in the bed beside me, if she minds the TV being switched on. Her reply is 'Bring on the dancing girls!' She then asks, 'Do you do a lot of riding here?'

'Yes,' I answer politely.

The newsreader talks about whether Robert Maxwell slipped on the deck of his yacht or was pushed, and whether or not the Mossad were involved.

Later I watch a marvellous documentary about the First World War, based on the letters a young French soldier wrote from the Front to his young wife in Paris. The film is made by Lubtchansky, whose father wrote the letters, before returning safely to his wife.

'The English soldiers go pounding through the rain, oblivious to it all.'

Among those reminiscing is one old lady: 'I never saw my Billy again. He used to give me jam.' Tears run down her cheeks.

I remember that I, like the film-maker, have a whole chest of love-letters, written by my grandfather to my grandmother; he, though, never came back from France. Seeing this old lady, who, like my grandmother, lost her chance of happiness so young, I start to cry myself.

7 November
In the morning we have to go to the day-room to get our own breakfast. I have Corn Flakes. When I get back, Maggie is sitting beside her bed reading today's copy of the *Sun*.

I am still possessed with a manic energy. After breakfast I go up to the next floor, in my night clothes, to visit Joan. She is in the same small room and her mental condition seems to be worse, but the operation on her hand was successful. She is again wearing no clothes and is now shouting and swearing at the nurses, who have fed-up expressions.

Five newspapers are spread out on Joan's bed, all opened at pages showing the latest news about Robert Maxwell. But one paper, which Joan wants, is missing; the *Sun*. Joan begs me now to go and get her a copy, saying that she is desperate to find out what the rival Murdoch paper says about Maxwell.

I offer to go downstairs and ask Maggie if I can borrow hers. I notice that I am extremely revved up. In a way I like this. All the excitement about Joan stops me from worrying about my own situation.

Coming back with the borrowed newspaper to Joan's floor, I meet Paolo, in the smoking area outside the lifts. I also recognize the woman who was always sitting with Caroline who changed sex. She's smoking a cigarette and wearing day clothes – a green shirt and jeans.

Paolo, looking rather distinguished with his black hair and beard, is having a cigarette before he goes in to visit his mother-in-law. 'Darling, you are very manic.' He tells me I must go and see a therapist during this traumatic time. He will arrange it for me through his contacts.

We then both go in to see Joan. I am touched by Paolo's compassion for this distraught woman. He takes her in his arms,

calling her, as he did me, 'darling'. I decide to leave them alone in
these moments of intimacy and take a little walk along the
corridor. I peep into the ward where I was with Pam, Jenny,
Rosemary and Carmen and where much of the time, strangely, I
was so happy.

Now five other women are in there, waiting to have their breast
lumps or lymph glands taken out. Suddenly we all seem like
products in a factory, objects about to be processed, or things
containing a flaw waiting to have the faulty part removed. No
wonder, with so many women in here every week for the same
operations, the doctors begin to treat this disease, this growth,
from which you can die, as so ordinary.

I go on up the corridor and glance again at the area where
Caroline's friend is still sitting smoking. I nearly ask how Caroline
is getting on as a woman, but at that moment Paolo returns from
visiting his mother-in-law. He kisses me goodbye and I go back to
Joan's room on my own, carrying the copy of the *Sun*, which she
grabs from me. She skims through the articles on Maxwell, then
says decisively in her high voice, 'Get me the hospital telephone!
I'm going to do something that will amuse you!'

I go along to the day-room and wheel back the telephone on its
trolley.

Joan dials a number from memory, asking politely, but with
considerable authority, if she can speak to either one of two female
journalists. She is immediately put through to one of them.

'I am ringing up to complain about this morning's article you
wrote in the *Sun* about Robert Maxwell. How dare you write this
about a dead man who can't defend himself? You scum-bag, how
would you feel if you got a broom up your bottom or a red hot
poker up . . .'

I'm shocked by the number of four-letter words Joan uses and
wish I hadn't brought her the newspaper or the telephone. I also
have the feeling that she has done this kind of thing before. I have
no control over her, however, and watch her passively while she
spews out expletives. Luckily at that moment Emily, followed by
Jackie, the blonde nurse, walks in.

'I think your mother could be prosecuted for making threats with violence,' I tell Emily. Jackie says that the doctors are now coming on their rounds, so all visitors must leave.

Back in my own ward I talk to the American lady. The elderly man who was visiting her last night was her husband, and the little boy was her son. She had him, her first baby, aged forty-five. She still looks extremely ill and I wonder if she's going to die. She comes from an area near Baltimore where Lilah, who is my American godmother and one of my mother's oldest friends, lives. My mother nearly married Lilah's brother Philip. She spent a great deal of time in America – she went to school there and had to salute the American flag every morning at prayers – and she returned there often as a young woman. She loved it.

At midday, after the doctors have seen me, Miranda comes and drives me home. I am carrying a bag full of pills – anti-sickness pills (Dexamethasone), my oral drug (Cyclophosphamide) and a bottle of sleeping pills. I have written instructions on when to take the Cyclophosphamide and the anti-sickness drug.

When I get home I realize I have left by my bed the beautiful flowers that Emily bought me yesterday. I hope the woman with the towel on her head enjoys them.

8 November

I am woken very early by my son running about in the room over my head. Ever since he was born he's woken early. I can't seem to enforce any penalties to stop him. He doesn't like toys and doesn't have the same pleasures as most other children. Instead he has obsessions, like watching the same video, *The Snowman* or *Robin Hood*, again and again, and repeatedly drawing the same set of pictures, often characters from these films.

Today, while my son's at school, his therapist rings up and tells me that Joseph is suffering from self-destructive urges and that I must hide all my pills in case he tries to swallow them. I put them on the highest shelf of my cupboard. This new anxiety about my son is the last straw.

I have been having outbreaks of sweat since I came home

yesterday. I have been told to drink as much water as possible. I sent Maureen out to buy six bottles of Evian, and have them now beside my bed.

Paquita, the Spanish lady Cynthia recommended to do shiatsu, rang up and said she had thought about my problem and decided she could help me. She could come and see me today.

Paquita, who arrived on a bicycle, is a dignified young woman with long brown hair and a pale face. She comes from Avila, a walled town in Spain where I went with my mother when I was seven.

First she made me lie down on the bed and tried a few movements of shiatsu, hitting me with sharp little strokes. As I lay there I had the impression of a golden light coming over me. But then Paquita said I was too tense for the shiatsu to work. She said she would like to cook healthy food for me instead. She had worked for a long time in a health-food restaurant in Dublin.

Paquita, like everyone else, said it was very important for me to relax. (I told her I had to finish a short story by Monday and she seemed to think this was crazy. She said I was far too wound up and should calm down. I did not tell her I was tempted to go to a reading at the South Bank Centre tonight.)

We arranged that she should return on Monday and prepare healthy food for my lunch, with enough over to last for several more meals.

Friday

The children have gone away for the weekend with my ex-husband to the house in Sussex. Lucy begged to see her pony. I must now write the short story for the anthology *God*. I know exactly what I want to write.

I sit at the big desk in my daughter's room, among photos of herself in school uniform, her pony and the dog, a chart of an imaginary riding-school with comments on each child rider and letters from her cousins at boarding-school.

I'm going to write about Jill, who died last February. I went to stay with her in the States in December 1989, just before she found she had a second recurrence of cancer, and I also visited her there again twice before she died.

I had known Jill for seventeen years. Her death was the first occasion on which I had felt real grief, or allowed myself to feel it. I'm not sure why this was. Was it because she was the first of my friends to die? She was my age, my contemporary. Or was it simply that she had touched my heart?

Before, I had pretended not to mind all the deaths that had occurred in my family. At my brother's funeral I remember laughing and joking with my cousins.

As I drove away from Jill's grave in Connecticut with Liza, who'd flown from California for the funeral, I said to her, 'We're grown-up. There's no one to look after us.'

When I got back to London three days later I lay shivering in bed, not with cold, but with shock. Each day, for weeks after Jill's death, I would wake up with a terrible pain in my chest. I realized this must be what was meant by 'heartache'. I kept having sudden overwhelming urges to lie down, at odd times of day, sometimes even while walking in the street.

All this was only nine months ago.

Then in August my mother fell over.

I have been writing the short story all evening. I used some experiences from my own childhood, such as visiting a church in Avila with my mother and having to put my hand down a hole to touch a relic.

In my story I've also written about R, a man I was in love with who looked like my brother. I now recognize that this man, who's so handsome and so like my brother, is extremely weak. I suppose I would still find him attractive, but I never see him. I don't know where he is.

After leaving all his possessions at the house in Sussex for eight months he never got in touch with me. He eventually sent a removal van to collect them. He came for meals with me and my husband regularly for a whole summer, autumn and part of the winter, but since I separated from my husband in September 1989 he has refused even to have a drink with me. The fact that he looks like my brother, whom I loved so much and who committed suicide, makes this abandonment worse.

Saturday
I woke up a few times in the night. Each time my sheets were soaked and I had to change them. I rang up Liz Whipp, my doctor friend, and she said to experience these hot flushes after chemotherapy was normal.

I did some more work on the short story and at about 11.30 I finished it.

I then walked to the local photocopying shop, five minutes away. I felt extremely frail, but my mind was buzzing. While I was in there the ex-wife of R, the man I had put in the story, walked in. She asked about my health. Her own leg was in plaster; she said she had broken it falling down a staircase when she had visited her ex-husband in a dilapidated cottage in Wales during the half-term. I think she guessed that I was curious to know where he was, so she told me. He is in Snowdonia, trying to sort his life out, I suppose. She said he was probably soon going to South America to make a film. I then posted the story and went home.

I realized that if she knew I had breast cancer, then so did he. He couldn't even be bothered to send me a note saying he was sorry I was ill. Even that woman who I had thought disliked me had sent me a get-well card.

Julian rang up later and asked if I wanted to go round and have supper. I said I was too tired. Maureen was upstairs watching a video. I asked her if she would mind putting one of the frozen foods that Miranda had brought me into the oven. I then collapsed into bed.

Sunday
My daughter phoned several times. She had been to a little horse show in the village in Sussex and fallen off three times. She said

people clapped when she got on again for the third time. She is very brave.

I also talked to my son. His voice sounded remote, as though he were speaking from a spirit world. He asked if I believed in Heaven. He said, 'I'm a very scared child.'

Athena has invited me to a party, and I have asked Julian to escort me. He came to collect me in his smart car at 7.30. He refused a drink, but helped me change a light-bulb. I told him of the documentary I'd seen on the hospital television about the First World War and how I had a whole crate of love-letters belonging to my grandmother and my mother's father. I said it was awful that my grandfather had not even been killed in action but on leave: the shafts of a farm cart, hit by the car his companion was driving, went through his body. (Lucy had found a newspaper cutting about this last summer in an old photo album and shown it to me.) Julian agreed that my grandmother had probably suffered even more through his not being killed in action.

We then drove to Ealing, where Athena lives. We were early; only three other people had arrived, one of whom was an elderly Austrian princess.

Athena seemed ill at ease with me. She was behaving like a star at her own party. She was wearing a bright, spotted dress, low-cut at the front and back.

Piles of delicious-looking Greek food, made by her, were arrayed on a table. After we had been there ten minutes a guest arrived bearing an oil-painting of Athena, which he then hung up in a prominent place in the room, so that anyone entering could see it at once. People crowded round admiring the painting. I thought Athena's behaviour was a bit vulgar. Surely the only reason for ordering an oil-painting of yourself at your own party would be if you were an out-of-work actress or model, desperate for a job?

I did not feel well and had to sit on a sofa, instead of circulating as I normally would. Julian sat with me most of the time. Once he talked for a few moments to a frizzy-haired woman, whom he

later said reminded him of his second ex-wife, then he chatted
with a blonde woman. The Austrian princess's husband was
wearing a white jacket with a stripe across it, which Julian said
made him do a double take as it was like a Nazi uniform. His
mother is Jewish.

M, the writer who had told me about the short-story anthology,
was also there with her husband. She was very considerate and
kept bringing me food and water. Halfway through Edward
turned up, panting and revved up with emotion over his affair
with the Turk, which seems to have gone wrong already. After an
ecstatic evening out with him last week he wrote him a love-letter,
but hasn't heard from him since.

Mr Goat was also at the party, without his wife. His new play is
being put on at a theatre in Richmond. He said Athena was going
to it with a group of friends on Thursday, and would I like to join
them? I said unfortunately I couldn't. (I am having chemotherapy
again on Wednesday.) Mr Goat danced with Athena in a very
uninhibited way, then they went into a bedroom to smoke grass.

I enjoyed myself, but found Athena's behaviour very odd. Every
so often she veered towards me like a bee attracted to a flower, a
buzzing, aggressive bee, but at the last moment spun away to talk
to other guests. I couldn't decide whether she was being sadistic,
gloating over my weakened state, or was genuinely terrified of
illness.

We left at midnight. On the way home Julian bought me a
carton of milk in a supermarket in Westbourne Grove. Five men
were standing in the middle of the road trying to get a taxi. I put
all the locks down in the car as I waited for Julian. I felt very
vulnerable.

I asked Julian if he wanted to come in and read my article about
the house-swap in Los Angeles. He said, 'Oh, I thought you were
in Santa Barbara.'

He got out of the car and stood there uncertainly. He seemed to
hesitate, so I did not invite him in again. I'm not sure if he is
contemplating having an affair with me or not.

Monday, 11 November
Lulu is concerned about Joseph, who is her godson. She thinks he should be having proper religious instruction. She is going to arrange it through her church, the one where the priest is always visiting Gorbachev.

At midday Paquita came round, bringing strange Japanese foods with her – seaweed, a large jar of brown paste called misu, special thin noodles and other ingredients I didn't recognize. She made a delicious soup, to which she added seaweed. She also cooked some noodles. An hour afterwards, however, I had violent diarrhoea.

Afternoon. Lulu rang up and said she had spoken to the American nun who arranges religious instruction classes for children. She told me to telephone her at once.

I called Sister Angela and explained that my son didn't like being in groups; I thought it might be better if he had instruction privately. Sister Angela waved this objection aside, saying that the point of the Sacrament and Service of Reconciliation (the modern term for Confession and Communion) was that the child must be 'part of the community'. She told me to bring him round today to the beginners' class at 3.30. I am willing to try anything to help Joseph cope better with life.

Later. Joseph and I went to the Community Centre next to the church. Sister Angela, who had cropped hair and an eager expression, introduced me to the Irish mother of six who would be teaching the class. She also dismissed my reservations about Joseph's shyness. Joseph himself then said he didn't mind being part of a large group. She swept him into the room with the other children, telling me to come back in forty minutes. I could see that she thought I was an over-anxious mother.

When I returned, Joseph came docilely out of the class. In the car going back he was silent and when I asked him what had gone on, he refused to tell me.

Later that evening he said, 'The lady showed me a picture of a very unhappy black boy.' He added that the boy only had a spoonful of rice a day and that his stomach was sticking out. He asked, 'Does he go to the lavatory?'

I said yes and that his stomach was sticking out because he was starving. I asked, 'Are you very worried about it?'

'No, I'm not very worried about it,' was the reply.

Tuesday, 12 November
This morning I went to see the therapist Paolo has found. She is Lithuanian and practises in Camden Town. She was late as she was delayed at Victoria Station on her way from her home in Streatham. She'd had to sit in the train while twenty policemen boarded it.

She is a shortish woman with a very round face. She immediately offered me a drink (Aqua Libra with water) and placed some green grapes before me on a plate. She then made herself some herbal tea and put three ricecakes in front of herself.

She is a convert to Catholicism. She moved from the Russian Orthodox church after she met the Pope on a skiing trip in Poland several years ago. (She calls him Pope.)

I told her I was separated from my husband and tried to give an account of our marriage and present relationship. She asked me questions about my childhood and quickly found out my mother was an alcoholic. When I told her about my mother falling over, she seemed excited. It turns out that she specializes in alcoholism and the effects of it, both on the alcoholics and the people close to them. She told me I should go to meetings of a group called Adult Children of Alcoholics and gave me a printed list of their venues all over London.

As I was leaving I told her I had breast cancer and she looked very shocked. She said she thought it might be partly a result of my not being able to express anger against my mother and the events in my earlier life. She talked about her own childhood in Lithuania and how she had once run away from school and got lost in a forest of birch trees. This is different from my son's therapist, who won't tell him how many children he has or even whether he has a dog.

This afternoon I went to a meeting at Joseph's school. My ex-husband was there as well and Joseph's therapist, a morose man with dark, saturnine looks. We sat on shabby chairs in the main room next to a tiny kitchen. Joseph's form teacher was dressed in a tomboyish way in jeans and T-shirt. She chain-smoked throughout the meeting. She said that her priority was 'to contain Joseph in a group' and to manage his aggression towards the other children. She said he found some of the other children's weird behaviour – hand-flapping, screaming and so on – very disturbing. Sometimes she had to put him in a room on his own to work. His friendship with a boy called Peter was discussed. His therapist said lugubriously that Peter was Joseph's *alter ego* and that Joseph enjoyed it when Peter did naughty things.

When I later told Miranda about the meeting, she said that Joseph's not liking the other children's behaviour was a sign of sanity. If he didn't notice that their behaviour was abnormal, it would be far worse.

Evening. I have just returned from a meeting, chaired by Sister Angela, for the parents of the children about to take the Sacrament of Reconciliation. I drove to the Community Centre in pouring rain, feeling rather weak. When I walked in I was surprised to find a group of pregnant women doing an exercise class. Luckily a smart blonde Belgian mother in a Jaguar had also gone to the wrong place, so I followed her car through the streets and we eventually wound up at the local primary school. There was a terrible smell of feet in the room.

Sister Angela had been showing a video of a modern version of the Prodigal Son, but the video had broken down halfway through. I gathered that, in this version, the Prodigal Son's father was a lorry driver.

Sister Angela was not daunted by the breakdown. She asked a parent: 'What did he finish up telling him, Lola? What about the hesitation of the son?'

Lola, a thin dark woman with bags of exhaustion under her eyes, said that the film was about forgiveness.

Sister Angela said knowledgeably that in the Bible story the Prodigal Son had reached ultimate degradation in eating pig, food that was 'abhorrent to a Jewish boy'. In the modern version of the parable the father, instead of waiting at home, was already on the road waiting for his son.

'When you want to come home, there's going to be someone there with their arms open for you. In this life and the next.'

I realized that the only person who had been like this for me was my grandmother, and she was dead.

13 November

Day of second chemotherapy. Joseph bursts into my room at 5 a.m. and spends the rest of the night with me. He sleeps soundly; I do not.

At seven he starts describing dreams he had in the night. One dream, he says, was 'half nightmare, half OK'.

My daughter has started bringing me breakfast in bed. This morning she brings up a bowl of cereal, but without a banana, which she knows I like. Instead, two of Toby's dog biscuits are on top of the cereal. He then eats them on my bed, making a lot of crumbs.

I ring a local mother about a second-hand school coat. But I've got the day wrong. Lucy's meant to meet her at the school tomorrow for the coat, not today. The mother asks gruffly if I'm all right. She seems to know I have breast cancer.

The *Independent* is delivered. This is the first time I have had a daily paper delivered in my life. There's a postcard from the *Spectator* saying that my letter about Diana Cooper's nicknames will be published shortly, and a letter from a woman who lives next door to me in Sussex and wants to buy a tiny strip of my garden where our fences join. (Lucy advises me not to sell it.)

I wait anxiously at the window for Clare to take me to the hospital. She said she'd come at 8.30 but it's now nearly nine. Suddenly I see her in her Volvo in the middle of the road, talking to another local mother.

I am very tense as we drive off.

Clare drops me at the main door and goes to find a parking place. I go alone to the oncology ward. I'm the only person in the waiting-room, apart from a retarded man. The notice about Bernie going skiing is still up on the board near the water-dispenser.

Bridie, the Irish nurse, greets me, saying it's a good thing that I came early as I won't have to wait so long. Then a New Zealand nurse takes me in to have a blood test. While I'm waiting again, Clare, who's now arrived in the room, casually tells me what for me is a shattering piece of news. She works for a radio programme and had been asked to find people who wrote diaries during the Gulf War. She did not know anyone who kept diaries, so she asked my ex-husband if he did.

I exclaimed, 'That's incredible. *I've* been writing a diary regularly since I was seventeen. He knows that very well. Several years ago he edited some of it and showed it to a writer friend, hoping I could get it published.'

I said that the fact that he had not mentioned to me that the radio programme was looking for diary extracts was terrible. Surely I need a break? Clare apologized, but I said of course it wasn't her fault. She didn't even know I wrote diaries. It is now too late.

I feel very bitter.

A nurse came to see if I was all right, so I had to explain an allergy I had developed. When I said the word 'bottom' I lowered my voice, in case the retarded man heard. I heard the nurse say: 'He's scarpered!'

He didn't seem able to decide whether to have his treatment or not. He left suddenly.

The Sloane Ranger oncology nurse then arrived and asked me about the allergy. Another man was in the waiting-room with us. I said, 'I think I'd rather go into a private room as it's embarrassing.'

We went into a side-room. The nurse did not seem to know what could have caused the allergy. She went out and returned with a doctor with a brown moustache and a dreamy manner. He also did not know what had caused it, but prescribed some cream.

I went into the oncology ward and waited for the chemotherapy injection. Clare joined me. There was also a volunteer, a woman of about sixty, with a plummy voice, who brought us both cups of tea.

This time the injection was administered by Bridie's colleague, Nurse Blair. She wore her name on her lapel. It was the same surname as R's, the man I had been in love with. This gave me an unpleasant *frisson*. As the various chemical mixtures were going into my veins, Clare started talking about our children's school coats. (Later she said she had done this to distract me; normally we talk about more abstract subjects.)

Then an enormously tall person came into the ward and stood beside the nurse who was calmly pumping the different drugs into my veins. This person had a man's voice, a man's legs and a man's knobbly wrists, but wore a short curly wig of hennaed hair and a skirt, and had a red poppy in her buttonhole. She was called Rowena. She seemed very matey with the nurse and had obviously been in the chemotherapy ward several times before. I even got the impression that she was excited about having cancer. I found the way she stood over me as I had the injection a bit creepy. I wished she would go away.

When she'd gone, I whispered to Nurse Blair, 'Has that person had a sex change?'

Yes,' she answered, but tactfully refused to say any more.

Clare and I went to hand in my prescription at the pharmacy, where we waited for the pills. I showed her the short story I'd written for the anthology and asked if it was all right. As she was reading it, tears began to run down her face. I remembered how she had silently cried once in a restaurant when I had told her about the deaths of my brothers. I had been touched that she had minded so much for me.

After I got the pills, she drove me home and I went to bed. I drank water all afternoon.

In the evening I rang up Duncan and told him about the sex-change person who had stood over me while I had had my injection. I said she had seemed elated about having cancer. Had I imagined this? He said it was possible. Sometimes when a person had a serious illness, it gave him an identity. A man who had a sex change was trying to convince himself and others that his fantasy – that he was really a woman – superseded the reality of having been born with a man's body. It could be difficult to carry on this fantasy, even after the sex change. Having cancer, however, was irrefutable; it was bricks and mortar as opposed to dreams.

15 November
At five o'clock I was in the kitchen with Maureen and the children, playing back my answerphone. Suddenly I heard a message from a man at the *Independent*, referring to my 'extremely funny article' and saying that as he hadn't been able to get hold of me earlier, it was going in the paper tomorrow in the section called 'My Week'. I would be getting a cheque shortly.

My daughter's reaction to this exciting piece of news was extraordinary. She looked scared and tried to ring up my ex-husband. When she couldn't get hold of him she said it was all a trick and the man's voice on the answerphone was Daddy pretending to be a newspaper man.

Maureen, shocked, asked Lucy, 'Don't you want your mother to have success?'

Lucy said she had a headache, so I got out the Phenergan bottle. She refused to take any, declaring grandly, 'I don't go to psychiatrists and I don't take drugs.' She pointed out that she was the only member of the family not going to a therapist.

Later Joseph woke me at 3 a.m., saying 'It's a bit creepy when a child saves up its Saturday sweets.'

In desperation I grabbed the Phenergan bottle, gave him three doses with the plastic spoon and swallowed several gulps myself straight from the bottle. Joseph thought this terribly funny.

Emily has offered to accompany me to Sussex this weekend as I am still feeling ill from the chemotherapy. She says she will help me look after the children.

The children and I arrived at the station terribly early. There was nowhere to sit as all the benches that used to be at Victoria have been removed, because of IRA bombs, I think. I felt weak and unreal after the drugs I had had two days before. Having stood around for some time, I bought the children croissants.

Then Paolo arrived, not Emily. He was holding a pile of glossy magazines, a suitcase and a plastic bag with an odd smell coming from it.

Emily had still not appeared at the barrier where we had agreed to meet. Paolo was reluctant to get on the train without his wife. I said I did not want to travel without another adult as I felt so ill. The train was a commuter train and was extremely crowded. At last I got on with the children. I couldn't walk any further and slumped into the first carriage I saw, which was first-class. Suddenly Emily appeared, saying she was already sitting in another carriage further up. Paolo was still looking for her on the station. Emily stuck her head out of the window and began yelling his name hysterically. Paolo jumped on just in time, looking very dramatic. He proudly opened his plastic bag and showed me three lobsters for our dinner.

Emily went off up the corridor to look for seats so we could all sit together. She returned saying she'd found some. We then had to walk almost the whole length of the train, passing enormous numbers of commuters standing up. I dropped a full bottle of Evian water on the floor of a crowded carriage. I rushed on as there was nothing I could do.

When we arrived an hour later at our station in Sussex, both the doors near us on to the platform were inexplicably locked. After we'd finally got out, Emily realized she'd left her bag in the original carriage I'd been sitting in. She had to dash back along the platform and grabbed it just before the train left.

That evening we ate the lobsters Paolo had brought. The children had spaghetti. Joseph asked Emily over and over again if she believed in life after death. She said she kept an open mind.

I dream that I am going to Paris for the weekend. I pack a very light bag, almost nothing in it, except the shoes I bought with Jill when I visited her in Key West. I'm nearly ready to go. In the middle of the dream I'm woken up abruptly by Joseph. I realize that I can't go to Paris after all; I can't go to the place where I've always been so happy. I start crying bitterly.

16 November
I am not in control in my own house. Also, I feel extremely ill. I am in a panicky state and I keep feeling hot and cold. Emily is doing her best, but Paolo is very selfish and has grand ideas about country houses. He constantly refers to 'your little cottage, darling' and is obviously annoyed he is not being waited on hand and foot, as he is at his parents' house in Italy, according to Emily.

This morning I went into the kitchen, where Emily had valiantly cooked eggs and bacon for four of us. She herself doesn't eat a cooked breakfast. She was just sitting down at last to a tiny piece of toast when Paolo strode in in a blue kimono and swiped it.

The Douthwaites, pensioners who live in the bungalow next door, came over later. Mrs Douthwaite had kept me a copy of *Bella* magazine, with an article on breast cancer. She stressed how important it was that I finish the course. She is sure that the statistics about women dying apply mainly to those who haven't done the recommended treatment.

Joseph loves Mrs Douthwaite, who was brought up in Peckham. She is a lively woman, and thinks she has Spanish or even gypsy blood. Well over sixty, she puts on elaborate make-up each morning and wears bright colours, as I do. This morning she is wearing a scarlet T-shirt with a picture of a white kitten on the front.

When Mrs Douthwaite's there everything seems calmer. Joseph does his homework at the kitchen table with her and Lucy goes off to ride her pony. Then Molly, the young woman who's working two mornings a week for my mother, arrives, and comes up to my bedroom where I've retreated. (I must be looking odd, because Mr Douthwaite, a man of few words, asked 'Are you all right?')

I'm so relieved Molly's working for my mother. Molly tells me that my mother's very sorry; she wishes she had breast cancer instead of me.

Just before supper Paolo starts making an awful fuss about a shepherd's pie Mrs Douthwaite's made, saying he can't eat it, and that he'd rather go out to a restaurant. I say I don't feel well enough to go out, and anyway there's nothing wrong with the pie. A few weeks ago a man who stayed here – an elderly doctor – ate three helpings.

Paolo becomes more and more bad-tempered. I think he's annoyed that I'm the centre of attention because I'm ill. In the kitchen he says, 'Darling, you are very angry with me. It's good for you to focus your anger.'

Surely *he's* very angry that we're not having lobster again for dinner?

Meanwhile Emily has done all the washing-up. She has also drunk three-quarters of a bottle of vodka that I bought when I last went to France on the ferry to see Hal. I'm annoyed about this.

Sunday
3 p.m. Paolo is striding about the house saying he wants to leave. There are trains every hour back to London, but Paolo grandly decides he would rather order a local taxi to drive him and Emily back. He doesn't bother to tell Emily, who's been out walking Toby, of his decision until five minutes before the taxi comes.

After they've gone I slump in the sitting-room and try to read the Sunday papers. The children are fighting over a tub of chocolate ice-cream. Suddenly Julian turns up at the front door. He's been visiting a friend in Brighton. I'm so relieved to see him. I realize that I am overcome with exhaustion. I am so tired I nearly start to cry. Julian looks at me very kindly. Later he drives me and the children back to London. The children seem jealous of my friendship with him and Lucy remarks; 'Julian's not very good with children, is he?'

Monday, 18 November
First day of radiotherapy. My appointment is at 2.30. Maureen drives me to the hospital, then goes on to fetch Joseph from school.

The Radiotherapy Department has its own entrance, near

Accident and Emergency, in St Dunstan's Road. The waiting-room is in a self-contained area, up some steps. The usual enormous container of water with paper cups is there, as well as a machine dispensing coffee and tea. Down the steps along a little passage, past a garish oil-painting of a racing driver, is the area where radiotherapy is administered.

I have brought in the booklet I was given in the hospital last week called 'Radiotherapy, Your Questions Answered'. Under 'Radiotherapy to the breast' it reads:

> Do not wash the treated area at all. The skin in the treated area will temporarily change colour and texture about seven to ten days after treatment begins. It feels and may look a little like mild sunburn. Sometimes it can become quite sore, especially if rubbed when washing. So, until treatment has finished and the doctor, radiographer or nurse has advised you personally, please do not wash the treated area . . . Treatment also stops perspiration occurring as it affects the sweat glands.

I am ushered into a small cubicle and told to put on a dressing-gown hanging there. It is scarlet, my favourite colour.

I go into the room where radiotherapy is delivered and am given a short speech by a woman with a halo of brown hair and burning green eyes that are outlined by a thick black rim of mascara. I don't much like this woman.

First, she marks out the upper part of my body in purple. It must stay like this for the duration of the treatment, she explains. I will have radiotherapy to the right breast and under the right arm where the lymph glands were removed every day for six weeks. Towards the end of this period I will get extremely tired. The treatment will end just before Christmas. I may get a bit burnt, but luckily I have a dark skin so it may not be so bad.

I lie on a trolley and look around me at all sorts of machines. There is a low, humming noise. I feel none of the apprehension I had in the chemotherapy ward, except there are sinister notices warning of the harmful effects of radiation. But somehow, perhaps because of the absence of pain and the fact that there are no obvious after-effects, the dangers involved in the high doses of radiation are not quite real.

When I returned home, there was a message from Athena asking if I'd like to go to Mr Goat's play with her and her husband. I rang back, leaving a message giving several dates when I can go.

Then Duncan came round and cooked me supper, Pasta Capricciosa, with capers, garlic, cream, tomato, red wine, mint and parsley. I showed him a few pages of the diary I had written about being in hospital. He laughed a lot and said I should get it published. He suggested sending it to the *Evening Standard*. He is composing song lyrics for an opera of *Gormenghast*. He has called one song 'Time the Dream-killer'.

2.30 a.m. I can't sleep. My whole arm where I had the operation is tingling and the head-banging child next door has started banging its head in full force. It is absolutely ghastly.

2.45 a.m. I have just written a letter to the woman next door to ask if her child's bed could be moved away from the wall. I explained that I had breast cancer and wasn't sleeping very well. I put a PS: 'If you want the name of a good child psychologist, I suggest Mrs Lewensteiner at Great Ormond Street. She is absolutely charming and very good with children.'

Eventually I go back to sleep and have a disturbing dream. I am in hospital with several women in nightdresses. Most of them are American. One woman refers to when my mother came to the hospital on a previous occasion, I think to visit me. One of these women is hostile towards me.

I leave the hospital building and set out on my own into the country on some quest. When I've finished what I went to do I turn round and start walking back along the main road. I'm nervous I might be run over by a car. I'm alone. I come to a gate, barricaded with barbed wire, across the road. There's no way I can go on. What shall I do?

Then a woman with black hair comes, pushing a child with black hair in a pushchair. This woman helps me. She walks with me and shows me a way I can go up by the side of the fence. Suddenly the whole fence opens up and we easily pass underneath the wire. Now we're walking very high on a hillside, somewhere like the Sussex Downs. I'm free.

When I tell the therapist this dream the next morning, she says it is very positive and hopeful.

19 November

The mother next door came round. She said she was very sorry about my being ill and that she had moved the child's bed so that I wouldn't hear the banging. She did not refer to the PS in my letter. She *did* say firmly, 'I don't believe in difficult children.'

Later. Second radiotherapy appointment. I go to the hospital in a minicab in pouring rain accompanied by flashes of lightning. The cab's driven by a Pakistani called Johnny who zippily shows me a short cut to the hospital.

Since yesterday I have developed a very bad sore throat and am sure this is caused by the radiotherapy. The radiographer, the woman with vivid green eyes whom I dislike, insists that it isn't. She says it is flu.

When it's over, I call another minicab from the hospital telephones. A bad-tempered, impatient Moroccan driver takes me back via the same short cut, but this time one of the side-roads, next to a cemetery, is blocked by three police cars. Several policemen get out with Alsatian dogs and rush into the graveyard. We sit there in a traffic jam for fifteen minutes. I am very excited.

5 p.m. This afternoon I went to my Spanish class for the first time for five weeks. I did not tell anyone there that I had breast cancer. The teacher seemed pleased to see me and photocopied several batches of homework for me so I could catch up.

A Japanese student, with very thick black hair, came and sat next to me. (The teacher had told us to form groups of two or three and try to discuss in Spanish whether we preferred living in the town or the country.) The Japanese man had a very strong guttural accent, and neither I nor the blonde Englishwoman in our threesome could understand what he said.

He asked me in Spanish, 'Do you like drinking in the town or the country?'

I replied, 'That depends on the drink.'

However, it turned out that he had said 'vivir' (the verb meaning 'to live') and not 'bebir' (the verb for 'to drink').

In the same guttural voice he said that he preferred living in the country, in a place with mountains. Then he used a strange word, 'silviculture'. I saw that he was holding a technical book on forestry, written in English. I realized that he was probably describing an idealized Japanese landscape.

The Chilean teacher told him that the word with which he was describing forests was not suitable, but the Japanese man stubbornly went on using it.

It was a relief to me to be in a normal situation, without anyone knowing I had had cancer. The only unpleasant reminder was that the coffee and tea dispenser was like the ones I use all the time in the hospital and offered the same revoltingly weak tea and coffee.

8 p.m. Paquita came round at six and cooked some dishes of macrobiotic food. She insisted on giving me seaweed again, even though I said it had given me violent diarrhoea. She also prepared a weird Japanese tea made from the bark of a tree, and a dish of lentils. Afterwards I got terrible diarrhoea again. I'm sure it is the seaweed. I will refuse it next time. I must be more assertive.

20 November
My son's therapist has suggested that Joseph should spend two nights a week with my ex-husband so I'm not woken up at five every morning. I am desperate for sleep, but am worried that Joseph will think he is being thrown out. He is already very anxious because I'm ill.

Lucy said, 'Daddy won't have any sleep then. He'll be asking us to take Joseph for extra nights. Daddy'll probably have a nervous

breakdown. He'll get writer's block and he won't be able to write
his articles.'

When I went to the Radiotherapy Department later, Betty, the
woman who was first in the ward with me when I had my lymph
glands removed, came in through the side-entrance. She looked
ebullient and said she had purposely started her radiotherapy a
week late because she and her husband had wanted to go to a
dinner-dance.

She did not once ask about *my* situation – she doesn't have to
have chemotherapy – but went on and on about a lump that had
appeared under her arm as a result of the operation.

I was called in to get ready. This time there was a navy-blue
dressing-gown with scalloped edges. I liked it almost as much as
the scarlet one. The radiographer, with her crisp curly hair and
heavily outlined angry cat's eyes, seemed annoyed that I hadn't
been waiting meekly outside the cubicle, but had been talking to
Betty next door instead. She asked about my sore throat, which was
still there; in fact, it's worse. She was determined that it was not
caused by radiotherapy. I am absolutely sure that it is. She told me
to wait till Friday, when I would be able to see the doctor about it.

I am in a very weak state today and sometimes can hardly stand
up.

In the morning I send a copy of my story to R, the man I used to
be in love with. As I sealed the envelope I burst into tears. Is it
because he looks like my dead brother that this man causes such a
reaction in me?

Emily comes to lunch. She tries to make instant coffee, but there
isn't any. Instead she uses the real coffee-pot, making an awful
mess. (I have not drunk coffee myself since getting breast cancer,
as it is supposed to be unhealthy.)

Emily then took me to the therapist. I told my therapist about R.
When she asked my why I had married my husband, I couldn't
remember the reasons, except he had been nice to me. She seemed
a bit disappointed that he wasn't also the child of an alcoholic.

When I came out, Emily drove me to the photocopying shop
and waited while I got another copy of my manuscript on the

sixties that Duncan helped me edit. I can't wait any longer for a
reply from the publisher who has it now. I must send it
somewhere else.

On the way home I suggested that Emily go to a therapist like
mine to discuss her marriage, her drinking and her anorexia. She
refused. She had caught a glimpse of my therapist in the waiting-
room. 'That woman looks as if she eats far too many cream cakes.
She must go on a diet,' Emily declared militantly. She said she had
recently realized that in her forties a woman must decide between
her face and her figure. She has chosen her figure.

Later Mary Killen rang up saying she was definitely going to
publish my letter about the incident in the Catholic church on her
problem page. It should come out in the New Year. She is going to
ask a priest for a satisfactory answer.

21 November
I have got an extremely sore throat. I woke at 4 a.m. and started
sobbing. I was absolutely desperate, about my throat and about
my situation.

Last night Cynthia took me to a play at the Royal Court, *Death of
a Maiden*, about torture in a South American country. A woman
who was tortured is confronted by her torturer in her own kitchen
years later. She recognizes his voice.

I found the play too intense, and this was made worse by there
being no interval. Cynthia said I could leave if I wanted, but I felt
guilty at spoiling the play for her.

On the way to the theatre in Cynthia's car I saw a dwarf in
Kensington High Street. This dwarf, who appeared to walk with
incredible difficulty, limped slowly into the traffic and held up his
hand for the cars to stop so he could cross the road at his own
pace.

When I saw him determinedly getting on with his life in spite of
his impediment I felt encouraged. Before I got breast cancer I
would probably have hardly noticed the dwarf. Or I would have
felt vaguely sorry for him, without thinking what it was like to be
him.

The mother with the head-banging child has moved out. At two o'clock a removal van arrived and furniture was loaded for several hours. The house is now empty. She didn't tell me they were leaving.

Tonight Rosemary the Vegan rang up and said she was coming to Radiotherapy tomorrow at twelve o'clock and she had a present for me. We arranged to meet there.

22 November

My father's birthday. He died soon after his sixty-fourth birthday.

I went to the hospital early to have a blood count. Even then I was number nine and had to wait forty minutes.

I talked to the woman beside me. She was pregnant and wearing a light-pink dress. She was an Indian from South Africa. She had come to England a year ago and started a shop in South Ken. with her husband. She missed South Africa and the sunshine and wished she had never come to England.

I said, 'Could you persuade your husband to go back?'

She was trying to.

She was having the blood count because she might be diabetic. She hadn't eaten since six yesterday evening.

As I made my way towards the ground floor I met Di, the oncology nurse, in the corridor. I told her about feeling very manic after chemotherapy. She said, 'Oh, that must be the anti-sickness pills. They have that effect on some people. We have to give them to patients the first time because they're cheaper. I'll make a note that you must go on Dom Peridone next time you have chemotherapy.'

When I arrived at the Radiotherapy Department I met Rosemary as arranged. She gave me a wrapped parcel containing a book she'd bought for me called *Getting Well Again*. She said she'd also bought copies for Pam, Jenny and Carmen. She told me that she believed in a Higher Power and He was on our side. She advised me to visualize myself in places in the future when I was well, and to think positively. I said I had done this instinctively

during the half-hour before my last operation (when I had
imagined myself with my children on the Sussex Downs), but that
now I couldn't do it.

Rosemary then told me the same relaxation technique that
Cynthia had told me last month. She had also heard that the anti-
sickness pills could make you feel manic. She said a friend of hers
who'd had chemotherapy and was on the pills had cleaned her
whole house at one in the morning.

Later I thought that I should have asked Rosemary why, if she
believed in the Higher Power, was it necessarily His will that we
should get well?

I then saw Dr W, the young woman with reddish hair, about my
sore throat. She said that she thought it was due to a bug going
round, but couldn't be sure. She did not try to humiliate me as the
radiotherapist did. I liked her very much indeed. She treated me as
an equal. She has a baby and her husband is also a doctor in the
hospital. She said, 'It may take you a year before you feel perfectly
well. I had a Caesarean six months ago and I still feel the effects of
it.'

When I returned home, another family had already moved into the
house next door. I stared at them out of the sitting-room window
as they moved in and out carrying lampshades, books, saucepans
and small items of furniture. The woman has a long black plait
and was wearing a blue tie-dye skirt. A teenage boy was with her,
and a lanky husband, who has white hair and glasses.

23 November

Sussex. I was woken very early by Joseph watching TV in the
room below my bedroom. On the screen were harrowing pictures
of Kurdish child refugees. This made Rosemary's trust in a Higher
Power seem oversimplistic and self-deceiving, though of course I
half wanted to believe in it.

I rang up Emily after breakfast and explained that the anti-
sickness pills had made me manic the weekend that they were in
Sussex. She took the news graciously and didn't say, 'Oh, that's

why you behaved so oddly.' I suppose she knows that Paolo was
also very difficult that weekend.

Tomorrow is my forty-second birthday. On my seventh birthday
my brother was drowned, so I always think something bad will
happen on my birthday. Once, ten years ago, I ran over a dog. I
was on the way to supper in a village near my grandmother's with
some Polish friends. One of the guests was from my grandmother's village. Unwittingly, he started talking about 'the
tragedy' of 1956. After a few minutes I said, 'That was my brother.'

He said, 'We all have our tragedies.'

Today, the day before, the children and I are celebrating. I do not
feel at all well and think I have flu, as well as chills and sweats, the
after-effects of chemotherapy.

The von Strandmann family come to my birthday tea. They, like
me, stay in the village during school holidays and weekends. They
bring a professor from East Germany, where Hartmut von
Strandmann has been teaching history at the University of
Rostock. Their East German guest is a handsome courteous man
who bows low over my hand when he arrives and again when he
leaves.

Mrs Douthwaite has bought a chocolate cake for me in the local
town. Joseph, who put some candles on it, explains, 'She's not a
cake-maker.' (Yorkshire pudding, which he loves, is her forte. So is
apple pie.)

Michele, a local mother who's kindly taken Lucy riding several
times with her own children since I've been ill, also comes to tea,
as well as my old friend Tessa, an artist from Brixton. She's having
an exhibition of her pots in Brighton tomorrow.

I've known Tessa since I was eleven. When the others have
gone, Tessa, who's offered to help me with the children this
weekend, talks about her father's recent death and how she's
pleased to have been there when he died. Her mother committed
suicide when Tessa was eighteen. I know that Tessa and I have a
strong tie partly because the two people closest to us killed
themselves. Tessa's one of my few friends who knew my brother.
She liked him.

Tessa said that when she went to her father's funeral she felt that there was nothing in the coffin. I said I had also felt this at my father's funeral. I suppose you could say that the soul had already left the body. Although Tessa and I went to the same convent, she is now anti religion.

This evening my son came into my bedroom, where the dog was standing on the window-sill. He said, 'Toby's only got one fault. His penis is too big.'

25 November

London. Hal turned up from Paris yesterday, on my birthday.

It was very difficult to get a babysitter at the last minute. Maureen had planned an outing with friends who'd just arrived from Australia. As always Hal didn't tell me his movements till the day he arrived.

I rang round. A neighbour in Notting Hill offered me her cleaning-lady, who was psychic and a professional tarot card reader. She told me not to mind this. She did look a bit starry-eyed, but was entirely reliable. The psychic babysitter could only stay till midnight, however, and I wanted to spend the night with Hal.

I rang Miranda and begged her to stay the night in my house after the babysitter left. Having agreed to this, Miranda then rang saying she had a very bad period and couldn't come.

Then I saw my new neighbour, again wearing her blue tie-dye skirt, out of the window. I rushed out and asked her if she knew a babysitter. I explained it was my birthday. I thought she might have an au pair who would help out. She told me to wait a minute, went into the house, and came out saying that her husband would stay with my children until Maureen got back from her party. I warned her that Maureen might not get back till one, but she said her husband wouldn't mind. Their kindness is quite staggering.

My flu was worse, but I was determined to see Hal and go out. Hal's energy infected me. I suppose this is one of the reasons I like him. I feel when I'm with him that I can do anything, even rise from the dead, were it necessary.

He is nearly an hour late, as usual.

I obediently drive him to the BBC studios in Portland Place to meet a young man with whom he's recently made friends and he wants me to meet. It's a disc jockey called Andy Kershaw.

Andy's about to broadcast his Sunday night record programme, which we watch. Afterwards, Hal immediately tells him I've got cancer, and even jokes about it, calling me 'The Cancer Girl'. Strangely enough, I don't mind this. It's a relief to hear the word spoken out loud, the taboo word that you don't mention normally in front of strangers.

Hal's mother died of leukaemia a few years ago. She was sixty-six and had just retired to the seaside. Two weeks before she died Hal had her to stay in Paris, where he took her round on the back of his motor bike. She told people matter-of-factly that she had been pronounced 'incurable'. Hal said that she seemed to have accepted this, in a forthright way, without self-pity.

Over supper with him and his girlfriend, Juliette, Andy told us about staying in a hotel in a black township in Zimbabwe where he was the only white man. One morning at 4 a.m. he was woken by a loud knocking on his door. A waiter stood there bowing. Andy asked what he wanted. The waiter simply said, 'Good morning!'

Andy replied, 'Goodnight.'

The waiter bowed again and went away.

He had first asked Juliette out by going into the Crouch End restaurant where she worked as a waitress and saying, 'I've got two tickets to Zimbabwe on Wednesday. Will you come?'

She had said yes.

In the middle of the night Hal asks, 'Admit that I'm the only man in the world you can't control.' He then asks me if I love him.

I don't answer. I nervously drum my fingers on the bedside table. I know that there is an element of conquest in his request. At the same time he is extremely affectionate. I almost feel the heat coming off his hands, like I did when Paquita first touched me. Nevertheless, he is a bully.

26 November

I told my therapist about Hal and she said he sounded like a sex addict. I also told her about my other lover, the man with the enormous penis whom I have not seen since August. She said *he* sounded co-dependent or alcoholic or both.

She asked, 'Do you know who you are?'

I said, 'Well, who does know who they are?'

She said, 'I do.'

I thought this was rather conceited.

She showed me a cartoon of a woman in a mini-skirt with long hair and a leather belt. The woman was looking at the reflection of a child in the mirror in front of her. The child was crying. My therapist explained that the woman in the mini-skirt appeared to be adult and wanted sex, but had not yet come to terms with 'the child within her' who wanted something else. She said that while I had not reconciled the child within me I would always unconsciously be looking for men who catered to that child. She asked me to write an account of my emotional life as a child before the next session.

I thought, if I wait for all the right conditions and until I fall in love, I might be waiting for the rest of my life.

I told Emily what the therapist had said about Hal being a sex addict. She replied, 'How exciting!'

27 November

My son at 8 a.m.: 'I want you to die so I can get all your money.'

Me: 'In that case you won't get any.'

My son: 'Sorry, sorry. Do you want some water? Do you want a sweet to make you feel better?'

'Who the hell cares whether Diana Cooper was called Baby, Bubbles, Honks, or whatever? This kind of letter puts one off the upper classes for life.' My letter about Ali Forbes's letter has been published in the *Spectator*.

28 November

Duncan's gone to Moscow for two days to write an article for a magazine. He's never been to Russia before and is very excited about it.

Jacob and I went to three Pinter plays at the Almeida Theatre. The first was *Mountain Language*. I was irritated by the command on the door of the theatre, forbidding any member of the audience to leave during the one-act play. Since the play's about oppression, surely this self-important notice is particularly inappropriate? Audiences used to eat and talk during Shakespeare's plays.

After all the plays were over, we had a Turkish meal in Upper Street. Jacob, who normally likes Pinter, was disappointed. He confided that he is also thinking of doing therapy, on the National Health, to get rid of his depression and make him more assertive. He went for a preliminary interview with a psychiatrist at his local hospital yesterday. Jacob's now waiting for the result of this assessment to see whether he's depressed or disturbed enough to merit therapy on the NHS.

We talked about some girls I'd been at school with, whom Jacob also knows. He said, 'Most of the highly disturbed women in central London went to that convent.'

29 November

Today when I went to have radiotherapy I saw Pam from the ward with an elderly man – her boyfriend, I think. She looked very perky and well. She asked how I was getting on and I talked about my son and said he was very aggressive. Pam was sympathetic. She said it must be good for him to be with his dad. I then asked after her daughter. Pam said she was fine, but even when your children were grown-up you never stopped worrying about them.

I then saw Rosemary again, waiting with her daughter, who must have come down from university to be with her.

At teatime Vivian came over and we discussed the Pinter plays. She said the trouble with his 'political' plays was that the 'threat' in them was too obvious. In his earlier ones there was an

atmosphere of menace, but the menace was never named, and was
thus far more terrifying. I thought this rather clever of her.

30 November

Duncan is back from Russia. He loved Moscow, though he only
stayed one and a half days. He went with a boy called Bruno to a
market where Turks with huge moustaches sold lemons. He was
asked if he wanted to buy marijuana and went up a side-street out
of curiosity to negotiate, but didn't buy any.

He's now longing to go back to visit St Petersburg.

I took down notes of what he had said: 'In the Savoy Hotel in
Moscow it costs six US dollars for two cups of tea. The marijuana,
which he did not buy, cost twenty dollars an ounce.' This made me
feel I was doing something positive. If I don't write things down
regularly I feel unstable.

Duncan said I should be writing my own column and that I
ought to try to get one in a magazine or newspaper. I said I would
like to write one like Zenga Longmore's in the *Spectator*.

When I told Emily this later, she said I should get my friends to
write in complaining about Zenga Longmore's column. Then with
any luck she would get the sack and I might get her job. She
offered to write a letter saying she didn't like the column. I was
rather shocked, but said OK. My normal standards of behaviour
seem to have dropped because I have a potentially terminal illness.

Athena has not answered my message about going to Mr Goat's
play.

December

Sunday, 1 December

Weekend in Sussex. I have stupidly allowed my friend and neighbour to buy the small strip of my garden that she wanted and she has taken down most of the trees. Now, staring out of my bedroom window, I see houses that before were hidden by trees. It's like some ghastly parallel of my own situation. I'm exposed and denuded.

Lucy says, 'I told you not to sell it.'

Luckily Cynthia's here. On Friday night she cooked delicious pasta she'd brought from London.

She's very good with the children and they like her; she plays games with them. I stay in bed much of the time, only getting up in the morning to talk to Mrs Douthwaite and to watch a bit of *Jaws 3*, with Lucy.

This morning Cynthia brought up my breakfast on a tray. There was a boiled egg and, in a tiny cup, a white rose from the garden that had lasted into winter.

In the evening we invited some friends of Cynthia for a drink, but only the husband could come. This man, Robert Skidelsky, is a brilliant historian who was made a lord this summer, I think on the recommendation of David Owen. (He was once in the SDP.) He and I talked about California, where he'd just been to give some lectures. He doesn't know I've got breast cancer.

I gave an account of some of my experiences in America as a nineteen-year-old, when I had stayed in a hotel for disadvantaged women outside the Loop in Chicago.

Robert seemed to be waiting for me to finish each time I spoke so he could resume his account of his own visit. He had stayed with Milton Friedman somewhere near San Francisco. I asked,

'Was his house a luxury villa near the sea?'

Robert said it was on the sea, but was not a luxury villa.
Milton's wife, he said, in answer to another of my questions, was
an academic in her own right and they had been married fifty
years. Robert had also been to a town called Tacoma near Seattle. I
asked, 'Were you in an Alamo or a Hertz rented car?'

He smiled mysteriously and said, 'One or the other.'

Mrs Mortimer, my mother's friend and mine, also came for a
drink. Her two ex-husbands, talented rakes and womanizers, were
once in the London literary world. Mrs Mortimer, who's been
reading the *Spectator* for years, started complaining about Zenga
Longmore's column. She said the magazine should be 'pitched at a
higher level'. I asked if she would be prepared to write a letter
saying she didn't like the column, as I was longing to do it myself.
She balked at this, so I asked if I could write a letter on her behalf.
She said yes.

I have now written it:

Sir

I am seventy-six and have led a somewhat bohemian life, not
always of my own choosing. However, I cannot relate to
Zenga Longmore's life in south London with Rottweiler dogs
and characters with names like Clawhammer Jones and
Bingo. I feel that the *Spectator* should be pitched at a higher
level.

> Yours faithfully
> J. M. Brighton

I rang up Mrs Mortimer and read out the letter over the
telephone. Her only objection was that she was seventy-four, not
seventy-six. I posted the letter in the village post office.

I then had an argument in the kitchen with Cynthia about
Pinter's play *Mountain Language*. She thought it was brilliant,
much better than his earlier plays.

The next day we went to Charleston and its shop, where there
was an exhibition of pottery. Cynthia decided to go on a tour of the
house. Lucy and I then set off for the Skidelskys' on foot, passing

by Nicholas Mosley's cottage. (I haven't seen him since the Booker evening.) It was getting dark. Toby was very excited about some rabbits and went round and round in circles. We met the Skidelskys' fifteen-year-old son walking their black Labrador, Tosca.

Augusta was out. Robert seemed nervous without his wife. He was watching an exciting tennis match on television. The match was in Lyons and was eventually won by a Frenchman. Another member of the French team cried with emotion while being interviewed – Lucy was fascinated by this as she had never seen a man cry – and a player with a Rastafarian hair-do was carried round in triumph.

Robert gave Lucy a numbers puzzle that she solved at once and he was very impressed by this. She couldn't do it a second time, though. He took some scones out of the oven, made by his wife, and spread them for me and Lucy.

Cynthia turned up, looking very perky after her tour, then Augusta with her daughter. Augusta told us that three shops in Tottenham Court Road had been blown up last night near the Skidelskys' London flat, which is just behind Cynthia's house. The two Skidelsky children who'd been in the flat hadn't heard anything.

2 *December*
London. Maureen is leaving. She always said she would go before Christmas, but I hoped she might stay on till I finish my chemotherapy treatment in mid-May. She is determined to go to California at once.

It is the worst time possible. I am getting more tired every day. Apparently at the end of the six-week radiotherapy you can hardly move for exhaustion. The children, particularly Joseph, will be upset about Maureen's departure. I am too proud to beg her to stay.

I have started writing an account of my hospital experiences, with a view to getting them published somewhere or other, perhaps as part of a column.

Paquita came round after twelve and cooked some more macrobiotic food. She showed me how to steam fish in its own juice in a saucepan. She was insistent about giving me more seaweed, though I told her it gave me terrible diarrhoea. She seems obsessed with laxatives. I said firmly, 'Paquita, I never have any trouble going to the lavatory.'

Later I told Maureen I was worried that Paquita didn't have a sense of humour. Paquita, however, thought I was more relaxed this time. I privately attribute this to Hal's visit from Paris.

I have rung up an agency and said I would like a nanny for a few months.

Tuesday, 3 December
My daughter has taken to teasing Joseph in my bedroom, before they go to school.

This morning Joseph said, 'It's like Squirrel Nutkin teasing the Owl. Is it? Is it?' He added that eventually he would lose his temper and, like the owl in the Beatrix Potter story, bite off Lucy's tail.

Several friends have offered to drive me to radiotherapy appointments in a rota. This morning Sally, who was at the convent with me, took me. We were both at dinner at Julian's last night. Sally seemed tense and buttoned up. She also looked exhausted, far worse than I do. I said hypocritically, 'I was afraid you thought I was having an affair with Julian when I stayed behind after the dinner-party. When you came back to get your coat you saw I wasn't.' Sally didn't comment.

Sally's father died of cancer in his fifties. I remembered her telling me how shocked she had been to see babies in the cancer clinic that she had attended with her father.

At the hospital the radiographer whom I dislike has had a perm. She looks better with it, less like a doll's house doll. I have moved on to a more bland level with her. I'm not so keen to argue as I was last week.

Now when I stand outside the cubicle there's always a man in a wheelchair, aged about fifty, with a young male companion, I think from the Philippines. The older man is waiting to have radiotherapy at about the same time as I am. He has heavily lidded eyes, which are half closed, and scaly skin. I think he must have skin cancer. The young man is either a paid manservant or his boyfriend. He seems devoted to the older man. He carefully pushes his wheelchair down the ramp to the waiting area, then sits close by him before he's called in for radiotherapy. I find the older man's condition, and his possible blindness, frightening. I could get like this one day if my cancer spreads. The medical word for cancer spreading is 'metastasis'.

I went to my Spanish class as soon as I returned from the hospital. We had to write an account of our day in Spanish and read it out. I did not want to say that my days were abnormal at the moment because of my hospital appointments. I wrote: 'During a typical morning I dedicate half an hour to reading the newspaper or a book. I eat my breakfast in three minutes.'

I'm sure the rest of the class thought I was very lazy, particularly as I'd arrived late, after my treatment. Marie-Ange, the French-woman with long tawny hair, still seems to dislike me and I find her flirtatious manner with the teacher and the way she wants to be the centre of attention extremely irritating.

During the tea-break I made friends with another Frenchwoman in the class. She had lived for years in Africa and knew the aunt of an ex-boyfriend of mine, now in her eighties. She said she admired her tremendously because she had been very popular with the Africans and had run her own farm there since the age of eighteen. I wished I had visited my old boyfriend there when I had the opportunity in 1975. Now I'll never go.

After the Spanish class I interviewed two nannies the agency had provided. One was Irish and had worked for three years with the same family in Dublin; the other was an occupational therapist from New Zealand who's working temporarily at a London hospital. She said she was shocked at the inefficiency of the NHS. She has none of the helpers she's supposed to have and has to spend much of her time on the phone to the Social Services. When she wanted to dry a patient with a towel, there weren't any, only pillow cases.

The Irish girl came with me to Joseph's religious instruction class. In the car he started screaming that he hated it. When I asked him what was wrong, he said that the teacher ignored him and that he was afraid of the other children. The girl, who, like me, had been brought up Catholic, said it was better to stop the classes as they would put him off religion for life, so I took him home.

Joseph then sat on the sofa while I interviewed the nanny. He butted in, asking again about Squirrel Nutkin and the Owl.

'Was it *nice* of the Owl to pull Squirrel Nutkin's tail out? Was it *nice*?'

No, of course it wasn't nice, I decided, and told Joseph so.

The girl from New Zealand wanted the job but for the wrong reason, to get away from working at the hospital. Both children preferred the Irish girl, who's twenty-seven and said disapprovingly that Roddy Doyle's book *The Commitments* had portrayed 'the worst side of Dublin'.

At five I telephoned Sister Angela and said I didn't think my son was ready for the Service of Reconciliation. She arrived at my house half an hour later on her way to a Filipino wake in Linden Gardens, gave me a booklet and urged me to read it with my son. I, however, am too cowardly to do this. Also, I am unconvinced by the booklet, which is all about loving people and forgiveness. The only person my son loves, apart from me, I hope, and his father and sister, is Mrs Douthwaite.

4 December

This morning Andy, Hal's friend whom I met on my birthday, rang up and said he was going to Africa. I was pleased to hear his Lancastrian accent on the telephone. He sounded very robust and straightforward.

At lunchtime I dashed off a letter to Sister Angela saying that my son wasn't coming to the Service of Reconciliation tonight. I said I was afraid that if we forced him he would be put off religion, and that I would attend the service instead. (I felt guilty Joseph wasn't coming and was also genuinely curious to see what happened.) I took the letter round to the Community Centre and left it there.

I got back to find Julian outside my house, reading a book in his car. He had arrived early to take me to radiotherapy. At the hospital – Julian stayed in the car, still reading *War and Peace* – I had to wait longer than usual. The radiographer I previously disliked, whose name I have discovered is – improbably – Bob, is now very friendly.

Afterwards I suggested having a cup of tea in my house or Julian's flat. He did not reply, but drove straight to his flat. As we went down the basement steps, he said, 'This is the place where I have been happiest in my life.'

I asked, 'Is it because the woman you were desperately in love with for ten years used to live next door?'

He said, 'No.'

I suggested it was because the flat was womb-like. I had lived in a similar place in Paris – Hal's old flat in the Latin Quarter – and I had often longed to return to it and even dreamed about it long after I had left.

Julian then toasted some teacakes and there was an awful crash in the kitchen. He did not say what had happened. We had apricot jam and butter, and several cups of tea. Before we'd arrived I had thought of saying, 'Let's go to bed immediately!' but I did not do so as I was afraid of being rejected.

Julian picked up a book and read out a sentence. It was about a man who had made a pass at the sister of the girl he was really mad about. The sister took his pass seriously and the author made an observation that went something like this: 'In the working classes a flirtatious gesture, which would be interpreted by the middle and upper classes as a game, would be taken . . . as a preliminary to sex.'

What was the point of Julian's reading this out to me? I am not working-class. Was he saying that I was to interpret his 'mildly flirtatious' gestures as a game and nothing more?

I said I would have to leave, to go to the Service of

Reconciliation, and Julian offered to drive me there.

Julian said he wasn't impressed by Jesus, as he'd died at thirty. I said this was irrelevant. Surely one's conduct and the state of the soul are the main things, and the after-life? Julian said Jews did not believe in the after-life.

The service was at six. Lulu had said she would try to join me there later, when she returned from the hospice. Sister Angela grabbed me in the aisle and said, 'I got your letter. Good that you had that perception!'

I found myself sitting next to the mother of six who had given the religious instruction classes. A little girl I recognized from my son's class left her mother and crossed the aisle to snuggle up beside her teacher. Why couldn't my son be like this?

The church was full of children about to make their first confession. Father Sam, the young priest, said that the main thing to remember was that God loved us. He advised the children to 'pick one thing you are really sorry for'.

He announced to all of us, 'Three friends of God are going to come forward now, and everybody can see that you are really sorry.' This would have made me squirm as a child, but hosts of children came forward in threes and made their confessions to one of the three priests on the altar. A woman called Dulcie played softly on her guitar.

One girl seemed particularly to enjoy the occasion, looking all around her like an actress on stage before she knelt down to make her confession. Only one little dark girl in a beautiful red dress seemed to find it embarrassing and could hardly get the words out.

Father Sam then gave a short sermon, saying that we must 'love the people we find it difficult to love'. God was forgiving: 'He's not a big man sitting up there writing down the nasties.'

We all sang a hymn, 'Walk in the light', and the service was over. I had enjoyed it and was impressed by the priest's attempts to make the Sacrament accessible to children, but I did not think it would suit a child like Joseph, who was withdrawn and solitary.

As I left I met Lulu standing at the back, wearing a very short skirt, black tights and a scarlet bow in her hair. She had her bad-tempered Yorkshire terrier, Gilbert, with her on a lead.

She has started going out with a man who runs a bingo hall. She is giving a drinks party tomorrow, after which everyone is supposed to go and play bingo in Shepherd's Bush. I am invited.

5 December

I have received a letter from Cynthia, thanking me for the weekend, though she did all the work. She wrote: 'You are a first-class invalid and I think you could elevate it into an art form. Just think how awful it would have been if I'd found you each morning at 9.20 hunched and grey in your bedjacket on the edge of the bed, tense and tearing at your fingernails . . . It seems to me that you are in a high state of tension and anxiety, not without reason past and present. Disaster lurks round every corner, catastrophe at your back. Why not stop frigging about trying to turn out amusing pieces for the glossy mags and address your real interior fantasies?'

Later. Joseph and I go to a homoeopath in Wimpole Street recommended by Mrs Evans, the charming woman who teaches him music and is a friend of Lulu. The homoeopath is dressed like a nurse, or even a nun, with a high, stiff Victorian collar and plain grey clothes and grey-black hair. She's a small, neat woman and seems to know exactly what she's doing.

Joseph talks very freely to her and says he's afraid of ghosts. He tells her he has nightmares and sometimes sleeps in his sister's room. (I don't think he does, but perhaps he would like to.)

She prescribes some homoeopathic remedies for the white spots on his nails and his sleeplessness.

Joseph then asks her to guess what colour of hair his nanny has. She answers, 'Red.'

Joseph says, 'No, it belongs with B.'

'Blue.'

He likes this idea and says yes, but then tells the truth and says it's blonde. 'Why's it blonde?' he asks.

Maureen then comes to take him to school and I have my own appointment with the homoeopath. She doesn't seem at all fazed by the fact that I've had cancer and says that the radium brom that Lulu gave me last week, passed on by her friend who had cancer last year, is very suitable to counteract the effects of radiotherapy.

I, like Joseph, talk freely to her and tell her about my family history. The homoeopath thinks that developing cancer could be partly due to trauma.

I go down to Ainsworths Homoeopathic Pharmacy and get the various things she's prescribed. The little bottles come up from the basement on a string, like on a fishing-line, pulled by a soothing plump woman with a New Zealand accent.

I'm meeting the young man from the *Tatler*, the one who liked my house-swap article, in Soho at 12.30. He finally rang last week. Afraid of being late, I leave my last prescription at John Bell and Croyden, saying I'll return after lunch.

The club's already crowded. The journalist is not there. At a quarter to one I use the bar telephone to ring the *Tatler*. Then one of the waitresses remembers that he rang earlier to say he couldn't make it. I am annoyed, as I could have waited for my prescription instead of taking taxis all over the place. I now race back to collect the homoeopathic pills and take another taxi back to the club to meet Edward, whom I'm having lunch with at 1.30.

Edward orders two glasses of champagne. He describes a young woman who was in love with Miranda's husband, Alastair – she worked on the floor of the Stock Exchange with him. Once, while this woman was having an intense discussion about stocks and shares with Alastair in their kitchen, Miranda said bitterly to Edward, 'Alastair should have married a rich wife.' Edward now thinks Alastair probably had an affair with this young woman. He says what a pity it is Miranda never had children.

The Turk who was to be the new love of Edward's life has ditched him. Edward is mortified, and afraid he might bump into him in the local sauna. I tell him, 'Look, falling in love is nothing to be ashamed of.' I am saying this to convince myself as much as him.

We agree that the people who treated us badly should feel guilty, and indeed often they do.

A girl has answered the ad about cookery that Lulu put up weeks ago in the cookery school. I had forgotten all about it. I have now invited her round for an interview.

She is blonde with green eyes, very pretty. She has recently been working on a yacht touring the West Indies and normally cooks business lunches. I realized it would be ridiculous to ask her to cook for me alone – far too expensive, and anyway Paquita's doing it – so I asked if she could cook for a dinner-party on 18 December. (My children will be away with their father, I will be fed up with my radiotherapy treatment and too tired to cook for so many myself. This will give me something to look forward to.)

Larissa, a woman I have known for some time but with whom I never really made friends, came round for tea. She has one arm. She got cancer when she was ten. She had a lump in her arm, and the cancer spread to her lungs. She went in and out of hospital and had chemotherapy, then her arm was amputated. After she learned she had cancer on the lungs, her mother, a strong Catholic, took her to Lourdes. When she was examined later, there was no trace of anything on her lungs. Her cancer has never returned.

Larissa told me that one of the chemotherapy drugs she was treated with had been flown over from a children's hospital in Boston. A young pilot had been given special charge of it. Years later, by complete chance, she met the pilot. He remembered the incident, and the importance of the package.

She seems to want to make friends with me without making a lot of fuss about it. She is extremely good-looking, with bright-blue eyes and light-brown hair. She has a direct gaze, almost a flaming look. She started her own bookshop several years ago. She has just successfully sold it and now wants to travel to exotic places and do writing and journalism.

I think she will become one of the people who have made friends with me because I have cancer. I am pleased about this.

*

Letter today from Liza from Los Angeles. She has started going to AA meetings at a quarter to seven in the morning. The evening ones are too social, she says. Normally Liza is avid for contacts that might launch her into stardom. Los Angeles is full of alcoholics, narcotic addicts, bulimics, sexaholics, compulsive spenders, anorexics and even compulsive exercise freaks, judging by a recent article I've just read. Most of these addicts seem to be powerful people in the film business.

Later. I went to Lulu's drinks party. Lulu's new boyfriend was playing his guitar and singing sixties songs, plus songs invented by himself. Lulu had also invited her ex-husband.

At the end the boyfriend started handing out bingo cards to the people who were going on to the bingo hall. I decided not to go as I was too tired. Also, I have always hated bingo, a game entirely without skill.

Lulu's mother, Nancy, and her second husband were also there. Both in their eighties, they still love social life. Lulu says they will cross England for a sandwich.

When I got home I went to bed for the first time without sleeping pills. I woke about five, then slept intermittently. I dreamed vaguely about R, the man I had been in love with, the man who looks like my brother. I woke up feeling exposed and vulnerable, like a snail without its shell.

7 December

Paquita came this morning, but was half an hour late. She again refused to do any healing, saying I was far too tense. She did some more cooking, however. This time I was quite strict about telling her not to cook any seaweed. She said that the brown drink made from tree-bark was most important for my recovery. I said I found it disgusting, but agreed to drink it.

Miranda came round with some miniature daffodils. She said she had just met R, in the street outside his ex-wife's house. I said guardedly, 'He doesn't live there.' I added that his wife had thrown him out. I tried to talk in a detached way about him, so as not to let Miranda see how much he had hurt me. Miranda said she didn't particularly like his wife, though she hardly knew her. A great friend of hers had invited the wife to dinner twice, but had never been invited back. She had then pushed in front of Miranda's friend early one morning to get a taxi.

After Miranda had gone, Emily rang up and said she had heard last night in a new club in Soho that Miranda was having an affair with a rich Spaniard and that Alastair was about to divorce her. I was shocked, but decided I did not want to know about it in my present situation. I must have one friend whose life isn't in a state of chaos, and I thought Miranda was this friend – Miranda, who has appointed herself my main helper during my illness. She hasn't told me about her private life and I'm not going to ask.

Later. Miranda is trying to help me get another nanny as the two I interviewed a few days ago didn't work out. (The Irish one didn't want the job, and I thought the New Zealand one, despite being an occupational therapist, wouldn't be able to handle Joseph.)

Someone in Miranda's office knows another nanny agency. Miranda talked to them this morning and said it was important that I have an older person who can take responsibility, as I am in the middle of treatment for breast cancer. The woman at the agency seemed to understand the situation and said she was sure she could find someone quickly.

She later rang to say they had found an Australian girl, Margie, who was interested in the job. She was only eighteen, but was a very 'caring' person. I agreed to interview her. It seemed too much effort to look for anyone else, and I was worried I would be left with no one in the worst stages of my treatment, just before Christmas. Maureen is leaving in a few days.

8 December
I told my therapist about Miranda and she asked if she was co-dependent. I said I wasn't sure; she had no children and she did spend nearly a whole year looking after a man with cancer of the

prostate. The therapist then gave me an enormous list of books I should order.

The number of titles made me quite giddy: *Men Who Hate Women and the Women Who Love Them* (Tessa had already made me read this one two years ago); *Of Course You are Angry*; *Adult Children of Alcoholics*; *If Only I could Quit*; *Marriage on the Rocks*; *Going Home – a Re-entry Guide for the Newly Sober*.

To please my therapist I agreed to go to a meeting of Adult Children of Alcoholics. I said I was going to persuade my friend Emily to come, since her mother was also alcoholic.

This evening about six Emily telephoned and asked if I could have her mother to stay for Christmas. I said, 'Don't be ridiculous. My own mother will be there. That's bad enough. Anyway, I will just have finished radiotherapy. I'll be exhausted.'

I told Miranda, who said it was the most absurd thing she had ever heard. Emily must be off her head. She said Emily and her mother should be having *me* to stay: 'If I were you I'd book myself into a hotel for a week and go away and have a rest.'

The idea of spending Christmas alone in a hotel seems morbid. I want to be with my children.

I rang Emily and suggested we go to a meeting of ALCOA together. I said there was one in Chelsea at seven tomorrow night. Surprisingly, she agreed.

Then Julian drove me to Highgate, where Jacob was giving a party in a borrowed house. In the car Julian started complaining about his first ex-wife, who divorced him ten years ago. Taking a cue from my therapist, I suggested he take her out for a meal and express his anger to her directly. He said she wouldn't agree to come out with him anyway.

Several of Jacob's 'convent casualties' – women who had been at school with me – were also at the party. Kate, who claims that being at the convent made her have a nervous breakdown, tried to bring her bicycle up two flights of steps, then rushed into the hall shouting, 'Are there any menstruators at this party?'

It turned out that she wanted to borrow some Tampax. She and another guest had just been to a memorial service and had brought a lot of left-over food with them. Jacob's teenage niece, who works in Liberty's, offered Kate some Lil-lets. (Jacob whispered that this was his niece's first introduction to London 'society' and he hoped Kate's uninhibitedness wouldn't put her off.) Kate then introduced me and Julian to a drunk blonde actress who immediately asked for Julian's telephone number. He is always being propositioned by women.

Another of the 'highly disturbed' convent women came over to us and started talking about her daughter, who was at a school 'where people were Jewish and said "toilet".'

I was disgusted by her snobbery and said, 'You're suffering from feelings of acute social inferiority and should go to psychoanalysis three times a week.' I was rather pleased with myself for being so direct and thought my therapist would have applauded.

Later Julian said that this woman was 'a floozy', but that another ex-convent girl we had met there was 'a lady'.

Mr and Mrs Goat were also at the party, and Mr Goat told me you could fly to Cuba through a company called Progressive Tours. I liked hearing this as it made me realize I may have a future life, where I don't have the week filled with hospital appointments and where I might be able to travel to faraway places.

Later Julian drove me home. It seemed an ideal opportunity for seduction. Maureen was out and I had told Julian this. As we arrived at my house, however, Julian said, 'I might go home and watch a late-night movie.'

I invited him in for a drink, which he accepted. He sat opposite me on a chair, occasionally looking at me intently. When he left he asked, 'Will you be all right?'

9 December

I asked Miranda whether she thought Julian had a normal sex drive and she said, 'Has it occurred to you that he might not want to have an affair with you as he's married?' She also said he might think I didn't want to have sex after my operation. This, however, is not the case.

Today Lulu's mother, Nancy, and her husband took me to
radiotherapy. Nancy came in with me and chattered loudly while
we waited outside the cubicle. The ill-looking man, the one with
heavy-lidded eyes like a lizard, was there again with his Filipino
companion. Nancy speculated loudly on their relationship in the
waiting area.

In the car going home Nancy, whose knowledge of the English
aristocracy is encyclopaedic, though she says she doesn't feel
English, being a quarter Peruvian, a quarter English and half Irish,
kept pointing out obscure houses in side-streets where fallen
members of the aristocracy lived. Once she said, outside a hideous
Victorian house in West Kensington, 'The ground floor is Charles
Fenbottom's flat. His father had an affair with the maid and was
thrown out by his father, old Lord S. A respectable nephew
inherited the title. It's one of the oldest Catholic families in
England.'

She commiserated with me over my marriage breaking up and
quoted one of our American cousins, who a generation ago had
told her mother in Virginia, 'I didn't know marriage could be so
GHEAASTLY!'

When I got back, Jacob rang, jubilant because he has been
accepted to have psychotherapy on the National Health. This
afternoon he went for an interview with another psychotherapist
in his local hospital. He had to wait in a room with six middle-
aged women. They were all talking about someone called Pat
Long. One of them said, 'Pat was so depressed at the group last
week she wouldn't even go on the mattresses.'

The psychotherapist Jacob finally saw, an older woman with a
grey bun and a squeaky voice, said he was probably suffering
from unexpressed grief at the death of his mother, who died when
he was nine.

Evening. Emily and I have just been to the meeting for the
relations of alcoholics. I could tell from the start that Emily was
ready to be critical. We sat in a circle and were welcomed by the
group members in a superficial way, then a visiting American

woman took the chair and went on and on in a very long-winded way about her past life.

Later a few people 'shared'. A handsome young man started to tell of how he had visited his alcoholic father in his father's country house. Emily and I perked up. Unfortunately, just as he was getting into more personal details he lapsed into bland jargon and we fell back into a stupor. Then a woman with curly hair explained that she was still living with her alcoholic boyfriend, then went into a long story about how her car had broken down that day, but she had survived it because she believed in a Higher Power. Afterwards Emily whispered, 'If she thinks that's a bad day, I could tell her a thing or two.' On the way home she told me that Ben, her lover, had been beating on her door most of the night, but she had refused to let him in.

10 December
I went to my Spanish class this afternoon. Pedro asked us to imagine we were going on a trip round South America and to plan our route, making short sentences about each country. He pinned a map on the blackboard.

When it was my turn, I read out a sentence in Spanish about Peru, saying I was frightened to travel in the mountains of Peru because I might meet the Sendero Luminoso. I said if I met them I would pretend to be on their side.

Pedro laughed delightedly at my rather sophisticated example, but Marie-Ange was furious. Only she and one other member of the group knew what the Sendero Luminoso was. Pedro asked me to explain it to the class. I said in English that they were a Maoist guerrilla group who killed people. Marie-Ange said scathingly in her strong French accent, 'You 'ave been seeing too many films.'

I had resolved not to ask Miranda anything about her private life, but curiosity overcame me. I rang her and said I had to write a letter in Spanish to a South American tourist board for my Spanish homework and asked if she knew anyone who could help me. She said yes. I then dictated a short letter to her on the telephone,

including the phrases 'Shining Path' and 'luxury hotel' to see how
linguistically versatile her lover was. She said she would find out
and bring me a translation.

12 December

Margie, the new nanny, came for a few hours' trial. She was
supposed to arrive at nine, but was twenty minutes late. Her
brother is getting married on Saturday, and she said she'd had to
go to the Home Office for him. She has short black hair and seems
energetic. I like her and so do the children. She says she can drive a
car.

Both the children are on odd routines as it's nearly the end of
term. Lucy went to school today at noon, in home clothes, and
Joseph finishes tomorrow at noon. Lucy's carol service tomorrow
coincides with Joseph's play. It is not very clear what part Joseph
has. At first he told us he was Father Christmas. Now he says he is
a fox.

Miranda brought round the Spanish translation. It was on smart
office writing-paper, from an address in Mayfair. I noted her lover's
surname, which seemed to be that of a noble Spanish family.

13 December

I was able to go for only a few minutes to Lucy's carol service,
which was up the road from our house. My ex-husband stayed
there throughout and Maureen and I went on to Joseph's school
play. He *was* a fox. I was worried that the Father Christmas story
was another of his fantasies, or a way of self-aggrandizement, but
when I asked his teacher, afterwards, she said he *had* originally
been Father Christmas. Another boy had wanted the part so badly
that Joseph had stepped down.

16 December

My aunt, who's eighty-two, came to visit me on a bus from
Oxfordshire. She is my late father's sister. She dislikes my mother,
partly, I think, because she's jealous that my mother has more
money than her – she often refers to my mother's wealth – but also

because she genuinely believes that my mother wasn't a satisfactory wife to her only brother. I am fond of my aunt. At least she has taken the trouble to come and see me, even though she hates travelling alone.

When my aunt visits, which she does once a year, she comes with me to collect the children from school and helps with other such chores. My mother has never done this.

Although my aunt disapproves of my mother, she admitted today that she was sorry for her because of my brothers. She told me how she had been summoned by my father the day my brother was drowned. (The telegram had said 'Raymond accidentally drowned', as though he would have drowned on purpose.) My aunt and her husband had then driven several hours across country. That evening the vicar had come and told my father that his son was in Heaven. My father had shouted, 'I don't want my son in Heaven, I want him down here.'

My mother, according to my aunt, had sat in frozen silence, unable to express herself. When she told me this, I too felt sorry.

At about 6.15, while I and my aunt were both drinking whisky and water, I got a telephone call from Lulu's new boyfriend, who wanted to drop in as Lulu was working late at the hospice. I explained that my aunt was here. A few minutes later he arrived with his guitar. My aunt initiated a discussion about women being superior to men. He agreed, grabbed his guitar and started yelling out a song of his own composition: 'Women are for loving: da da da!' My aunt laughed a great deal at this and seemed to enjoy herself.

The next morning she accompanied me to Joseph's swimming gala at a local pool. Joseph won a race, swimming incredibly fast, his arms moving by his sides like a water-beetle. My aunt whispered, 'How many of those children do you think have been abused? Should we believe what we read in the papers?'

She then became so nervous about missing her bus home that she left the gala an hour early. My ex-husband, whom I sometimes think she prefers to me, escorted her to the bus station.

*

Today I started writing an account of the first time I had
chemotherapy. I might send it to a column in the *Independent* called
'The Best of Times, the Worst of Times'.

I told Miranda I was doing this and she said, 'Surely the worst
time must have been when you were actually told you had
cancer?' In a way, however, that was so unreal that I scarcely
believed it; or, if I did, I tried to overlay it with frenetic activity. I
suppose to some extent I am still doing this.

18 December
Cynthia had a party last night. It was full of people who've
rejected my manuscripts. Deborah, who used to be my agent
before I had children and stopped writing, asked how I was
getting on. I told her I had a manuscript with a publisher.

A publisher who'd rejected my book on childhood last summer,
saying it was 'beautifully written' but she couldn't publish it in the
recession, was also very friendly. She looked like Titania, in a green
dress. A neurotic and attractive older man took me out to dinner.
He kept complaining about his insomnia.

A woman keeps ringing up trying to clean my carpets.

I am having seven people to dinner tomorrow. The blonde girl
who answered Lulu's ad came round yesterday and we discussed
menus. Everything she suggested seemed to have coulis with it –
raspberry coulis, cucumber coulis, even salmon coulis. She
suggested salmon *en croûte* as the main course, with watercress
coulis. She seems very professional. She insisted on having two
waitresses to help. They cost twenty pounds each. The last course
is 'brandy snap baskets filled with fresh fruit and cream, served
with a mango and passion fruit coulis'.

19 December
Julian took me to radiotherapy. While I was inside having the
treatment, he sat calmly in his car, again reading *War and Peace*.

Later. Mr Goat messed up the numbers at my dinner-party by
coolly asking if he could bring a strange female, a woman he was

obviously having an affair with. I tried to refuse, but didn't manage it.

I did not ask Kate, my most highly disturbed Catholic schoolfriend, but instead invited her sister, Bev. (Kate invited my ex-husband and not me to her party a year ago when we first split up. Her sister is single, like me, and has invited me to two parties.)

Another woman, Jo, whom I'd met recently, came bringing me several of her own books on cancer, including yet another copy of the Bristol Programme. She also brought an amaryllis bulb in a plastic bag, with instructions on how to grow it. She herself had cervical cancer two years ago, but is now all right. Jo has four children and is very involved with politics in Latin America. She often travels there on her own and is very courageous. With her tonight was a fifty-year-old painter called Lucia, from Guatemala. Lucia spends half the year in Paris and regularly has exhibitions of her paintings in galleries in Europe. Jo whispered to me before dinner that Lucia was right wing and, another fault in Jo's eyes, didn't like children. I rather liked Lucia, who conducted herself with aplomb. After dinner, when we were having coffee, she complimented me on my clothes (I was wearing red Turkish trousers and a black top I had bought several years ago) and said, 'You would be good – in Guatemala.' She begged me to visit her there one day.

I also invited my new neighbours, who had helped me out that night when Hal came from Paris. The man, Richard, works in the City and his wife, Annie, runs a small picture gallery and is very involved with the local Labour Party. Annie mentioned to me just before the meal that she found men intimidating and preferred sitting next to women. She begged to sit beside Lucia. This was impossible, however, as the other women wanted to sit next to men. I put Annie next to Julian, whom many women find charming and sympathetic – he is a good listener – but after dinner she said he didn't seem to like her and hadn't responded to her overtures of conversation. She repeated that she found Lucia, who was sitting across the table from her, absolutely fascinating.

I realized that Annie could become a friend. I also liked her ·

husband, who has a gentle manner and dramatic black eyes under his glasses.

Lucia wore a leopard-skin shirt, black silk trousers and high heels. She had long gold ear-rings and three gold bangles. As she left with Jo she said again, 'You would look good – in Guatemala!' Annie said later that Guatemala was under an awful dictatorship, but admitted that she longed to be invited there too.

I had not asked Emily to the dinner since she usually collapses drunkenly at the table, sometimes even before the main course.

Jacob, another guest, asked to stay the night on the sofa. He has started therapy with the lady with the grey bun and squeaky voice – he has to bicycle three miles to her house on Friday evenings – and is very excited about his new Christmas job – an ugly sister in *Cinderella* in Bromley. He is keen for me to go and see him in it. It involves taking a train from Waterloo Station, then a taxi. I have told him I do not want to go as I might fall over a post.

At midnight Mr Goat asked for the number of a minicab firm, then sent his female companion off alone in it. He left shortly afterwards with Kate's sister. He will obviously stop at nothing to 'get a leg over' a new woman. His new play, an avant-garde version of *King Lear* set in an imaginary Middle Eastern country, is coming on shortly at the Royal Court's Theatre Upstairs. He did not suggest giving Jacob a part and Jacob is too much in awe of him to ask.

20 December

The man with the enormous penis has re-entered my life. He rang up and said he wanted to take me to a party. I told him I had had breast cancer and he said, 'You poor baby!' At the party, in Bayswater, I had to leave early because I was exhausted. I found myself leaning against the wall talking anxiously to a sympathetic woman in television about my son. JB did not offer to take me home, but said he wanted to stay on longer.

I couldn't help comparing his selfishness with the kindness of Julian. Why won't Julian have an affair with me?

Before meeting JB I had had a drink with Julian in the wine bar near where we live. I felt rather emotional. I asked, 'Julian, what do you think is going to happen to me?' He looked at me very kindly and made a noncommittal reply.

This morning my new friend and neighbour Annie rang up and came round for a chat. She says she has fallen head over heels in love with Lucia and wants to have an exhibition of her paintings in her gallery next month.

21 December

A friend who works at the Museum of London and is married to a painter, came round to cook me pumpkin soup. I told her how I was sick of wearing the same T-shirt at radiotherapy – the one I bought in Taos, New Mexico, with my son last summer, and smelling the strange, unwashed smell under my armpit. (It is not like BO; it's not that bad. I'm just sick of not being able to wash.) I said I was afraid I would always associate this T-shirt with being ill. She said when I had finished all my treatments, the best thing would be to burn it in a ritualistic bonfire. I do not think I could bring myself to do this. I might get to like it again years later.

After only an hour of her visit I was so tired I could hardly speak, so she went home.

22 December

The birthday of Nicky, my brother who committed suicide. I hate this day.

23 December

The house is full of carpet-cleaners. (I finally gave in to the woman who kept telephoning.) Mr W, the builder, is here too – there is bad damp in the corner of Joseph's bedroom – as well as Emily's current boyfriend, a Rastafarian who is sixteen years younger than her and is doing gardening for a living. Maria, a 66-year-old Spanish lady who used to clean our house, is also here. She now spends six months of the year in her luxury villa near Alicante, but is doing occasional cleaning while Patricia, my normal helper, and her sister are away for Christmas.

To escape from all the people in the house I went round to buy some Christmas presents in the nearby French delicatessen. I then met Julian in the street. I took him up to Miranda's flat to introduce them. While he was in the loo, Miranda whispered that he reminded her of a character in Nancy Mitford's book *The Pursuit of Love* who, whenever he went abroad, had to wear dark glasses because his eyes were so kind that all beggars rushed towards him.

I went home and rang up Kate, to ask if she knew whether Mr Goat had been to bed with her sister. She loyally said that she had no idea.

24 December
My last day of radiotherapy.

All the nurses and radiotherapists are wearing Father Christmas hats. In the distance I see the man with hooded eyelids and his Filipino companion.

I go in to see Dr W again, the doctor whom I like. Her doctor husband rings up from another part of the hospital and she tells him to buy some special herbs and a Christmas pudding in Marks & Spencer on his way home tonight. Their gentle domestic conversation makes me wish I was married again.

Tessa's waiting for me outside with a red van. She's offered to drive me down to Sussex as she's spending Christmas with her Polish cousins half an hour away.

Emily is to be in the Grand Hotel in Brighton with Paolo for Christmas, perhaps in another last-ditch attempt to save her marriage. She said that Paolo has pointed out callously that this is probably the last Christmas he and Emily will have together, so they might as well spend it in luxury instead of watching Emily's mother get drunk.

Emily is staging some kind of performance in a local arts centre near Brighton the day after Boxing Day. She asked if she could borrow my car to bring down some of the equipment, but, knowing what she's like with cars, I said no. Ben is on holiday in

Israel with a black model he met in a bar two nights ago. I did not ask what has happened to the Rastafarian gardener.

Her mother is now in an old people's home in Eastbourne and she is going to visit her there on Boxing Day.

I am more tired than I have ever been in my life. Even now I am still not allowed to wash my right breast or under my right arm. I have to wait at least ten more days. My nipple is still raw and I keep having to put purple paint on it, using rubber gloves. When the paint dries, it makes my skin very stiff. I feel like an armadillo. Also I itch all the time.

When I went into my bathroom tonight to put on more of the purple stuff, Joseph was there wearing the rubber gloves, which were much too big for him. He asked, 'Are these what nurses use to poke children's – gentlemen's – you know what?'

'Yes,' I said wearily.

Christmas Day
I was woken at five by Joseph singing 'The Holly and the Ivy'.

My ex-husband is here, for the children's sake, and because I couldn't cope with this Christmas on my own. He has cooked the turkey, as he has done every year since we were married. Last night I helped him fill the children's stockings.

Christmas morning. My mother arrives in a local minicab. She is still walking with a stick, after the hip operation. Her teeth look very bad – two are missing – and her hair is straggly, though most of the time she insists on wearing a red woollen hat, even at lunch. Her present to me is a silver ship. A few weeks ago she and Molly went to London to a vault where some family silver was stored. The ship, about a foot long, has little figures and silver rigging. It's on a separate silver base on wheels.

The ship is very beautiful and the fact that my mother has given it to me means a great deal – to her. My mother thinks possessions will save her. She hoards things like a child refusing to give up its toys. When I was at boarding-school, she sent me presents from far-off places. Once she sent me a butterfly paperweight. The lovely butterfly was trapped in transparent plastic. I mislaid it and

she wrote me a long letter scolding me for not looking after things.
I didn't want the butterfly. I would have preferred to have my
mother.

Before lunch we were all invited to the Douthwaites' bungalow
for a Christmas drink. Their sitting-room looked very festive, with
wrapped presents, nuts, paper-chains and boxes of chocolates
everywhere, and a small silver Christmas tree. Mrs Douthwaite's
sister and brother were visiting. Mrs Douthwaite gave the children
fizzy drinks and filled their glasses with tiny pink plastic balls of
ice. My mother and Mr Douthwaite talked about the last war. He
was in submarines for four years with three Frenchmen and my
mother was in the WAAF, decoding at Bletchley. Mr D likes a
drink himself and made jokes about giving my mother something
stronger than lemonade. I thought, considering her broken hip,
this was rather tactless. We did not offer my mother champagne at
lunch and she didn't ask for it. She had brought some fizzy apple
juice as a substitute.

After lunch Lulu and her mother rang up to wish me Happy
Christmas. Lulu's bad-tempered dog has bitten a man from Parcel
Post and he may sue.

Boxing Day
I am spending most of the time in my bedroom. I am at a low ebb.
I can't bear looking at my breast, covered with purple. I'm sick of
sitting in the bath and not washing the upper part of my body. I
hate looking in the mirror. I feel very unattractive and also very
tired. My breast itches and burns the whole time. I wish the von
Strandmann family were here, but they are all in Austria with
Hilary's parents.

At teatime Paolo and Emily came over from Brighton and we
ate some Christmas cake. Paolo said something about a woman he
knew who was dying of cancer. When I hear about people dying
of cancer I am terrified. I know what being 'in the grip of fear'
means.

After tea, instead of Emily going to visit her mother
immediately as she had planned, we played Trivial Pursuit in the

kitchen since Joseph was watching *The Snowman* on television next door. Mrs Douthwaite and her sister Fee-Fee came over and joined in. Paolo sulked because he didn't understand some of the references, such as BBC programmes from the fifties and British sport. He went into the sitting-room and Emily went in after him to see if he was all right. By the time we had finished, Emily had got at the gin and was lying asleep on the sofa while Paolo had disappeared. My ex-husband carried Emily up to the spare room.

Paolo turned up again at about nine in a taxi to collect her. He woke her up and half carried her downstairs. As usual, she was dressed inappropriately for the time of year, in red stiletto heels and a black mini-dress. She allowed Paolo to lead her out of the front door, then suddenly broke free and threw herself across the taxi's bonnet. Paolo and the driver tried to coax her into the car. Eventually I went to bed. My ex-husband told me later that the taxi had taken them both away at midnight.

27 December
My ex-husband has gone back to London to write his book. I am left here with the children and Margie. The children like her and she is doing her best, but she keeps complaining about her own ailments, particularly headaches. I think she would prefer an employer who gossiped with her more about emotional problems. I can't do this.

Mrs Douthwaite saw her romping with Joseph in the garden, however, and said she was the only girl who had done this with him. Maureen had been far too lazy. Margie also makes more effort with the children's food. Yesterday she served tacos stuffed with minced meat, which they enjoyed.

28 December
Joseph comes into my room early and talks about his dreams: 'The only dream I didn't have very clearly was about Daddy's two shoes – the big shoe trampled on the little shoe. All my other dreams are very clear.'

He then tells me, 'I've got another mobile tooth.'

Lucy is out every day riding the piebald pony. Joseph is very jealous of the pony. He wants to have a spider as a pet.

31 December

Dear Elisa
Just a brief note to say how much Stephen and I like your story and how delighted we will be to include it in *God, an Anthology of Fiction*.

All the best
Sarah.

January 1992

1 January

'Saw big black cloud and thought it was going to snow, but it didn't. I hate Mum.' I have just reread this in an old diary. I was thirteen when I wrote it. At first, when I read those words, I couldn't remember hating my mother. I assumed that my violent emotions were a result of adolescence.

But perhaps I really did feel like that. Even if I don't 'hate' my mother now, I hate the chaos that was so much a part of my childhood, the sense that all the time we were waiting for another disaster to strike.

When I first realized I had breast cancer I knew I was engaged in a battle with my mother. It may sound melodramatic, but I know that this time I have to get the better of her or I will die. This time it has to be me.

Last night, New Year's Eve. I did not go to any of the parties in London that I'd been invited to. I felt too weak.

Instead I stayed in Sussex and went at the last minute to the Skidelskys', where I had been invited by Nicky, a local landowner, to see in the New Year. Nicky, the only person I know who's read *The Satanic Verses* and Nicholas Mosley's *Hopeful Monsters* straight through – they're both 'difficult' reads – had told me to phone if I wasn't doing anything on New Year's Eve. When I rang, he said he'd decided to go hunting in Northants early the next morning. Then he changed his mind, perhaps because he felt sorry for me, and told me to meet him at the Skidelskys' at about eleven.

I got there before he did, in my own car. (Margie, who was babysitting, luckily – as she's only just arrived in England, she didn't have a party to go to – seemed surprised he wasn't coming to fetch me.)

The Skidelskys had just finished dinner. Besides their three children there was Simon, a blond man who rents one of the cottages under the Downs, another teenage boy and a rather depressed-looking man in his fifties. I had brought some truffles.

We all went into their sitting-room, where there was an enormous log fire. Nicky then arrived with a bottle of champagne, which we drank. Nicky said he wanted a wife and was going to advertise for one. She must be a good cook, he said, and must give him candlelit dinners. Everyone except the depressed man and me seemed amused by this. I did not find it amusing, because, except for the Skidelskys' daughter, I was the only unmarried woman in the room.

Simon, who's very funny and looks like a grown-up Little Lord Fauntleroy, 'with golden lovelocks waving on to his shoulders' and big blue eyes, suggested that Nicky should advertise for an upper-class wife. He said more 'characters' would reply.

At 11.30 we went upstairs and played knock-out ping-pong, which involved rushing round the table after you had hit the ball once. According to Nicky, the Skidelskys, high-powered intellectuals, are mad about sport. Once they'd been on holiday in Morocco with some friends. As soon as they'd arrived, Robert, despite the heat, had embarked on a highly competitive game of squash with the biographer Michael Holroyd.

I thought I wouldn't be able to run round the table because of my operation under my arm. I did do it, but not with my usual strength. I was out before their nine-year-old daughter.

At midnight Augusta brought in a plate of nuts and raisins covered with brandy, which she set fire to. We were all supposed to stick our fingers into the flames, though I didn't. Nicky got me a raisin out of the flames, and I ate it.

We toasted each other with champagne. I was kissed warmly by Robert, Nicky and Simon, but I was too shy to kiss the three teenage boys, and they didn't kiss me.

Nicky then left for home with his dog and Robert embarked on a discussion with his son Edward about IQ tests and original thought. Robert said that recognizing existing 'patterns' was a requirement for an IQ test and that all kinds of other exams, including scholarships and Oxford entrance, often precluded original thought. An original thinker like Keynes – Robert is writing the second volume of his biography – wasn't so good at recognizing orthodox patterns and therefore had to think of alternatives.

I liked the way Robert argued intimately with his son. I liked the family atmosphere in the Skidelskys' house. I wished my own family when I was a child had been like that. I kept getting up to go home and then sitting down again. Then I lost my handbag. Perhaps I didn't really want to leave this agreeable place. I eventually found the handbag beside the ping-pong table.

2 *January*

New Year's Night. I dream I'm in a house in Notting Hill with Mary Killen and R's ex-wife. We're in a beauty session organized by Mary, a complicated event connected with her problem letters.

There's a wedding anniversary party, given by R and his ex-wife. In the dream his wife says what other people have said in real life, that he can't communicate.

I wake up with a feeling of sweetness and hope. I look out of the window and see that Paula, the girl who sometimes comes to do the garden, is planting bulbs in the earth.

I ring Miranda in London. She reveals that there *was* a party at R's ex-wife's house last night. On her way back from a New Year's Eve party she passed the house and saw children tumbling out of the front door. One was on a skateboard. She thought she saw R himself, but wasn't sure.

Later I walk with Joseph and Lucy to the local stables. Michele has offered to take both our daughters in her trailer to ride on the Downs today. We load the ponies and she drives slowly towards the Downs, me following in my car with Joseph.

We park near some beautiful old farm buildings, near where

Toby fell into a slurry pit. (He nearly drowned, because we
thought his hysterical barking was that of a farm dog.)

Michele and I then follow the girls on foot along the old coach
road under the Downs and back through the park.

Joseph charges ahead of us, following the ponies. He's very
jealous of the whole expedition and even tries to hit Spinet, Lucy's
pony. After half an hour Michele offers to take Lucy back to the
stables when the girls finish their ride so I can go with Joseph to a
lunch-party.

At the lunch I drink a lot of champagne – Lee, the American
host, and his wife are very generous – and forget momentarily that
I had breast cancer.

Evening. My breast still seems infected in one area. I am sick of
being covered with purple. I hate the English winter and I hate this
time of year.

3 January
Clare rang from London, saying there was a very optimistic article
in the *Independent* about breast cancer. Although I had the paper I
hadn't seen the article. I read it carefully.

'The statistics show that in women whose cancer has spread to
armpits, 62 per cent who had extra treatment survived at 7 years,
compared with 50 per cent who did not . . . 35 per cent of treated
women survived at 15 years compared with 23 who did not.'

Did this mean that 62 per cent survived who'd had treatment
and 50 per cent who'd also had treatment did not survive, or did it
mean that the 50 per cent who'd not had treatment did not
survive? I became frantic with worry.

I rang Miranda and she said not to take too much notice. I then
read out a paragraph to her, trying to make a joke of it: 'The three
beneficial treatments identified by the research are the hormonal
drug Tamoxifen, which blocks oestrogen; a cocktail of cyclotoxic
drugs (chemotherapy); and ovarian ablation to turn off the
oestrogen supply.'

I said to Miranda, 'I'd better say when I next see the professor in that club in Notting Hill Gate, "Now please may I have my chemotherapy cocktail?" '

When I put the phone down I saw an optimistic paragraph that made me realize why Clare had alerted me: 'Richard Peto, head of the Imperial Cancer Research fund's Cancer Studies Unit, Oxford, had never seen cancer results so good in terms of saving lives.'

However, when I reread the preceding paragraphs, they seemed to refer more to the benefits of Tamoxifen than chemotherapy. I read the whole article through again: 'Chemotherapy gave 5 extra survivors'; 'chemotherapy' (wrongly spelt twice) 'and Tamoxifen gave 12 extra survivors'. The word 'survivors' sent an unpleasant chill through me.

That night I rang Liz Whipp in Bristol and she said she would read the whole report in tomorrow's *Lancet* (the seven-year report on which the article was based) and talk to me in detail about it tomorrow evening.

4 January
My comic letter about the incident in the Catholic church has been published in the *Spectator*. I am delighted.

Mary's reply is as follows: 'In the circumstances it would have been quite in order for you to approach the celebrant and interrupt him firmly and calmly. For future reference, however, you should acquaint yourself with the telephone facilities adjacent to your church so that you can move swiftly on your own initiative should something similar happen again.'

I rang Liz again and she tried to summarize the results of the report in the *Lancet*. She said that until the results of the report were published a few days ago, no one had been sure about the beneficial results of chemotherapy. It was still not absolutely certain how much survival rates in pre-menopausal women with breast cancer were due to chemotherapy itself or to ovarian ablation, which normally occurred anyway after chemotherapy. More studies, comparing these two groups of women, were still needed.

I took notes as she was speaking, jotting phrases all over my
notebook, and tried to make sense of them afterwards.

I am having my next chemotherapy injection next week.

6 January

Back in London. Beginning of the school term. I have received a
letter from a man called Andrew O'Hagan of the *London Review of
Books*, rejecting my diary account of my hospital experiences.

Three other items of mail this morning:

1 A joint in an envelope, from my friend Kay in New York.
   She's heard that smoking dope can stop the sickness after
   chemotherapy.
2 A new American novel from Geraldine Cooke, *Closing
   Arguments*, about murder and sado-masochism and sex in a
   small US town. She hopes I can review it.
3 Clippings from Hal, from the *Washington Post* and the *New
   York Times*, about the results of the recent study published
   in the *Lancet*. These articles are clearer and more optimistic
   than the ones I've read in the English papers.

The *Washington Post*:

Whereas recurrences of most types of cancer appear in the
first five years after surgery, breast cancers can recur decades
after an apparently successful treatment. For that reason,
researchers are hesitant to set a time at which a woman can be
declared 'cured'.

Nevertheless, the new findings show the benefits of
hormone treatment or chemotherapy in breast cancer are
more noticeable ten years after surgery than five years after.
The finds have prompted some experts at least to raise the
possibility that the drugs may have permanent effects.

The *New York Times*:

In findings that have startled even the most optimistic
experts, the largest analysis of breast cancer patients ever

conducted shows that the life-saving benefits of widely used hormone or drug treatments prevail for at least ten years, long after therapy has ended.

Hall enclosed a cheeky note with these, saying that he was trying to preserve my body for the future, for his own purposes as much as mine.

I go to see my therapist. I now sit on a padded black chair beside her instead of opposite her on a hard brown one. Today she wants me to discuss sexuality. She also wants me to do some boring old yoga or t'ai chi. I don't want to do this.

I talk about my dream about R at New Year and his odd behaviour in real life. She said there was no doubt that R had been attracted to me, yet for some reason had decided not to do anything about it. She herself knew a priest who was attracted to her, though obviously she wasn't going to seduce him. She then described how she had just fallen into the arms of her new lover. She said they had not made a conscious decision, but their bodies were too strong for them. When she told me this, I was annoyed as I felt she was putting me in a position of inferiority to her, i.e. she was ready for a proper relationship and I wasn't.

When I returned home I'd forgotten my key and had to wait on the doorstep for fifteen minutes for Margie and the children to return from their schools.

A neighbour had popped a *Times* article through my letter-box. It said that fifty women die of breast cancer per week, that it's more prevalent in England than anywhere else, that doctors are complacent and that it's the only type of cancer whose treatment hasn't improved in the last few years. I can't imagine why my neighbour, whom I like, gave me this pessimistic and discouraging article. She probably hadn't read it.

10 January
6 a.m. A few hours before chemotherapy. I will now have it regularly twice a month until it ends in May, except for a three-

week break at the end of January, when I'm going to America.

I woke at four in a state of dread, despite a sleeping pill Miranda had given me.

I dreamed the following unpleasant dream. I was in a big swimming-pool in a sports centre. I was about to go to hospital. Miranda was there and several of us were swimming about in the pool. I lost Joseph in the changing area. I was desperate. Then my mother turned up unexpectedly, with an escort, to take me to hospital. Molly was also there; in fact, there were too many people there altogether. I eventually found Joseph.

The scene changed to a meeting in our Sussex village. My ex-husband was there. Someone came by on a hay-cart, or maybe I was on a hay-cart. It was announced that Mr Mainwaring, who works for my mother, had died.

Somebody else had also died in the dream, but who? I hope not me.

Chemotherapy again. Miranda took me in her car. Just as we were leaving, my neighbour Annie came walking down the hill. She smiled and kissed her hand as we drove off.

I showed Miranda the short cut that Johnny, the minicab driver, had shown me and we parked this time at the side of the hospital, very near the radiotherapy building. We each put two pounds in the meter, four hours' worth of time. To get to the main hospital from here we had to walk past a hut with an intriguing notice outside: Emergency Psychiatry Unit.

Getting off the escalator, we met a blonde woman who was also about to have chemotherapy. She said we had to go to Clinic 4 first, not straight to the Oncology Department.

In Clinic 4 – a large dark room with benches covered with cracked grey plastic – several people were waiting. I was immediately given a blood test to see if I was HIV positive. This was too sudden for me to be alarmed. Also, in a way I was relieved to have the test. Occasionally I had wondered, when one of Hal's contraceptives broke, whether I would get AIDS. As for JB, he had been very stubborn and hated using condoms, though the last couple of times I had seen him I had insisted on it, saying I already had cancer and wasn't prepared to get another terminal illness.

After having a few words with Di, the cheerful oncology nurse with the pony-tail who had appeared in the waiting-room, Miranda and I were called in to see the professor. A blonde nurse was in there with him. The professor looked more friendly than he had at the last appointment, when my angry letter had been lying in front of him. The professor is handsome in an actorish way. He looks Celtic, with floppy black hair, pink cheeks and blue eyes. He said immediately, 'Didn't I see you in a club in Notting Hill Gate?'

He explained that he had recognized me, but couldn't remember where we had met. He had thought perhaps I worked in the hospital. I told him I had recognized him too, but had decided not to say anything. He had found the club too smoky. I said I had found it claustrophobic (particularly after *he* had appeared, reminding me of cancer, but I did not say this) and that I thought the club's main function was as a place to drink after closing hours. I added, 'Though you and I were both there at the respectable time of 9 p.m.'

He asked me some questions and tapped a lot of information on to the computer screen. He then examined me behind a curtain. I found him more attractive than when I had last seen him in the hospital.

I got out my notes and asked him about ovarian ablation. I wrote down what he said so I could ask Liz about it. I mentioned the various articles on breast cancer that I'd just read, and said that the one in the *New York Times*, on the recent *Lancet* survey, had been very good and thorough. The professor said that American journalists tended to take more trouble to understand what they were writing about, but that most articles he read about breast cancer were 'full of rubbish'. He had been asked recently to appear in a TV programme on it, but had refused. He said, 'I don't want to be recognized in some seedy bar and have someone think, what's a top cancer doctor doing in a place like this?'

(When I discussed this offbeat remark with Miranda, she said he wasn't making a joke about the club; he really meant it.)

Miranda and I waited on one of the benches outside for the results of the blood tests. The blonde woman who'd told us where to go earlier was also waiting for her results. She was reading a Danielle Steel novel and asked if this was my first chemotherapy. She said that it was her seventh.

Then the oncology nurse brought back the results of our tests. Neither of us was HIV positive. Instead of feeling overwhelmingly relieved, I just thought, well, that's that under my belt.

Miranda and I walked with the blonde woman along the corridors to the Oncology Department. On the way she told us she had four children and that her husband had died the week before in a plane crash in Eastern Europe. She was waiting for his body to be brought back to England. When we arrived at the Oncology Department, she went straight into the chemotherapy room.

Miranda and I sat outside, appalled. Her situation seemed so awful, yet there she was, calmly reading Danielle Steel, not even a mother, sister or friend with her. The injustice of her double misfortune was staggering.

I was told by Bridie, the Irish nurse, that I would have to wait a while for my injection. Miranda said we preferred to wait outside rather than in the ward, which she knew I hated. At last I was called in there by the Scottish nurse, Mrs Blair. Bridie was now busy with other patients, and so was Rosie.

The blonde woman was on the bed by the window, still intently reading Danielle Steel. I whispered, 'Is she all right?' to Nurse Blair, who replied that she thought her husband's death hadn't 'hit' her yet.

I was in the end bed, in the darkest part of the room, beside a man speaking French to a woman I thought must be his wife, but turned out to be a volunteer. I did not see this man's face. He was having his injection of chemotherapy and this made me turn away, nauseated. When he got up to leave a few minutes later he gave me a charming smile. Too late, I saw that he had lovely brown eyes and wished I had engaged him in conversation.

Saturday, 11 January
Miranda is going to a movie tonight with her Spanish lover. She has still said very little about him. I do not know if I will ever meet him.

I have deliberately asked to have my chemotherapy treatments on Fridays rather than midweek as I had before Christmas, so I can recover at weekends while the children are away with my ex-husband. This means I will be on my own in the house, however, which is depressing.

I am taking many different forms of medication – acid phosphorus and foresight minerals and breast cream from the homoeopath, Ondansetron anti-sickness pills, instead of the ones that made me manic – these have now replaced the Dom Peridone – folinic acid tablets and Cyclophosphamide tablets, the third drug of the chemotherapy 'cocktail'. (The other two are injected.)

Last night I smoked half the joint that Kay had sent me from New York. I don't know if it made me feel less sick or not, but I was certainly calmer.

I woke about one covered in sweat. I changed my nightdress, moved to the dry side of the bed and lit up the second half of the joint. Then I started to cry.

I went to sleep again with the help of the joint. I woke again around six, then at 9.15.

Maria, the cleaning-lady, arrived at ten. (She prefers to come on Saturdays.) By then I was talking to Lulu on the telephone. Lulu loves speaking Spanish, so I gave her the phone. Later Maria said that Lulu had told her she was very worried about me, that she prayed for me every day and had told Maria to pray too.

I like Maria. I feel well when I see her. I like the way she dresses so smartly and I like her self-respect. Last week two teenagers in her street told her off for wearing a fur coat. Maria had retorted, 'You don't tell me what I can wear. Are you jealous?'

At 12.30 I went to have lunch with Vaneeta in a restaurant near Portobello Road. I decided that I would get suicidal at home on my own after Maria left. Just as I was leaving my house, a tree-surgeon arrived to trim the pear-tree and the cherry-tree in my garden. My new neighbours had kindly organized it, as their trees also needed trimming.

Vaneeta looked exhausted. Her husband died suddenly a year ago. They had only been married ten months. Then she had a miscarriage. A few years before that her brother, like mine, died of an overdose, but I think in his case it was an accident.

After lunch we went into the local bookshop, and I immediately saw a new book by R on the front desk, about South America. There was a flattering introduction by a friend of his, saying he was a terrific guy.

When I got home I read some of it. I found the mock-modest 'Aren't – I – honest?' tone of it absolutely infuriating. The fact that I fell in love with someone I don't respect is maddening.

I spent the rest of the weekend writing my review of *Closing Arguments*, the novel Geraldine had sent me. By concentrating on the words I was writing I tried to forget that I felt sick and weak. I wrote most of it in longhand, lying in bed.

On Sunday Cynthia rang up. She had written to Richard Ingrams suggesting an idea for his new magazine, the *Oldie* – reviews of memorial services. She proposed that she and another journalist friend should do this. He hadn't replied to her letter, but had rung this other woman asking *her* to do it.

12 January

My American cousin Dita rang up. She has offered to come over and fly back to the States with me when I go to stay with her and her mother in ten days. I am touched by this, particularly as she hates long flights. She says she hasn't been to England for years and is looking forward to staying with me in London for a few days first. Normally I would have discouraged her from spending the extra money; I would have reassured her that I was perfectly all right to fly alone. I didn't do this, because I really would like her to come with me; I'm at a very low ebb and have never felt more hopeless – I mean without hope.

The expense does not mean that much to Dita, who is well off. It is important that she has offered to help me when I need it and that I accept it. (A New York fortune-teller told me when I was twenty-five, 'If someone offered you a silver spoon, you'd dash it to the ground. You must learn to accept help, child!') Now I have had to.

I am very fond of Dita. Our grandmothers were sisters. She is one of the most kind-hearted people I know. Katherine, who worked for my grandmother for fifty years, told me that years ago, when she was having a thyroid operation in a London hospital, arranged by my grandmother, Dita was in London and sent her flowers every day. When I flew over to New York last February for Jill's funeral, my plane was seven hours late because of snow at Gatwick. I finally arrived at Dita's apartment from Newark Airport to find she was still waiting up for me. She hugged me and said, 'I'm so sorry for you, Elisa, that you've come on such a sad occasion.'

Vaneeta rang up this morning and told me James had a big article in the *Sunday Telegraph* about the treatments for cancer, so I went out and bought it. In it he attacked the conclusions of the recent report in the *Lancet*. He wrote that there was no real proof that chemotherapy worked any better as a preventative or 'cure' of breast cancer than simple ovarian ablation.

> The obvious reason was that the cytotoxic drugs had not in fact killed off the micrometastases but had instead lowered the levels of circulating female hormones by destroying cells in the ovaries. Breast cancer is hormone-dependent and a similar therapeutic benefit can be obtained much more easily and with less toxicity with X-ray treatment aimed at the ovaries or hormone-blocking drugs.

James rightly emphasized that chemotherapy had terrible side-effects:

> nausea, vomiting, hair loss and general debility, which on top of the trauma of being recently diagnosed as having cancer leaves many women seriously depressed.

He also attacked trials, implying that most of the experts didn't know what they were doing. Was he trying to be controversial or did he really believe this? He had always been a rebel; when I had met him in 1971 he had been a member of the Communist Party of Great Britain, intent on working with patients in the East End.

Evening. I have written a letter to the *Sunday Telegraph* about James's article:

> Sir
> I have breast cancer and have just completed six weeks of radiotherapy and three out of twelve treatments of chemotherapy. I am forty-two. I therefore read Dr James LeFanu's article 'Cancer: the Choices' last Sunday with considerable interest and attention to detail.
> Dr LeFanu alleges that most of the experts in this subject are in a state of confusion and do not know what they are doing. If he really thinks this, surely it would be better to publish his article in a medical journal rather than in the national press, where it will terrify numbers of women who will now think they are getting the wrong treatment?
> He also criticizes cancer specialists for asking women 'to take part in clinical trials to make sense of this confusion'. He has omitted to mention the one reason why these trials do and should continue to take place; that is, there is still no known cure for cancer.

I rang up Clare and read out the letter, to make sure I had got it right about cancer trials. She said she would ask someone she knew whose brother was involved in cancer research.

I also rang Shabu, Vaneeta's friend, the one who used to work as a doctor at the Royal Marsden. Shabu said that James has always had 'a bee in his bonnet' about chemotherapy.

Clare called back and said that her contact had been very interested in my letter as it had alerted him and his brother to James's article, which they'd missed. (I was confused about who

was the friend and who was the brother, but one was Richard
Peto, who had pioneered the important statistical research of the
study whose results James was attacking.)

13 January
A local mother left a message on my answerphone saying there
was an item about breast cancer on *Woman's Hour* this morning. I
began listening to it when I should have been finishing my review.
I then started to cry. I was sitting on the floor of my daughter's
bedroom. I simply couldn't bear to hear yet another woman
describe how she'd tried self-help remedies, another how she'd
been treated badly by the doctors and so on. I couldn't bear to hear
anything more about the subject. When I went downstairs to the
kitchen, there was a message from Duncan on my answerphone. I
immediately felt more cheerful.

I rang him back and told him about Richard Ingrams hijacking
Cynthia's idea of reviewing memorial services. Duncan said
Cynthia should 'attack back in an unrestrained manner' and print
the story in the *Standard*'s 'Londoner's Diary'. He said that
freelance journalists should meet every week and discuss self-
defence. He had just had trouble with a glossy magazine refusing
to pay him for an article that they had commissioned. Also,
another editor had made him rewrite an article and, when he had
done it, had sent him the proofs of the original one she'd rejected,
not noticing the difference. He is charging her two hundred and
fifty pounds for wasted hours.

I have arranged to meet Jenny, who was in the ward with me,
today at the hospital. She is having chemotherapy. I am having a
check-up.

Later. I am in Clinic 8, waiting for my appointment. I came into the
hospital through a forbidden side-entrance, meant for medical
college students only. I boldly passed the man at the security desk,
went up several corridors and, going through a door I'd never
used, found myself in the oncology ward. This little transgression
of the hospital rules gave me a kick and made me feel independent.

Jenny was sitting in the waiting-room looking woebegone. She told me she had been waiting for her treatment for over four hours.

At about two I went with her into the chemotherapy ward and the Scottish nurse, Mrs Blair, was there. Jenny is the first person to try out a new kind of treatment, which involves cooling the scalp first to prevent hair loss. After she was attached to the machine that cooled her scalp, Jenny complained that she was freezing. Mrs Blair admitted she must have put the machine on too low a temperature. Jenny then had her hair covered with conditioner, and a blue rubber cap attached to a tube was put on her head.

Leaving her there, I went upstairs for my appointment in Clinic 8. I was delighted to see Dr W, whom I'd last seen just before Christmas. She looked pleased to see me too. She explained to me in detail what was happening and readily answered all my questions. She made it clear that chemotherapy was a precaution, and admitted that there was no way of knowing whether there were other cancer cells in the body, unless I got another lump. Only 5 per cent of people get more lumps after radiotherapy and surgery, she said. She emphasized that I was getting the best available treatment. She also admitted, when I pressed her, that there was no 'cure' as such. She said that chemotherapy normally induces the menopause and if it didn't it would be induced anyway by ovarian ablation. I liked the way she answered my questions so conscientiously, trying above all to tell me the truth.

On my way out I visited Jenny again. She was still attached to the machine. It was odd being a visitor in the oncology ward. I wondered if I would ever be able to visit the place again when I was no longer a patient, like other ex-patients did, calling to say hello to the nurses and cheer up the new patients; or whether it would always make me feel sick.

I got on to the top deck of a bus in Fulham Palace Road, next to a woman picking her nose, so I moved. The conductor stupidly told me to get off at the bingo hall instead of at the underground so I had to cross several roads near Shepherd's Bush Green.

Suddenly I forgot the depression I had felt in the morning when I had heard the *Woman's Hour* discussion, and was excited. I imagined I could smell the spring.

When I got back, Hal had telephoned.

14 *January*
Julian rang this morning and complained about his wife and his wife's sister, who have both arrived from Tokyo. They are staying with him for several weeks. He said his wife keeps boasting that she is from a high-class Japanese family, so he asked her why, in that case, she spends all day window-shopping. When he buys her a dress, he says, she immediately gives it to her mother or sister.

I found this carping rather unattractive. In fact, it is the worst side of Julian. I suppose now his wife's here I won't see him.

I am still confused about whether or not I will get the menopause. After lunch I rang Sarah, Pete Ayrton's wife, who has done nursing, and asked her whether I will get it early because of chemotherapy; if I do, will it then last a shorter time than an ordinary menopause? I asked what the effects of the menopause were. She said one effect can be the lowering of sexual libido. I said, 'Well, that would make life easier.'

A few hours later I became anxious that I might not have much sex in the future, so I hastily arranged to meet JB at a secret destination. When he arrived he asked if I'd brought any whisky and I said no; why, hadn't he? He went out and came back with a bottle of Jameson's. We then made love after warming the bed with a blow-heater. He suggested going on a half-term spring holiday with me and my children and his children. I do not want to commit myself to a long-term relationship with him, however. Am I just using him for sex? Yes.

16 *January*
Margie seems to be getting on well in the job. Yesterday I overheard her talking on the telephone with great intensity to what I assumed was a member of the opposite sex about a 'relationship'. How has she had time to develop a relationship

when she's only been in England a couple of weeks? I hope she's not phoning Australia.

This morning the children came in to my bedroom, Lucy carrying the usual bowl of muesli covered with dog biscuits and a banana. They started wrestling on the bed. They seemed to be enjoying it.

At nine I left in my car to go to my therapist. When I got there, there was no answer. I waited on the street for twenty minutes then put a note through the door, saying, 'I can't wait on the street any longer. I am not well and am absolutely exhausted.'

I collected my tickets to Miami from a travel agent near Portobello Road. I bought suntan cream and other things for Florida from the chemist. I bought some freesias for Dita, who was arriving in an hour from Heathrow, and some pink tulips for the kitchen. Then I went and did some work on my typewriter. Since I've been ill I've been writing my diary in longhand. Using the typewriter again made me feel 'in the saddle'.

Later my therapist phoned and was very apologetic. Her train had got delayed on the way to Victoria as usual. She offered me another appointment in a few days, but I said I couldn't come as I was going to America. She advised me to try to relax when I was with my cousins and to 'cry if you feel like it'.

I rang up a local writer whom my poor brother had admired as a teenager in the sixties, when he had experimented with different drugs, and asked if he had any dope to spare. I said I wanted it ready for my next chemotherapy session in a few days. He had some grass and said I could come and get it.

I went round to his flat at midday and found him sitting drinking tea and smoking. I had the impression that he smokes grass all day. It doesn't seem to have impaired his mind, as he is very quick-witted.

I gave him ten pounds for the grass, which he said was very high quality, then he managed to make me pay five pounds for an out-of-print copy of one of his books, which I didn't particularly want. I was too weak to say no.

When I returned, Dita had arrived at my house by taxi after a ghastly flight. There had been no warning that there would be turbulence when they left New York. When they finally arrived at Heathrow, the pilot announced that it had been the worst transatlantic flight he had been on for years.

Dita said the good side of it was that she now knows how much an aeroplane can stand.

17 January

Last night Vaneeta gave a supper-party in her tiny flat in north Kensington. Jacob and I and Dita were invited, and JB (I cancelled a rendezvous with JB beforehand and arranged to meet him at the dinner. I now do not feel like sex. Instead I went to the club to meet Jacob, leaving a note for Dita, who was still asleep after the awful flight.)

Jacob was late arriving at the club and two women friends of his were there waiting for him, drinking whisky and sodas. One, whom Julian had called 'a lady' at Jacob's party in December, was unexpectedly wearing a leather jacket and had dyed her hair very black. I went to the bar and ordered a drink from the handsome barman. When I got back to the table I heard her and her companion discussing letters they had both had published in the *Independent*.

I said I had also just had a letter published, in the *Spectator*, and I whipped it out of my handbag. I asked to see their letters. One of the women had hers with her, but the other had to quote hers from memory. The first letter was very high-powered. It was about philosophy, science, religion and the nature of truth. The second letter was also extremely erudite and contained a quotation from a poem by Milton. I thought at first its author had made up the poem herself and said, 'How clever!'

At last Jacob arrived and soon we went off to the dinner at Vaneeta's. I was driving. I was a bit drunk after two whiskies and had to drive out into terrifyingly fast traffic on Park Lane.

I collected Dita while Jacob bought Vaneeta some wine in Oddbins. Dita had put on a green dress, some gold jewellery and her second wig. She was wearing new shoes and fell over in the front hall, but was good-natured about it. Margie helped her up.

Dita seemed to enjoy the supper, though she didn't like Indian food and just had rice. She did not seem impressed by JB, who had brought Vaneeta a bunch of pink roses – probably because I am always accusing him of meanness. Dita seemed to think JB was gay, which surprised me, as no one has ever suggested such a thing before and he has never shown any signs of it. Dita preferred a man called Desmond, who is often at Vaneeta's dinners and who talked romantically about lying under the stars in the desert.

At the end of the evening we began discussing reincarnation. Jacob said that he found the idea of it hard to accept.

Vaneeta said she *had* to believe in the doctrine of karma, otherwise things made no sense. She declared, 'I try to be a good person. I try to be kind to other people. My brother died; my husband died; I lost a baby. I have to believe this is to do with paying for the sins of a past life, otherwise it would be too awful.'

Jacob told me later that he had found Vaneeta's statement terribly sad.

17 January (continued)

I am writing this in hospital while waiting to have my blood taken.

It's Toby the dog's birthday. He's four.

Lucy came in this morning with Toby's biscuits and chocolate drops, which she had bought him specially. She said she had been very good with Joseph yesterday in the car coming back with their father. I asked her why she fought so often with her brother. She said she enjoyed it. I asked, 'Do you like the feeling of his little body on yours?'

She replied, 'That's some pervert thing. I just like fighting.'

Joseph is fascinated by Dita's wigs. This morning he grabbed one off her head. She was good-tempered about it and thought it rather funny. Dita has had problems with depression all her life and is on tranquillizers. This means she spends much of her time asleep.

This time I went to have chemotherapy on my own.

As I'm waiting now in Clinic 4 to have the usual blood test I notice someone I've seen before, both here and in the chemotherapy ward, the girl with dead white make-up and very black eyes and a bald head. She always has a baby with her, and the baby, though nearly walking age, is bald like its mother. I wish I could think the baby sweet, but I don't. I find this girl, with her white make-up and deliberately heavy black eyes and bald head, who may have cancer like me, terrifying, and I find it unnerving that she takes the baby in with her when she has her injections. Is she using it as a child would use a doll, to keep her company and make her experience less frightening, or is she a single mother and unable to leave it with anyone else? Her baldness is intentional; she could wear a wig. (You can apply for them on the NHS.) In other circumstances I would admire her baldness; it is a kind of defiance. But when I see this very young bald woman with her baby I feel sicker than ever. I don't want to talk to these other people having chemotherapy.

A gaunt Indian man, whom I have also seen before in the chemotherapy ward, is here too, waiting to have his blood taken. I have never spoken to him either. I'm avoiding him because I think he is iller than I am and, although this is heartless, I don't want to be associated with very ill people. He looks doomed. I want to survive. (I may be completely wrong about this – his being doomed, I mean.)

Just as I was leaving the hospital I met the American woman who'd had the towel on her head, outside the flower-shop. We exchanged addresses and said we would meet for tea. She lives five minutes away from my house.

Dita told me last night that Margie had said to her she would never leave me while I was still having treatment. I like Margie, but sometimes a mask-like expression comes over her face. She reminds me of a doll with china-blue eyes. She's often late when taking the children to appointments and collecting them from school, and this makes me anxious. I also feel she should not be in this job, which is a terrible strain for a young person. I feel a bit guilty about it. I should have got someone older and more experienced.

Saturday, 18 January
I have had an odd letter from Liza: 'This is to apologize for taking
your mother's sheets and china to my bedsit in Llandudno in 1975.
I am very sorry about this.'

I am mystified, and disappointed there is no news in the letter.
It was true that I had been to visit Liza when she was in rep in
Wales and had been shocked to suddenly see my mother's sugar
bowl on the shelf of her bedsit. But it had happened nearly
eighteen years ago. Why has she suddenly referred to it? She is
obviously trying to clear her conscience. Does she think I was
going to die?

Duncan and I are going to a wedding party tonight. Although it is
the day after I've had chemotherapy, when I normally feel so
weak, I am determined to go. I am resting most of the day to build
up my strength.

At teatime I went to see Vivian for half an hour. I took her the
copy of my book on the sixties. I want her to read it while I'm in
America.

I went with Vivian into her kitchen, where I'd visited Jill when
she first broke up with her husband. She had stayed with Vivian
then. It was spring and there was cherry blossom out all over
London. Vivian, whom I hardly knew, had had an ear-ring in one
ear that was supposed to stop her smoking; every time she felt the
urge she had to twist the ear-ring. She had seemed neurotic, sad,
sympathetic and humorous.

Today, as I sat at the kitchen table, she made me some herbal tea.
She told me kindly to try to relax, but I couldn't. I was revved up
about going to America and also anxious about all the arrangements concerning the children I had to make before I left. I talked a
bit about my therapist. I said I couldn't be aggressive with her.
Vivian, who's also been in therapy, said, 'You should tell her that.'

As I left I promised, 'I'll ring you from America. I'll ring you on
February 1st.' That was the day Jill died.

She said, 'Yes. Do that.'

Sunday, 19 January
The party last night. At seven o'clock I put on a red and black dress
I had bought three years earlier in a sale in Harvey Nichols. It is like
a Spanish flamenco dress. I asked Dita if she had a necklace I could
wear and she generously lent me a gold one. She went out to dinner
with her ex-husband's brother. I explained to her how to use my
front-door key – I only gave her the middle one, as last year she lost
my keys a few seconds after I'd given them to her – and promised I
wouldn't lock her out by double-locking.

I stuffed my handbag – one Lulu had given me for my birthday,
shaped like a small oval box – with my anti-sickness pills and my
chemotherapy pills, which I was due to take again at midnight. I
drank several glasses of water to keep me going. Then Duncan
arrived looking very handsome. He said he couldn't completely
do up his evening trousers, which he'd had since he was an
undergraduate, as he had put on weight, but I thought he was
very slim. I gave him a glass of apple juice.

I asked Duncan to help me put a transfer, like a tattoo, on to my
upper arm (the invitation had said 'Formal and Amusing'). I did
not think it went well with my dress.

We then left for the party in Duncan's second-hand sports car. I
was in a combative mood, perhaps because this was the only way
I could overcome my feelings of weakness and exhaustion after
chemotherapy. I was sure that R would be there. I was also excited
because of the party.

It was held in the Museum of Steam in Chiswick. Pipes and old
engines were everywhere. I felt like a young girl in my dress,
which had a stiff sticking-out skirt and a bunch of false fruit on the
front. Almost the first person I saw was Larissa, with a nervous-
looking thin elderly man. After saying hello to the bride and
groom we climbed up several flights of an iron staircase and
looked down at the guests below.

Mark, the brother of James, the doctor, was up there. He said he
had seen my comic letter in the *Spectator* and that it was 'post-
modern'. I was flattered by this, but did not really know what
'post-modern' meant.

At the drinks table I saw Tim, Jill's ex-husband. He behaved oddly, pretending not to recognize me. I thought it was probably because I was a friend of Jill and he did not want to be reminded of her. I had had lunch with him in a restaurant the day before Jill died.

We had all been placed at tables of six or eight or ten. I did not see R anywhere. I was at a table with married couples, except for the thin man who'd been with Larissa earlier. Tim and his second wife, whom he'd met soon after he divorced Jill in the early eighties, were also at my table. Before we sat down, I went up to him and said, 'You weren't very friendly to me earlier.' He did not seem very friendly even then. I found myself between a couple who are both in publishing. I suddenly became annoyed that I was at a table full of couples and said to them, 'You look very bored with each other.'

I moved round to sit next to a smiling blonde woman. She had written a book about Russia. She said that she and her husband were running an organization to send English books to Russia. I asked if she knew Mark's wife, who worked for an organization that allocated money to Eastern European and Russian writers.

The blonde woman replied that Mark's wife had reviewed her book, saying it was the best book ever written on modern Russia. I thought she was being absurdly grateful, so I reminded her, '*You* wrote the book; she only wrote the review.'

The blonde woman then gave me advice on my own writing. She advised me to go on trying to get an agent, otherwise I would end up in 'a sort of limbo'. She said it was difficult to promote one's own book; it was too personal and impossible to detach oneself from it.

Her husband suggested that I sit between him and Tim. Tim stubbornly refused to move away from his wife. I whispered to the other man, who was American, that Tim was refusing to sit next to me, for 'his own reasons'.

This man, Roger, had a bent, hooked nose and enormous charisma. He complimented me on my beautiful dress and tried to involve me in his project of sending books to Russia. I said I couldn't do it at the moment as I'd been ill and had no energy. He then talked across me to Tim about TV franchises. It appeared that he was going to stick his neck out on TV and say something very courageous. Tim seemed impressed by this.

I went with Roger and the thin man to get a pudding. I met Duncan over at the food table, saying he was fed up with all his table not drinking, though actually he never drinks much himself. He came to my table with me, but at that moment Tim at last decided to talk to me. Duncan said teasingly, 'All right, I'm going off to talk to Cassius.' Cassius was a young man with enormously long eyelashes like Bambi. I'd met him once before with Duncan in the Groucho Club.

Tim explained he had been odd to me earlier because he'd been embarrassed he hadn't telephoned me soon after Jill's funeral. He asked me some detailed questions about her novel, which is coming out later this year, and if I could get hold of an advance copy. I said I couldn't possibly do this.

He said he missed Jill terribly. He had recently had a conversation with her father, who had asked if he wanted a memento of her. Tim had put the phone down on him. I said it was a pity that her relations had taken all her possessions and that Vivian, who had done so much for her, hadn't even got a photograph.

Tim said, 'It doesn't matter, Elisa, it doesn't matter.'

Duncan and I went off to look for the loo. I took a folinic acid pill in the cloakroom, having first dropped it on the floor. We asked a young man in a suit, with long shaggy hair, where the lavatories were, and he told us, 'Outside.'

I said, 'But we can't go in the street.'

In fact, there were some public lavatories outside. They were freezing cold.

As a result of this detour – on the way back we saw other lavatories near the dining-room – we missed the best man's speech, which everyone later said was very good. We heard the bridegroom's speech, however, which was short and sincere.

Duncan and I then danced on our own among the steam engines. David, a friend of Duncan, also came on to the dance floor with a series of young women.

I whispered to Duncan, 'Did I tell you my erotic dream about David?'

Duncan said, 'Per-lease!'

A few minutes later I followed Larissa to the loos near the dining-room and asked her why R wasn't at the party. She replied that his ex-wife had said he was babysitting.

I said, 'That's absolutely infuriating!'

Larissa said, 'That's just an excuse for not wanting to come. He knew you'd be here. Also, it's very selfish, because it means there's an empty space at his table. Now some single woman has no one to sit next to her.'

I said, 'I must go back now in case Duncan dances with those gay men. I don't want to be left without a partner.'

Duncan was talking to the bride's mother, who had relations in St Petersburg. When he said he was going there, she gave him a list of things she wanted taken to her relations. Duncan said later it was practically the whole of Sainsbury's.

Duncan and I then danced again. Cassius kissed me and gave me a beautiful spray of pink orchids. I was pleased, though they clashed horribly with my red dress.

Later we went to say goodbye to the bridegroom. He was talking to the best man, who told us he had been best man already three times in his life, but was always extremely nervous about making the speech. He had had to make one recently in honour of Martha Gellhorn on her birthday. He said he had built the speech round her being frightening. He said this went down very badly, except that she herself had liked it. I said, 'The others were probably too frightened of her to laugh.' He laughed loudly at this.

As we got into Duncan's car, which was parked near enormous high-rise buildings, we heard a nightingale singing in the freezing cold.

Duncan said he couldn't see the point of nightingales; at his parents' house in St Tropez there were so many he threw stones at them to make them shut up.

When I got home I found a message from Dita on my answerphone saying I had locked her out – I must have double-locked by mistake – and she was up the road at the Kensington Hilton. It was 2 a.m.

I drove to the Hilton and gave her name at the reception desk. Poor Dita was already upstairs in one of the hotel bedrooms, which she had to pay for. (She refused my offer of payment.)

Monday
Clare rang up yesterday saying my letter about chemotherapy was in the *Sunday Telegraph* and I rushed out to get it.

I read it and proudly showed Dita. It had been cut so that it was now more succinct. My second point, about the necessity of clinical trials, had been taken out. Richard Peto, the expert alerted by Clare, had also written a letter, about the need for clinical trials. Of course, his letter was far more informed than mine. He accused James's article of being 'particularly silly' and explained that 'we need trials, because we need accurate information about matters that affect the life and death of 1,000 people a year'.

While Dita was out for lunch at a new hotel, the Lanesborough, which was owned by one of her English stepsons, Hal turned up. He was in England for twenty-four hours on his way to Africa. At two o'clock he came round to make love to me. By that time I was absolutely exhausted and my eyes kept closing, partly out of fatigue after the late night, but also because this seems to be the effect of chemotherapy. Perhaps I hadn't drunk enough water. I heated up some lasagne that Margie had made on Friday for the children. He seemed delighted by this meagre offering, probably because I don't normally cook for him.

Hal should have been bringing *me* lunch, I thought later. He takes a pride in not giving 'presents'; in fact, he's always boasting about it. At the same time, providing the lunch for him made me

keep going. I heard Dita returning at about three, but she went
straight upstairs to her bedroom. Later she tactfully said she had
heard a man's voice downstairs with me, so decided to make
herself scarce.

I am worried about the long flight to Florida tomorrow.
Although Dita is supposed to be looking after me, she will
probably forget something or get on the wrong plane. Last time I
flew with her in America she left a tennis racket on the plane and a
fur coat.

Tuesday, 21 January

Dita and I left the house for Heathrow while it was still dark. Just
before we left there was a drama about my blue and gold necklace,
which my ex-husband and my son had given me for my birthday
in 1990.

Margie thought she'd left the necklace in the glove-pocket of the
car. She ran out to look, but it wasn't there. I then told her to look
on the road beside the car, but she returned again saying she
couldn't find it and also couldn't see properly in the dim light.
Lucy then took charge. She went out on her own in the dark and
came back at once with the necklace. It was a bit squashed and
looked as if a car had run over it. However, I was delighted to get
it back and put it on at once. I was proud of her for finding it.

The excitement about the necklace distracted me from my
anxiety about leaving the children. Also, it had become a good-
luck symbol. If I had thought too much about leaving the children,
I probably wouldn't have gone. My ex-husband, however, will be
supervising much of the time.

Later. On the plane to Miami. I feel claustrophobic and am still
taking Cyclophosphamide. I brought a bottle of Evian with me,
but already I need more. I get anxious if I don't get enough water
and also feel sick and dehydrated. Dita kindly asks the stewardess
for water. As a result of drinking all this water I keep having to go
to the loo.

Luckily there are some seats free at the back near the toilets. I am reading a collection of stories by Simon Burt, a friend of Duncan.

About halfway through the flight I lie down on the empty seats. I always find it impossible to sleep on a plane. Finally I think I do sleep a bit. I have disturbed hallucinatory dreams.

I am being followed by Margie in our red car. I'm in my old Renault. Every time I try to park there are too many cars behind me and I can't do it, and she doesn't understand I'm trying to park. Later I turn round and see Maureen sitting placidly in a car, and wonder if she should become our nanny again.

When I wake up, we're flying down the east coast of America, over enormous fields of ice.

At Miami Dita's mother's chauffeur, a quiet, gentle man of about sixty, is there to meet us.

It's roughly two and a half hours from the airport to Hobe Sound. Almost as soon as we're on the highway I have to stop and get more water from a garage – they sell the familiar Evian bottles.

Most of the journey is through developed areas, past bungalows, retirement homes, McDonald's, marinas, mobile-home sites. As we finally approach Hobe Sound and then Jupiter Island, where the rented house is, the view gets wilder and along the main road of the island at last we can see the ocean and beside it russet-coloured sea-grape, cacti and wind-swept palm-trees.

We draw up at the house, and Tiggy (Dita's mother and my grandmother's niece) comes to meet us in a pale-blue dressing-gown. I am so pleased to see her. She reminds me of my grandmother, and looks like her – she's slender and petite, with grey-blue eyes and very good legs. She came to visit my grandmother often throughout my childhood. Tiggy is eighty-four and very alert. A masseuse, with jet-black hair, is standing behind her.

After supper Tiggy walks in the blue dressing-gown to my bedroom beside the swimming-pool. She says not to worry if I hear noises in the night. It will only be the chauffeur next door. He and I are in a building on our own, a few yards from the main house. I am touched to see Tiggy walking alone beside the pool to my bedroom. At last I am being looked after. I don't have to go anywhere or do anything.

22 January

The house is large and formal. Two ugly stone storks stand at the end of the pool near my room. There are hardly any flowers in the garden; it's all lawn and bushes. Tiggy, who loves flowers, has put two of her own plants – blue periwinkle – in tubs at one end of the pool. Unfortunately, these flowers are closed most of the time. She's also ordered pink geraniums and white nasturtiums to be put on the terrace.

There's a clay tennis court no one plays on and behind this are a few red and yellow hibiscus flowers.

The Irish cook, who's my age, asks what I want for breakfast. I'm still denying myself coffee, for health reasons, so I ask if there's any herbal tea. This self-denial makes me feel puritanical and like an invalid. I will probably start drinking coffee again soon.

Dita's still asleep. To get to the beach I go up a path beside another private house, where there's a notice saying 'No entry'. Just beyond is the white beach and the ocean. On the sand are cream-coloured shells, striped with brown, bits of driftwood and Portuguese men-of-war. They're like little narrow balloons, darkish blue, not pale blue or white as I remember them from the first time I came to Florida, aged five.

My mother took us to America in 1955. I was allowed to miss several weeks of school. We sailed on the *Queen Mary*, my two brothers, our nanny Doreen, and my parents. From New York we took a train down to Florida and stayed with my grandmother's sister, Tiggy's mother, at her house in Palm Beach. We were put in the guest house nearby – the Dream House. Every day we walked along the road to Great Aunt Dita's big house, with its white Spanish columns.

We played on the same stretch of beach as I'm on now, only several miles further south. There was no one on it then except a red-haired American boy, David, who, like me, was five. My brother Raymond was nearly four and Nicky was thirteen months

and could already walk. He was a friendly, bold little boy with
blond curly hair and brown eyes. The Americans called him Butch;
he was so courageous. When did my brother's character change
and become fearful? Perhaps it was after Raymond drowned. I'm
not sure.

Today old men are fishing with long lines, standing by the
water's edge, and people in shorts jog past, exercising their dogs.

Usually when I visit Tiggy, as I've done for the last two years, I
walk for an hour on the beach each day before breakfast. Today I
can only walk for about five minutes before I have to stop because
I'm breathing heavily. My weakened state is brought home to me.

23 January

I dream all the time here, perhaps because of the chemotherapy
drugs – I took the last ones of this course today – or perhaps
because I'm more relaxed and therefore remember my dreams
better.

Last night I dreamed that Bill, an old friend in New York who
has AIDS – he found out nineteen months ago when I was staying
there with Jill – suddenly arrives in a red car out of the sky and
says, 'I'm dying.' With some relief, I realize I must go and help
him.

After this dream I wake at four with a feeling of peace. Real life
seems so difficult compared with sleep.

In the late afternoon I talk to Mrs Slater, a friend of Tiggy, who's
also staying. Like Tiggy, she is a Long Island widow. She's
dignified, open-minded and quietly intelligent. She had a breast
off (a radical mastectomy) and her lymph glands removed over
thirty years ago. She's now in her eighties. She says it took at least
a year to recover and she had to do a lot of exercises. She advises
me to go on doing the exercises I learned in hospital, otherwise my
shoulder will get stiff. She shows me one that Dr K in
Radiotherapy showed me: a stretching exercise, with the hand
creeping up the wall as far as it will go.

I have to keep out of the sun, not that there is much, because of
having had radiotherapy. Normally I'm a sun worshipper. Now I

don't even feel strong enough to swim. No one else is using the enormous pool either.

24 January
The flag outside the island club is at half-mast again. This means another member has died. Dita says seventeen people have died since October. This is not surprising, as many of the members are in their eighties and nineties.

On the way to the Beach Club for lunch Dita and her mother and Mrs Slater discuss who could have died this time. Dita thinks it is someone called Walker.

Last week an old lady died. Mrs Slater said the husband had a girlfriend while his wife was ill and she's already moved in with him. Dita said women were crazy about widowers. She herself had asked a man to lunch soon after his wife had died. 'But he didn't like me,' she added ruefully.

'How long after his wife died did you ask him to lunch?' I asked.

'Oh, a few days.'

At the Beach Club, which is protected from the ocean by blue glass, we sit at a table outside. It's very cold. We shake hands with a very old couple. Dita says the man's over ninety and did most of the landscaping round here.

We have lunch with another couple, also in their nineties. We have to fetch our food from the counter; Tiggy drops her tray, but a young blond waiter clears it up very quickly. Dita says her mother minds very much about something like this, as it makes her think she's losing her faculties. It is humiliating.

The couple with us are so old that they make Tiggy and Mrs Slater look young. Tiggy is wearing an attractive cornflower-blue suit. She always dresses very well.

Dita whispers to me that Mrs Slater's son went gay at the age of fifty, after a thirty-year marriage. He is now living with a man.

26 January
I went to the local Catholic church, St Christopher's, with the

chauffeur and his daughter, who lives in Miami. It was packed. We got there rather early and sat near the front.

The priest was very bossy and made us rehearse the refrain of a hymn we were supposed to sing later. The sermon was about Christ's teaching and how we might not like what we hear, but we should still listen. He said from now until Lent there'd be readings from St Luke and we should pay attention. Everyone except me went to Communion.

When I went back I had breakfast with Dita. She is against most religion. Today she accused fundamentalist religions of taking poor people's money. (I'm sure many New York psychiatrists take rich people's money, i.e. hers, but I did not say this.)

There is a big article in the *Palm Beach Post* today about breast cancer. On 1 February there is a sponsored walk in aid of the Susan G. Komen Breast Cancer Foundation. These walks raise funds to provide mammograms for low-income women. Susan Komen died of breast cancer in her thirties. Her sister, Nancy Brinker, started the Komen Foundation to raise money for research, then, in her thirties, she got breast cancer herself. The Race for the Cure, which I think is the title of all the sponsored walks, is being held in seventeen cities this year.

There is a photo of Nancy Brinker, married to Norman Brinker, chairman and chief executive officer of Chili's restaurants, looking very attractive. She has had 'a modified radical mastectomy', 'reconstructive surgery', 'four chemotherapy courses that left her bald and weak' and a hysterectomy. So far she has had no recurrence.

Underneath the article is a list entitled 'Breast cancer facts every woman should know'.

Breast cancer is the leading cause of cancer death among women in the 15–54 age group.
The five-year survival rate for localized breast cancer has risen from 78 per cent in the 1940s to 91 per cent today. If the breast cancer is *in situ* (not invasive) the survival rate approaches 100 per cent.

Women who have never given birth have a higher risk of developing breast cancer. The risk is high among Catholic nuns.

I like the way the Americans tackle this kind of thing head-on. I like the way in this country there is still the feeling that one can influence one's fate, that the lay person can still do something. Also, people here seem more open about illness. (Of course, if you're not insured, you can be ruined. American doctors cost the earth.)

At last the weather has got warmer. I am invited to lunch with my American godmother, Lilah, one of my mother's oldest friends, who also comes to Hobe Sound every year. She met my mother at school in London when they were both eleven.

Lilah had a riding accident several years ago and was very badly injured. She is still lame and her hands are twisted.

I admire Lilah a great deal. I can see that almost every movement hurts her. When she had the accident, they thought she might never walk again. Although they've been friends since they were both eleven, I think of Lilah as an adult and my mother as a child. Lilah has faced up to the problems of life; my mother hasn't. Maybe she is incapable of doing so.

I was bitten by mosquitoes while I went to watch the sunset at the Inland Waterway. Dita and Tiggy are at a movie, *The Prince of Tides*.

Staying with Tiggy reminds me of staying at my grandmother's, where, even as a young adult, I was treated as a child, with no responsibilities. Today, for the first time for months, I have a real sense of peace.

This morning I told Tiggy I might give up chemotherapy – I hate it so much and it makes me feel so ill – but she said this was unwise. My chances of recovery after chemotherapy are 85 per cent, she said.

I then read the *Palm Beach Post* again and saw that this was the statistic given, 85 per cent. She probably read the figure there this morning.

*

Later. Tiggy has told Dita I was thinking of giving up
chemotherapy. Dita urged me to finish the course. She said she
might come and stay with me in London again in May, to keep me
company.

Walking along the beach this evening I thought about Jill and
my visit to her in Key West, a year before she died. Now I would
like to go there again. When she died, I thought I wouldn't be able
to bear going back.

28 January
My hair has started to fall out. I notice strands of it in the sink,
more than usual. I hope I won't go bald. I mentioned it to
Dita and she said she'd go with me to get a wig in New York, at
the shop where she bought hers. It's not expensive. Buying a
wig as a 'fashion item', instead of getting one through the
NHS, makes it more attractive, less of a last-ditch effort by an
invalid.

This morning Tiggy tried to persuade me to spend the whole
fortnight with her in Florida, rather than going to New York with
Dita. It's very tempting just to stay in this protected environment,
but I want to see my friends in New York.

At dinner tonight Tiggy and Dita mentioned a local couple
who'd recently committed suicide. The man was a doctor, and his
wife, who had had surgery that went wrong, was in awful pain.
They had inhaled the exhaust fumes of their car.

I asked, 'What about their children?'

Dita asked, 'Were they Beach Club members?'

I said her question was like a *New Yorker* cartoon.

There is a lot of talk about Governor Clinton in Arkansas; will
he be the next Democratic candidate? Now an affair he had while
married is being investigated by the press. The first time reporters
asked him if he'd committed adultery he replied, 'I wouldn't tell
you if I had.'

The next day, however, he and his wife were prepared to go on
TV to talk about their marriage. Apparently his wife had used her
own name in his first campaign, but this wasn't good for his

political career. Now she's going to use his surname and appear as the supportive wife.

29 January

Yesterday I had a massage with the black-haired woman I saw with Tiggy the night we arrived. Tiggy gave me her appointment as she said she found her too strong. She preferred another masseuse, who only did feet.

This masseuse is Cuban. She came into my room carrying a fold-up table and then gave me a very strong massage all over that lasted an hour. I told her I had had breast cancer and was still on chemotherapy treatment.

I asked her about Cuba, where I want to go next year. She said she had left the island as a small child with her parents. She would probably go back when Castro fell. She would like to 'help the country back on its feet'. This reminded me of the attitude young Cubans (and some young Americans and Europeans) had during the first years of the revolution, how they had voluntarily cut sugar cane, thinking that they also were helping Castro get the country 'back on its feet'.

I used the fifty-dollar bill Merrill had given me in London to pay her for the massage. I thought she would be pleased that I had given myself a treat with the money.

That afternoon Cynthia rang from England to find out how I was. She is going to Cuba in two weeks. I am very envious. When I told her about the masseuse, she said dismissively, 'Oh, a bad Cuban.' I found this over-simplification idiotic. Is Cynthia, an intelligent woman, pretending to be stupider than she is?

Yesterday Tiggy gave me a short story by her niece to read. It was about her father – Tiggy's brother – in Kentucky. It had won a prize, but Tiggy said she didn't like the way her niece wrote about her father. She had described him bringing whores to the house and being drunk.

Dita passed me a note that read: 'He was a right-wing Ku Klux Klan toothless alcoholic. Mother never faced up to it. His daughter had to.'

Later that evening we watched George Bush's State of the Union speech on TV. He used the phrase 'I know in my heart' three times. He also said, 'When Barbara holds a baby with AIDS . . .' The false sentimentality of this – the way it was said for political purposes – made me quite sick.

When it was over, Dita talked about Tsongas, an ex-senator who wants to be president. She said, 'He's had cancer, so I don't think he'll get very far.'

I said sharply, 'My friend Nick had Hodgkin's disease twice in his twenties. Now he's forty-one and he's never had a recurrence.' I didn't like the way she had condemned Tsongas out of hand, putting him on the death-list without giving him a chance and assuming that most of the American public would do likewise. It was also oddly tactless of her, particularly considering how kind she's been to me. Had she forgotten that I had had cancer?

30 January

Lilah has invited me and Lucy to stay in her house in Ireland this summer for the Dublin horse show. She said she'd also try to invite her granddaughter, who's the same age as Lucy. I like the idea of this, of making plans for the future.

31 January

New York City. Dita and I arrived here after a two-hour flight. She did not leave anything on the plane, thank goodness.

Will, a black American from Long Island who works for Dita, came to meet us at the airport. Will's wife, Allie, was Dita's nurse and companion for several years, and also helped look after Dita's son when he was a child. Allie died last summer of a heart attack.

Will was very talkative as he drove us to New York City. He reminded me of the time when he, Allie and I had travelled on a Laker flight from JFK to London for Christmas in 1977. We had had to stay up most of the night after we had bought our tickets in Queens. They had taken me back to their house on Long Island and Will had made omelettes. The plane finally took off for London at four in the morning. The day after we arrived I got a terrible cold and then we discovered that my brother, who was supposed to spend Christmas with my mother, had committed suicide. My grandmother caught my cold and never recovered properly from it. She died six months later. I did not mention these lugubrious events to Will.

February

1 *February*

Jill died a year ago today. I rang Vivian at 7 a.m. American time, but her answerphone was on. Then I watched seven different channels very quickly on Dita's huge TV – they included *Defense Spending*, a look-back at the Gulf War, a Jane Fonda work-out ad and a ten-minute advertisement, like a small play, for learning English.

Dita has kindly lent me her own bedroom and is sleeping in the smaller one. Her dog, Lottie, a Yorkshire terrier, seems confused about this and keeps peeing on the floor and barking at me hysterically.

At eleven I spoke on the telephone to Joan, a New York woman who had breast cancer two years ago. A neighbour in London had kindly given me her number. Joan was taking a kid glove out of the mouth of an English bulldog puppy while she was talking to me on the phone. She sounded ebullient.

She said that the thing to do while having chemotherapy was to keep on leading a normal life. I said I was trying to do this, but I was physically exhausted. Even today I had risen at a normal time then I had flopped back to bed, short of breath.

I phoned Vivian again in London and got through. I liked hearing her gentle voice. When I rang off, the bells of the church near Dita's apartment, the church where Jill's funeral service was held, started chiming.

An hour later I walked through Central Park to see Moira, an Englishwoman whom I'd met at the funeral. A journalist and professional cook, Moira now has a job supervising the food in the Tavern-on-the-Green restaurant in Central Park.

Moira is my physical opposite – extremely blonde, with very pale freckled skin and green eyes, one with a slight squint. Today at lunch, when I tell her I've had breast cancer, she says that she had cancer in that eye several years ago and now has a glass one. She had her treatment in England. She was absolutely terrified when it first happened. Now she hardly ever thinks about it. She has a husband and a child of three.

Talking to her brought home to me that there are people walking round everywhere who've had cancer, who may still have it, leading what appear to be perfectly normal lives.

After the lunch I forced myself to walk back through the park. I realized that in my weak state it would be easier for me to get mugged. The sun came out and the park looked beautiful; the air was crisp and clear in the way it is only in New York.

That afternoon I rang Bill, my friend who has AIDS. I'd already told him on the phone from Florida that I had breast cancer. When he heard it was me, he said, 'Hello, Miss Chemotherapy.' I found this charming and funny.

I went down to Greenwich Village later to meet him at a pizzeria. Bill is six foot six and when I first knew him in 1975 was astoundingly handsome, lean and tanned, with a finely chiselled face and big grey eyes. He had a temporary job in Gimbels store, in housewares, though he wanted to be an actor. He was brought up Catholic in the Midwest and for a short time was in a seminary training to be a priest. In the early seventies he came to New York, hit the gay 'scene' and must have got AIDS then. On my visits to New York as a young woman we often walked all over the city together. I felt protected by his enormous height, his knowledge of the streets and his kindness.

In the bus going down Fifth Avenue today on my way to the Village I remembered the first time I'd met Bill in an apartment he shared with three other young men on Central Park West. He had told me excitedly, 'There's a cult of youth in this city. Last night at a party I met a man who was after my ass.'

We were both twenty-five. Now we're forty-two. Bill, who was so handsome, is balding and his hair is whitish-grey. He has 'lesions' in one ear, one of the first signs of the physical deterioration caused by AIDS.

We share an enormous pizza at the only available table, near the door, which keeps opening, making us freezing cold. Bill talks very frankly to me, but he still hasn't told his parents. His brother and one of his two sisters know he has AIDS.

He seems cheerful, though he tells me he's on anti-depressants as he was waking up each morning feeling suicidal. A play he's written, *Mask*, based on the sadistic murder of a young Norwegian boy in New York a few years ago, is being shown at a theatre next week.

Bill says his illness could be worse. The lesions could be on his face. He is taking part in a trial at Mount Sinai Hospital, so most of his treatment is free. He is now on the drug combination AZT, but they don't know yet if it's working.

Bill never made it as an actor, but lived off jobs such as waiting on tables until recently, when he began writing the script of a weekly soap opera, which gives him a steady income. He lives in a subsidized building for people in the performing arts.

Bill says he's determined to go on writing his weekly script. He has deliberately not told his bosses that he's ill. A few weeks ago one of his employers rang him and asked him to change some things in his script that same evening. He sat up for several hours that night making the changes. He said if she'd known he had AIDS she wouldn't have asked him. He wants demands to be made of him; he wants to be treated like anyone else.

Sunday, 2 February
I spoke to Alexander, an old boyfriend of mine, on the telephone. He now works in Washington for an English newspaper. He was extremely friendly. He did not know I had breast cancer until I told him. He said patronizingly, 'I suppose you're handling your emotional life as badly as before.' (I thought afterwards, *you* can talk, but I stupidly didn't think to say this at the time.)

He asked hopefully if I'd discussed him in London with
Larissa, also an ex-girlfriend. I said truthfully, 'No, we haven't
mentioned you.'

I later had a dream in which my children and his were mixed
up in some domestic situation. I had some difficulty with a
nanny, I think Maureen. I was given a bowl of cereal to eat. At
first I was enjoying it, then I became aware I was eating sand.

When I woke I realized that I felt betrayed, by Maureen, for
leaving me and the children, and by Alexander, who had often
treated me cruelly. I still felt betrayed by him even after all these
years.

I went to meet Merrill and Patrick M, a writer to whom Geraldine
Cooke had introduced me in London. I went downtown with
Dita in a taxi, since she was going to an art exhibition. As we
approached the street where Jill had lived, where I used to stay
with her, I began to get an awful pain in my chest. I said to Dita,
'I feel terrible going near the street where my friend died.'

Patrick M was already at the Temple Bar. He had just got
married to an English actress in Reno, after knowing her only a
few months. I noticed his nails were bitten to the quick and that
he downed three glasses of Sauvignon Blanc rather quickly.

I tasted his wine to see if I wanted the same type and said,
'Ugh! No! It reminds me of my mother.' (It was the same acid
white wine as she always had in her house.)

Patrick laughed.

Merrill then arrived with a present for me – a beautiful grey
shirt. She had been at a poetry reading. She asked how Jacob was.
I did an imitation of him imitating her reading from her book at
Waterstone's, Hampstead, last October. (Jacob always does it in
an expressionless monotone.) I'm not sure it went down that well.
Merrill probably doesn't know that Jacob mimics everyone.

Merrill said she wanted to write a film-script of Patrick's novel
Spider, about a disturbed man in the East End. I wasn't sure if he
knew I'd had breast cancer and did not refer to it.

3 *February*

My ex-husband rang up to say that Lucy has passed her Common Entrance.

Later Dita took me shopping. We walked up Madison Avenue, normally a very expensive street but now, because of the recession, many shops are closing and having sales. I told Dita I had decided not to get a wig as I didn't think any more of my hair would fall out.

Dita was fun to shop with and very unselfish. She encouraged me to try on different clothes and complimented me. I bought a three-quarter-length navy-blue dress with a low neck that made me look both slim and curvaceous. (I know you're not supposed to get too thin if you've had cancer, in case you get it again. But if I think I'm fat I feel demoralized.)

As we came out of the last shop, Dita suddenly ran out of stamina and insisted on taking a cab home, though it was only three blocks.

10 p.m. I've just had dinner with Kay, who sent me the joint a couple of months ago and lives in a small walk-up apartment in the East Nineties; she cooked an extremely good chicken stew. Kay has recently completed a novel, which she showed to Pauline Kael, the *New Yorker* film critic. Kay used to work on the *New Yorker*, but now she's a librarian at the New York Public Library.

When I got back I rang Liza in California. She urged me to go and buy a book by Bernie S. Siegel called *Peace, Love and Healing*. She also urged me to start a breast cancer circle in London. She told me to ring up Sloan Kettering, the hospital where Jill had most of her treatment, and ask for the latest details about breast cancer. Liza is very determined, and she never gives up. She has spent years as an actress, often out of work. Now she's writing a novel.

I thought I'd better refer to Liza's odd letter apologizing about taking my mother's china. Liza explained that it had been part of the Sixth Step of her AA programme, 'Making Amends'.

When my brother died, Liza offered to come to the funeral with me.

4 February

I walked through Central Park again, this time to see my London neighbour's friend Joan, who had breast cancer and is writing a book on chemotherapy. When I arrived, the Spanish doorman said she was out walking her English bulldog puppy. He made me wait for her in the lobby.

She is a healthy tall blonde woman, very lively. She said she finished her treatment for breast cancer two years ago. She asked if I wanted to do any research in England for her 'how to' book on chemotherapy and gave me a recent article from the *New York Times* with tips on how to cope with it.

I then went to visit Diana, Dita's sister-in-law, in her large and beautiful apartment on Fifth Avenue. She is small and bony with red hair and green eyes. She seems in control of her life.

Diana said I had a hopeless mother and it was better not to be too involved with her. She said, 'I'm sure your mother loves you, but doesn't know how to express it.'

I asked her about the story, the one about Tiggy's brother that Tiggy had shown me in Florida. I said it was very good, but that Tiggy had been upset by it. Diana, who had had the niece to live with her for two years when she was younger, said one must remember that Tiggy was born in 1906 and also that she wanted everything connected with her family to be perfect. Her brother had had whores in his house while his daughter was living with him. Tiggy thought the story meant that her niece didn't love her father, whereas it was obvious from the writing that she did.

I went back to Dita's and read the article I'd been given earlier. It was helpful and informative, and the way it was set out, under sub-headings, such as 'Why Chemotherapy', 'Fighting Side-effects' and 'How Therapy Attacks Cancer', seemed designed to help the reader understand.

> A generation ago chemotherapy was used only as a last-ditch effort when other cancer treatments, namely surgery and radiation, failed to produce a cure. The treatments often made patients even sicker than they were already and, because their

cancers were usually well advanced when the drugs were
given, most patients died anyway. The effect was to give
chemotherapy a bad name in the minds of most of the people
who could now benefit from it . . .
Today chemotherapy is playing an ever-larger role as the
mop for cancer cells that may escape the surgeon's knife or
the radiologist's beam and lurk in hidden regions of the
body where they could seed a recurrence months or years
later.

Although I know that I'm supposed to think of the
chemotherapy as an ally, 'mopping up cells' and giving me a
higher chance of survival, I can't think of it as other than
traumatic and frightening.

Also in the article was the telephone number of where you
could get a free booklet called 'Chemotherapy and You'. This was
arranged by the National Cancer Institute. A book by Nancy
Brinker, who raises money for cancer research, the woman I'd
read about in the *Palm Beach Post*, was also plugged. It was called
Coping with Chemotherapy.

In a way I wished I lived in the States, where it seemed that
women who didn't even know each other were far more open
and helpful about illness. Then I remembered Jill's experiences of
having cancer in a New York hospital. Apart from the recurring
high medical bills and the added stress these caused her, each
time she had chemotherapy she had felt it necesary to hire a
private nurse for the whole night just so she could be escorted to
the bathroom to be sick. The hospital nurses were too busy.

I remembered too the way that Jill had referred to her treatment
as 'my chemo', as though, by using the abbreviation, she was
persuading herself that it was friendly, or, at any rate, not that
bad. In fact, each one of her treatments – she was having far
higher doses than I am, for a more severe and different type of
cancer – was appalling. I had stayed with her once after she had
spent all night in hospital after chemotherapy. She had come
home and been sick. White-faced, she had rushed in and out of

the bathroom all that day. The irony was that these horrible
onslaughts on her body were supposed to 'cure' her.

Once she admitted her revulsion. In Key West we had both
bought striped bags in a supermarket. A few weeks later, when
she found she had cancer for the second time, she began using
hers as an overnight bag on her visits to the hospital for
chemotherapy. She admitted the last time I had seen her how
much she loathed the sight of the bag because of this.

I now have an aversion to the red bag that I used all winter to
carry my hospital appointment cards, radiotherapy booklet, pills
and Evian bottles to and from the hospital. I deliberately haven't
brought it with me to America. (Dita has bought me another bag,
covered with shoes, which I like much better.)

Bill has arranged for me to attend his play rehearsal tonight, as
otherwise I will miss it. He particularly wants me to see it, partly
because I was responsible for getting his first play put on in a pub
theatre in London.

We're to have a quick supper before the rehearsal. I take a
cab to Bill's high-rise building on Tenth Avenue and Forty-
fourth Street. I'm five minutes early and have to wait in the
lobby.

When he arrives, I find I'm still shocked by his new
appearance. I can't get used to it. Although he says he hasn't
changed, to me his face looks emaciated and drawn and he's very
thin. He always was thin, but not thin like this.

Bill's very hyper as he's just handed in his soap opera script for
the week. We go up to his apartment on the fifteenth floor and he
plays his answerphone. There's a message from a co-writer of the
soap saying how pleased she is by his message complimenting
her on *her* script the day before.

I then start reading the script Bill's just handed in, about a
woman called Lillian with breast cancer. He says he wrote it soon
after we'd had pizza together the other night. I notice that this
character Lillian says something that Bill himself said that night,
in relation to having AIDS: 'I don't want people to treat me

differently; I want responsibilities and to carry on as normal.'

Bill feels this very strongly. I agree. I want to agree. I want to be as courageous as he is.

We go to the café in a health club next to the building. We sit at a table and are hailed by a couple who live in Bill's building and now have him to dinner every Thursday.

Bill insists on paying for my spinach salad. He's always looked after me, walked me home through New York at night, asked questions about my children and remembered what I've told him about them, even years later. When he came to England, I remember how he wheeled my baby son in a pushchair through the Sussex lanes at great speed. I have a photograph of him leaning out of the window there, bare-chested, tanned and happy. Today he says the lesion in his ear has healed since I saw him a couple of days ago, but I fear this is temporary.

Later, when the play is over, we wait together on Forty-second Street for a cab to take me back to Dita's apartment. As we're standing there, I have the sudden conviction that he will soon be a corpse.   Then I, who am normally undemonstrative, fling my arms round Bill and hug him.

5 *February*
On the plane going back to England. I'm reading the book Liza recommended, *Peace, Love and Healing* by Bernie S. Siegel, which I bought yesterday.

> The only thing I would lay claim to on my behalf is the ability to inspire hope in people . . . you have to wonder about doctors who worry about giving their patients 'false hope' . . . I believe in using hope to facilitate change in the healing of lives. Years ago I felt like other physicians about 'deceiving' people into getting well . . . Now it's ten years later and I have no difficulty using all the tools at my command, including hope, to help people live.
>
> We're used to the idea of disease as a punishment or a failure – but a gift?

Think about what I call spiritual flat tires, and you may begin to understand what I mean.

I couldn't help being to some extent persuaded by Bernie S. Siegel's boundless optimism and benign personality, but then I began to have the same reaction as I had had to the book *Getting Well Again*. As I read more and more 'inspiring' case histories in Bernie Siegel's book – a critically ill woman whose intravenous tubes and lines were removed so she could go to her son's wedding, a rabbi who suffered a stroke aged sixty-six and, despite being barely able to walk, every week commuted from his home in Chicago 'to a rabbinical class in New York in order to pass on his knowledge of the ancient Jewish texts' – I began to feel insignificant, as though my own situation was utterly unimportant.

I was also worried by Bernie Siegel's beaming face on the cover. He was completely bald, with a brown gleaming skin. There was a red rose at the bottom of the picture that framed his head and shoulders. The thought then crossed my mind that he had made enormous amounts of money out of writing these books. But was this so awful, if it helped people who would otherwise be desperate?

6 February
Lucy came to the front door in London to greet me; Joseph was already asleep. She was wearing an orange T-shirt and short pyjama bottoms. I gave her a present of a photograph frame with a horse's head on, which I had bought in a shop on Lexington Avenue the day I left. She stayed up late talking to me.

This morning Joseph came in and said, 'No one would like to marry me; someone with a hole in his head and no top lip.'

In fact, he's very handsome.

I'm delighted to see the children, but now I can't concentrate on them properly. I'm so worried about my next dose of chemotherapy, which is today.

I have received three letters from women in response to my letter in the *Sunday Telegraph*.

One was from Mrs J. S. Pollard in Solihull, who'd had breast cancer and was now very well: 'If you can imagine that you are on the other side of your illness and you are well on the way to full recovery and that every day is a bonus and to be enjoyed and lived to the full . . . all the best for the future and enjoy every minute of it.'

The second letter was from a Mrs Ansell in Fife, who'd had a mastectomy and no further treatment. She said she was worried at first not to be given Tamoxifen, but was told it wouldn't affect her form of cancer. 'Once more congratulations on your letter and keep your chin up. There's nothing else for it. Life becomes very sweet all of a sudden and worth fighting for.'

The last letter, from Miss Christina Marshall from Tayside, recommended a preparation called Mina-Mino that contained amino acids and vitamins; she said it had restored her energy after radiotherapy.

I was extremely touched by these letters.

Jacob rang this morning and said Liz Whipp had told him that this would be the worst stage of my treatment, the middle, and that I would naturally feel low.

Miranda joins me in Clinic 4. When I go in for my appointment with the professor, she offers to come in and take shorthand notes. He seems irritated by this, as if it's none of our business to ask so many questions. We ask about the anti-sickness pills. He says I should go on taking them for four days after I have the chemotherapy injection. I say that I felt sick for a week at least after the last treatment. He says it may not have been connected.

The most important questions we ask are about the menopause and about whether or not to take Tamoxifen. (Miranda knows someone who's taking it already, whose mother died of breast cancer.)

Dr W, the little red-haired doctor I like, had told me that the onset of the menopause was a direct result of chemotherapy and that chemotherapy would definitely induce it. The professor said, 'She didn't know what she was talking about.' He said there was only a 50 to 60 per cent chance of having the menopause after chemotherapy, and I would probably start getting periods again regularly.

Miranda then asked whether I should take Tamoxifen as a preventative, after finishing the course of chemotherapy. The professor said the benefits of Tamoxifen in my age group were not known. As for taking it on spec: 'As far as we know, the benefits are likely to be minimal.' He said that my tumour had been too small for them to discover whether it was oestrogen receptor sensitive, and the point of Tamoxifen was to suppress oestrogen.

When I said I sometimes felt faint in the mornings, he told me this was unheard of as a side-effect of chemotherapy.

After we'd left, Miranda and I discussed his irritation at her taking notes. I said he probably thought he was going to be sued or misquoted.

We then met the oncology nurse, in the corridor. She emphasized it was most important to take pills that were an antidote to Methotrexate – Fluorouracil. Otherwise I might get ulcers.

Saturday
I collected a book I'd ordered before I went to America, *To the Friend Who Did Not Save My Life* by Hervé Guibert. I ordered it without seeing it, something I hardly ever do, because I'd read a complimentary review of it in the *Independent*. It is about a man who'd been diagnosed HIV positive. I've become interested in how people deal with life-threatening illnesses since I had breast cancer. When I started reading it, however, I was disappointed. The writer seemed extremely unpleasant and misanthropic. Near the beginning he states that he has realized once and for all that he does not like his fellow men. After I'd read this I put the book down.

I am much calmer than before I went to America.

Emily came round this evening and I cooked some fish. She is now having an affair with her cat's vet. The vet comes to her flat only once a week, on Monday afternoons, as he is living with another woman. So far they have not gone out to a movie or restaurant together, but he bought her some ear-rings from John Lewis for her birthday. He owns seven TV sets and, according to her, is very funny and sexy.

Emily showed me some stories she'd written about her and Paolo on holiday in the south of France when they were first married. I thought they were quite good. Paolo now seems to have moved out permanently. He is living in Hampstead.

Sunday
I went in my car to the Catholic church. The Famous Writer's wife drove past me and I waved. I then parked behind her near the church. I said, 'I didn't ask you to drive me to Mass today as now I feel well.' I told her I had just been to America. I could tell that talking to me made her nervous – perhaps she thought I was getting too familiar – so I ran on ahead of her to post a letter.

In church I found myself again sitting behind the Irishwoman who had helped with the fainting woman all those months ago, and possibly even the woman who'd fainted, though I wasn't sure. Across the aisle was the disturbed man, in his usual place. He looked spectral. I remembered what Edward had once said about the Catholic Church 'fielding people who would otherwise be in mental homes'.

In Prayers for the Dead were the usual litany of Irish names. They're nearly always Irish.

Afterwards I went to meet Vivian in a restaurant in Notting Hill Gate. She had my manuscript with her, the one on the sixties that she'd read while I was away. I asked what she thought of it. She said it was like film-clips, like a movie by Jacques Tati. She thought perhaps I could improve it by 'wrapping it up', providing a commentary before each of the four sections, something like that.

I realized when I was talking to her that Vivian hardly ever talks about herself. She has given up her job recently to write full-time, but doesn't say what she's writing. She is intensely private. She feels more comfortable letting you tell her about your problems and being sympathetic. Or maybe I'm ruthlessly using this side of her because I need to at this moment in my life. She is extremely intelligent, kind and receptive.

I said to her, referring to the Bernie Siegel book *Peace, Love and Healing* and the other books like it, *Getting Well Again* and *Let's Get the Fear out of Cancer*, 'These books are really all dealing with the fear of death.' I thought that if you could get over that, there was nothing to fear (except pain, of course, but I would rather not think about that).

But even if I wasn't afraid to die myself, I wouldn't want my children to be left without a mother.

Monday, 10 February
Encouraged by Vivian's praise, I wondered about my manuscript that's been with the publisher nearly eight months and I rang up Miranda to ask if she'd done anything about it. (I'd asked her to ring the editor while I was away.)

She explained she'd lost her temper when the editor said she still hadn't finished reading it because her mother-in-law had died. Miranda had told her, 'In that case I think you'd better send it back.'

I was worried that I hadn't received it, but later this morning a card came from the Post Office saying that it was in their office at Earls Court Road. I rushed round there and collected it. Inside was a letter:

Dear Elisa
I am returning your manuscript as requested by your friend. I'm so sorry I didn't get to talk to you the week before you went away, but my mother-in-law died very suddenly, and as we were her only family, it was impossible for me to work that week.

I therefore only managed to read about half of the

manuscript before your friend requested its return. I think it is a real improvement on the other manuscript I read – I liked what I read a lot. I wish you all luck with it.

With best wishes

When I read this I thought it was better to swallow my pride. I dynamically leaped into a taxi and delivered it back to the publisher's office, which was only six streets away. I scribbled her a note saying of course I wouldn't have removed the manuscript if I'd known she was in the middle of reading it and I hoped she'd finish it.

Dr Isaacs, the young doctor I find attractive, was in Clinic 8 today. He examined me. What a delightful surprise! He also likes me. I could tell. How maddening I hadn't washed my hair or put on make-up!

When I got home, Lulu called. She said she was having a Leap Year Singles Party and I must come. I told her about the doctor and she suggested I invite him. I would have to send him a card saying 'Singles Only', or 'Only come if you're single'.

11 *February*
Another session with my therapist. I arrived half an hour late due to traffic in Bayswater Road. She didn't seem to mind. I'd been listening on the car radio to a discussion programme with Auberon Waugh, Mandy Rice-Davies and General Gow.

I told her I'd had a dream about my inviting her to a party for women in New York. She said this dream meant I should associate only with women for a while and they would heal me.

12 *February*
Duncan took me to his health club. I haven't seen him since I went to America. I told him I had already put on my bathing-suit as I hated changing in front of a lot of strange women – there are no cubicles – and I didn't want to see their bodies either.

Duncan told me my attitude was very bad and said, 'I'm so
glad we're having this little talk before we go.' He added that
there was much in favour of the German and Scandinavian habits
of nudity. 'In men's sauna, *in corpore sano*,' he said jokily.

He handed me a book he'd just bought on Catholicism and
sexuality. I explained that at my convent we had had to change
underneath dressing-gowns. When I had arrived there aged
eleven I had been surprised the first night to see the other girls in
my dormitory flapping underneath their dressing-gowns, backs
turned.

'Just what I thought,' said Duncan.

At the health club I had to pay six pounds to accompany
Duncan, who is a member. We went upstairs to our separate
changing-rooms. In mine there were several hostile-looking
women. One, in a white bra and pants, was carefully putting on
make-up. Exercises were going on in a gym.

I went downstairs to the pool, after painstakingly putting
everything into my small locker.

I saw Duncan sitting in a hot tub full of bubbles and I joined
him. I saw a man I recognized swimming up and down the pool.

Duncan then swam up and down the pool, first breast-stroke
then a powerful crawl. I was weaker than I thought and I swam
gingerly up and down near the steps, not even trying to swim a
whole length. I felt out of breath and my shoulder hurt because of
the last operation. At the same time I felt that, by taking me to the
club, Duncan was leading me back to life and health.

After a few minutes Duncan suggested we go into the steam
room. The same man that had been swimming earlier was in
there with his knees apart as though he were on the lavatory. He
said hi to me in a very friendly way. When he left, I gave the low-
down on him to Duncan. He is a publisher of unusual books and
the brother-in-law of a famous film director.

We went back to the pool, but I had no more stamina and left to
get changed before Duncan did. In the changing-room there was a
naked woman with a very serious expression. I felt vulnerable
because of my scars. Would anyone see my breast with the small

chunk taken out and think I was deformed? I had always had a good figure and long legs. Now, for the first time in my life, I could no longer take this for granted. I felt suddenly old.

I went down to the bar, which was full of mirrors, and saw a woman I recognized. At first I couldn't think who she was, then remembered she'd been the one who'd 'shared' at the ACOA meeting, about her terrible day. Today she looked very happy. I had an apricot juice and waited for Duncan.

We went on to our local health-food shop, where he became weighed down with purchases. I reached for one bottle of Evian water. I asked the man in front of me, whom I also recognized from somewhere, if I could go first as I had the correct money. He growled, 'I'm booorrred already.'

I was disconcerted and didn't understand if this meant no or not, so I gave the assistant the money anyway. Duncan said it was the actor Alan Rickman, whom I had last seen playing a dead man in a film. Duncan said he had spoken like this in an attempt to be 'cool'.

When I got home I found a note from my daughter:

Dear Mummy
Michele rang and told me there is a practice for the Prince Philip Cup on Saturday. You can ring Mrs Thwaite on Thursday about it, telling her my name, pony's name, where she is kept, and say she is a piebald. Her number is 0323 811 812. You can ring tonight.
PS PLEASE GO TO SUSSEX THIS WEEKEND AS DADDY WILL HAVE TO TAKE ME THERE OTHERWISE.

I felt very guilty that I couldn't go with her because of the timing of my chemotherapy.

I later saw a note she'd written beside the phone in my room: 'Some man going to call at six.' I guessed this was JB and rang him at his office, but he then telephoned from Victoria Station, saying he had just arrived from Vienna, where he had been on business. He would meet me at the club later.

Thursday, 13 February
I dreamed about Hal, but now I can't remember it.

Last night at the Soho club I arrive and JB is not there. Mrs Goat then arrived to meet a woman friend. She wore no make-up and looked depressed. Her husband is away, as usual. One of his plays is now having a revival in New York.

At last JB appeared, looking more bald than normal, but with his hair fluffed out at the sides in an odd way. He told some long-winded stories.

Jacob then turned up. As a result of his brilliant performance as one of the ugly sisters in the Christmas pantomime he has got another part, in *The Crucible*.

Everyone, including Mrs Goat and her friend, was made uncomfortable by JB's stories. I thought perhaps he was drunk. His humour seemed heavy-handed. Once he referred to my being strict when I was in bed with him and I found this embarrassing.

I was suddenly overcome with exhaustion and said I had to go home. JB, who had suddenly paid for everyone's drinks, accompanied me to my car, but when we discovered I'd parked the wrong way up a one-way street, he said he was going to leave me to it; he changed his mind, though, and saw me out.

Friday, 14 February. Valentine's Day
I did not get any valentines. The children have gone with their father for the first half of half-term. This morning I went to the hospital in a taxi. When I arrived I went straight to Accident and Emergency to see if my friend Nick was there. He had fallen off his motor bike. I found him in the Orthopaedic Department. By an extraordinary coincidence, my neighbour Annie and her teenage son were also in there. Her son had injured his foot.

Nick came out of a doctor's room wearing a multicoloured jumper with his arm out of one sleeve. His collarbone is broken and has to mend on its own. He has been prescribed strong painkillers.

We went to the hospital café and waited till it opened. Nick said because of his injury he has had to postpone his annual holiday. He still can't decide whether to go to Moscow in a group

or America on his own. I then offered to go with him. He said
yes. I said he should clear it with the woman he lives with, an
avant-garde photographer whom I like. I offered to share a room
with a woman in the group and not him. Nick said it might be
good for his girlfriend if I went with him as she takes him too
much for granted.

I realized that going to Russia with him was probably only a
fantasy – apart from anything else, I would be too tired to walk
and look at museums – but at the time it made me rather excited.
I get a buzz from making plans about future travel. And, of
course, it also makes me think that I *have* a future.

As we were sitting there, a woman I met last week in the
chemotherapy ward, who's disabled, came into the cafeteria and
sat with us. She told Nick to take Vitamin C Slow Release to help
his recovery after the motor-bike accident.

I said I had followed her last tip, to take Cyclophosphamide at
night instead of in the day, to minimize the sickness. I thought it
had made a difference.

The chemotherapy seemed to take a shorter time than usual. I
pretended to myself I didn't mind it as much as I do.

In the evening when I was in the house alone Annie came round
and rolled a joint for me. Her fingers are much neater than mine. I
showed her some of my manuscript about childhood and she said
each little section reminded her of a poem. She thought perhaps I
should send it to a poetry editor whom she knew.

After a while I had to ask her to leave as I kept falling asleep.

Sunday, 16 February
Last night I was in despair. I came back from Pete Ayrton's,
where I had been for dinner, and wept in bed. This morning,
however, I have woken up with a feeling of peace.

Pete and Sarah's dinner last night: there are three other guests.
One is an American sculptor from Brooklyn, whose agent recently
committed suicide because of the recession.

There's also a Scottish woman in exactly the same colours as

I'm wearing – scarlet and black. She's wearing black trousers and I'm wearing a black skirt. I'm also wearing new tights with bows on that I bought in 'Leg Room', a shop near Dita's apartment in New York.

The sculptor seems pleased to see me and doesn't talk as much as he did the first time I met him here. I find the other man, an Italian writer, particularly charming. He holds forth enthusiastically about the new Europe, the Romans' past and the influence of Latin.

Pete tells them I had a piece in the *Independent* about a house-swap. Pete wonders how Angela Carter is, and why she wasn't nominated for a recent literary prize. She's terminally ill, he says, and therefore won't have another opportunity. I didn't know she was ill. I suppose she has cancer, but I don't want to ask.

The sculptor says he's read Robert Bly's book *Iron John* and liked it. The book's been so 'knocked' here in England that it doesn't stand a chance. In America it's a bestseller. He says that the 'new' type of man can be a problem for some women, who suddenly find that they want a more assertive one after all.

Pete and Sarah and the Italian gossip about some Jewish friends who used to be left-wing and have now reverted to Orthodox Judaism. They then discuss some former members of the Socialist Workers Party who have become born-again Christians. The Italian says such people are often lost without their left-wing ideologies.

Afternoon. Joseph rang up from Sussex and said, 'This is Joseph – when you come please could you bring a blank video and the flickin' book I made with the picture of the castle – the one you like so much?'

I did not go there. Except for Pete and Sarah's dinner, I spent a horrible weekend on my own. I do not think I want to stay alone here for another weekend after chemotherapy.

17 February
I have completely changed my frame of mind from the night of

Pete's dinner, when I was in terrible distress. This morning Clare came round for coffee. I still felt very sick, but tried to ignore it. She recommended ginger as an antidote to sickness.

I talked to Clare about Bill's play and read out a scene in it where the murdered boy's sister says to his torturer, 'To see someone sad and confused and to take the time to stop and say, "You're right, you have no worth, you should be punished" is a crime of unspeakable evil . . . My brother's crime was despair, and I can forgive him that. I don't forgive deliberate cruelty.'

Clare seemed impressed by this.

Duncan and I then went to the health club. This time there was no one I knew there and I was more relaxed. The hot tub wasn't working, but there were two women in the steam bath. Duncan talked freely in front of them and gossiped about people in the media. I said Richard Ingrams was becoming a Catholic. Duncan said, 'He'd do anything to sell the *Oldie*.'

After we had changed, I joined Duncan in the bar. He was reading the papers.

Angela Carter has died aged fifty-one of cancer. This gave me a terrible shock. I do not like to have to admit that it's possible to die of cancer even if you're in the full flow of creativity. I read her novel *Wise Children* only a few weeks ago in Florida.

20 February
Sussex. Second part of half-term. When I get to the house, L's wearing the new yellow jersey I bought her in New York. It looks lovely, but she thinks it's too garish.

I have to go to bed as I still feel extremely sick. Margie's in charge. Later I go round the garden with Paula, the gardener, and I try to help Joseph ride the bike his father gave him for his birthday last September. He still can't balance and I'm too weak to support his body as he leans against me.

Joseph is overexcited and screams abuse at me. He then invites me into his little wooden house in the garden to look at the balloons he's put on the ceiling in honour of Margie's 19th birthday tomorrow. Later Margie, sitting on my bed, shows me photos of her family in Australia. She is the youngest of seven children.

Joseph clings to me several times in the night, saying, 'I love you, Mummy. Hold me!'

When I ask him exactly what he's frightened of, he cries, 'Don't say! Don't say!'

22 February

5 a.m. I woke abruptly at three and haven't slept since. I am full of anxiety, but what about? Being ill, my future, my lack of drive in getting writing finished? I am absolutely *sick* of my lack of energy.

I took the children on the Downs yesterday at about four. It was a beautiful day, we could see the sea in the distance. They both ran happily towards it. Joseph looked very handsome, as Lucy pointed out, in a green padded jacket one of his aunts had given him.

He now often rejects my maternal advances – trying to wash him in the bath, unbuttoning his clothes – and says, 'I'm not a baby.'

Last night he was in my bed clinging to me, but was frightened even in my room here, without the light on. When I asked him again what was so frightening, he repeated, 'Don't speak about it!'

I am absolutely exhausted.

23 February

Vaneeta arrived by train for lunch and in the afternoon Augusta Skidelsky came with her daughter and we went for a walk with the pony, leaving Vaneeta and Toby in the house. Vaneeta's eye was streaming, due to a detached retina.

Augusta did not know I'd had breast cancer, and when I told her I said it angrily, almost spitting the words out in disgust. How could I, who seem so energetic, have got something like this?

Augusta was talkative. She said she had had a pony as a child, called Queenie, which was kept at the local riding-school near where she lived. She had been very bossy and told the other children at the riding-school what to do.

Lucy let Joseph ride with her on the back of her bike, while Augusta's daughter was on the pony. Joseph looked sweet in Lucy's old brown hacking-jacket. Again my son seemed terribly handsome, with beautiful dreamy brown eyes. I let him ride the pony for a while.

Later we went back to London by train; Lucy and I played a board game, 'Battleships'. Vaneeta took us to the pizza house in Notting Hill Gate. Her eye was still streaming; she kept mopping at it with a handkerchief and in the process spilt her beer on the table. Vaneeta had immediately confessed to the waitresses, but Joseph kept saying: 'They blamed me.'

24 February

Zenga Longmore has got the sack. I now feel extremely guilty. But how could only two letters, Emily's and the one I wrote on behalf of Mrs M, result in the editor's terminating her column?

I ring up Edward, who despises the *Spectator* for being right-wing, but knows people who write for it. Edward says he has heard that the editor never liked Zenga Longmore's column and has been meaning to sack her for some time. I have decided to write in submitting myself as a columnist in her stead. I might die next year and so I have nothing to lose. Duncan has said, 'Go for it.'

At lunchtime I ring Joseph's teacher.

She says she was about to ring *me*. She asks, 'Does Joseph have a pet spider?'

I say yes, but it's made of cardboard. I then ask *my* question. 'Is it true that Mr Jamieson once brought in a giant spider to the school?'

She replies, 'No. Everyone would have vacated the building.'

I then ask if it's true that Mr Jamieson's left. She says yes.

Later Joseph comes home and says that the teacher called him a great big fibber'.

In desperation I ask, 'Why are you such a difficult child?'

He replies, 'I was a difficult child, wasn't I, even when I was a baby?'

I then feel guilty about saying yes.

25 *February*

This morning I went to court in the Strand in preparation for the decree nisi, which precedes the final stage of divorce. I had to formally finalize the arrangements for the children. My solicitor had asked if I wanted to put off the divorce because I'd had breast cancer, but I'd said no.

My solicitor, a young woman with blonde hair and bright red lipstick, was wearing a smart black suit. As soon as I arrived at her office I said I must have water. She went out and returned with a bottle of Highland Spring which we took in the taxi with us to the Law Courts in the Strand. Inside, I saw Miranda's husband in his City suit. When he asked why I was there I said, 'I'm afraid I can't tell you.' (I stupidly didn't ask what he was doing there.)

I was the first on the list in our court. My solicitor whispered that the judge was 'a sweetie'. He seemed amused by me. He asked if my husband had contributed any income from his writing. I said: 'No, not at all.'

He asked about my own income and I said that luckily I had inherited some money from my grandmother.

I will now have to wait about six weeks before I am finally divorced.

Last night. Party at a tapas bar beyond Finsbury Park to celebrate the launching of a book called *Fathers and Sons* published by Pete, in which men have written about their fathers. I talk to one of the contributors, who hopes his parents won't read his contribution.

The editor says that many of the men he approached wouldn't write about their fathers because they were still alive and their relationship with them was too painful. Would I be able to write a good memoir of my mother, I wonder?

Pete introduces me to a man who's going to be in the same anthology as I am, the one that's coming out in December.

An ex-publisher talks to me about having just been made redundant. He doesn't want to meet too many other men in the same boat as it brings home his own hopeless situation. (Is this like me not wanting to be associated with other cancer sufferers?)

Pete then takes me to a rock concert in Kentish Town for which he's got two tickets. It's a German singer called Nina Hagen. She wears a black wig and a sort of bathing-suit and black tights with false roses coming out of her bottom. At one moment she waves a book about AIDS published in Germany in 1988. She shouts that people say there isn't a cure for AIDS, but this book says there is. Several people raise their hands excitedly.

All around us is black. Everyone is dressed in black. The men have pony-tails and there are an enormous number of Japanese students. The sound is deafening. Nina Hagen changes her costume twice, and her wig. We are treading on spilt beer. We don't stay very long. Pete asks what I think of it. I said it's a pity that Nina Hagen is so concerned with special effects. Compared with someone like Leadbelly, for instance, her performance is tawdry and vulgar.

26 February

I go back to my work-room and rewrite the ending of the book about my childhood. To be working again properly, on a typewriter, in my own 'space', even for an hour, is liberating. The get-well books keep advising you to 'have time to yourself', 'create space for yourself' and so on. But the number of hospital appointments and the long waits at the hospital each time you go take up so much time that it's impossible. It is also impossible to feel calm, because of the physical after-effects of chemotherapy.

Jenny is determined to go on working during her treatment. She lives alone. Apart from liking to keep going, she may miss the social life of the office.

We've both been advised by the hospital not to go on the tube during rush-hour, for fear of catching germs during the period of our chemotherapy. Our resistance is down. The drugs that we hope are destroying malignant cells in our bodies are also killing healthy cells. Jill, who had had massive doses of chemotherapy, kept getting flu and colds.

Emily comes to lunch. Her new boyfriend, the vet, turns out to be an alcoholic and is now drying out in a hostel up the road.

Emily hardly eats anything at all, as usual. She is now preoccupied with Ben's dogs, which he keeps tied up for hours in a stable at his brother's house in Kent while he goes on trips abroad with the black model. Emily's going to drive down late tonight to Kent and feed and exercise them. This whole situation with the dogs infuriates me. Why can't she see that Ben treats the dogs in the same way he treats her?

I went to the health club again yesterday with Duncan. First we had caviare for lunch in his flat. He had brought it back from Moscow in December. Duncan is now determined to go to Russia this summer. He says he feels 'strangely compelled' to hang out there and start his next novel. He doesn't speak Russian, but may get a local bodyguard to act as interpreter.

Duncan's friend Patsy arrives for lunch with her six-year-old daughter. They've just been skiing in Poland. Patsy attacks the Catholic Church, saying it's a bunch of screwed-up bachelors led by the Polish Pope. She can't think why some of her more liberated women friends are returning to Catholicism and even sending their daughters to do their first Holy Communion. I daren't admit that Lucy did hers two years ago.

Duncan thinks that anyone who believes that they are munching on flesh when they take Communion must be round the bend.

An old friend of Duncan's has just been made Poland's deputy minister of defence and has stated that he wants Poland to invade Russia and take back stolen land. Duncan says that at Oxford this man was rather 'a lightweight'. Also, one of his best friends here has just been imprisoned for fraud.

As we're leaving Duncan's flat, two policemen arrive. Someone in the flat dialled 999. It must have been Patsy's daughter, while we were all arguing about Catholicism.

27 *February*

Visit to my therapist. I think she was disappointed I didn't cry in
the session. I started complaining about Emily and Ben and his
dogs. My therapist told me I should express my anger instead of
withholding it. I shouldn't be passive with people, like I was with
my mother.

When I got home I rang Emily and shouted, 'I'm sick of your
sentimental attitude about those dogs! Ben's treated those dogs
like shit for years! What do you expect from a man who's
abandoned his own son?'

Emily asked, 'What's wrong with you?'

28 *February*

Lulu's Leap Year Singles Party is tonight, although Leap Year's
Day is tomorrow. Numerous people have rung me asking what to
wear. Miranda said she might wear 'a short smart cocktail dress'.
Penelope, Lulu's anorexic cousin, told Lulu she will be 'dressed to
kill' in black. She doesn't really qualify for an invitation as she is
engaged to a man who is a candidate of the Monster Raving
Loony Party. That evening he will be busy campaigning in
Reading, so will not be available.

Duncan can't come because he's having dinner with a
woman from a recusant Catholic family who's sued her brother
in New York. Now she can't visit the family stately home
except disguised as a tourist. The staff have been told not to
admit her.

Jacob also wonders what to wear. He is now on crutches after a
motor bike fell on his foot. He is sure that he is going through the
male menopause as he's so accident-prone. Last night he went to
another meeting for disadvantaged gays. He became interested in
a Chinese man, but nothing came of it. A man from south London
offered him a lolly in the shape of a pink foot.

I told Jacob to wear jeans and a jumper. Lulu has now said she
hates men in jumpers.

Meanwhile Sarah has left a very sophisticated message on my
answerphone, saying, 'Ring me back with your sartorial

costume.' I did not know what 'sartorial' meant and thought it was something to do with monkeys.

I rang her back and discussed cellulite with her. (I think I have the first signs of it.) She goes every morning to the gym at the health club, but hasn't lost much weight yet. A survey has just been published in which American women were asked their main priority in life. Eighty per cent of them replied, 'To be thin.'

I told Vaneeta to wear a sari, but she says she doesn't want to look like a Christmas tree. Someone else has rung saying she's going to wear trousers as she thinks she's very fat. Surely trousers are the last thing to wear if you're fat?

I'm going to wear the navy-blue dress with a low-cut neck I bought with Dita in Madison Avenue three weeks ago.

I have invited Dr Isaacs to Lulu's party. Emily's mother, who of course is single, is coming up from the old people's home for it. I am not sure this is a good idea.

I spent all day trying to find out if Dr Isaacs was married, but failed. This morning I rang one of the nurses at the hospital to get some more anti-sickness pills; then I asked, 'Is Dr Isaacs married?' She seemed astounded and didn't know who Dr Isaacs was.

I got Lulu to ring one of the two Peter Isaacses in the London phone book but she said each time a young female Sloane Ranger answered so she put the phone down.

I then got Miranda to ring his secretary at the hospital, pretending to be an old friend of Dr Isaacs who had just come back from abroad and wanted to know if he was married. By mistake the hospital receptionist put her straight through to Dr Isaacs's bleeper while he was attending an operation, so she rang off in a panic.

I got Margie to drop the invitation off at the hospital, and don't know if he'll turn up or not. I have explained on the invitation that the party is for single people. How will I ever face him again during an examination if he doesn't answer?

29 February

Lulu's party did not go well as she'd asked too many single women and people she felt sorry for. Besides myself, there were two others with cancer. Then there was an Irishwoman with six children whose husband has just left her, a social worker from Southall who was beaten as a child and is now a nymphomaniac, Lulu's anorexic cousin, a retarded man who works in a hospital morgue (also Lulu's cousin, I think, and probably mine), Miranda, who now qualifies for Lulu's guest list of hopeless cases as she is about to divorce, and Dick, the man with prostate trouble whom Miranda knows already. (He's the one she looked after when he was hospitalized last year.) Larissa was invited because Lulu had discovered she's without a boyfriend at the moment.

Emily's mother got drunk and threw herself at the retarded man, who is handsome in a rugged way. Then she broke her hip falling downstairs. She is again in Charing Cross Hospital. I may see her when I go for a check-up next week. Dr Isaacs did not come, nor did he answer my invitation.

Only Emily, out of all the single women, met a new suitor. This was Miranda's old friend, Dick. Emily whispered to me in the middle of the party to keep Larissa away from him; she did not trust her as far as the opposite sex was concerned. She said she had once had her to supper and Larissa had made a play for Emily's current boyfriend, the only respectable one she'd ever had and the one her parents had wanted her to marry. Emily claimed that Larissa had shoved her leg against his under the table and gazed at him intently with her burning blue eyes.

Emily rang me early this morning begging me to find out anything I can about Dick, to see if there is any future in a relationship.

I have just phoned Nancy, Lulu's mother, who knows everyone who is remotely connected to the upper classes. I asked her to give me a run-down on Dick, then grabbed a pen and frantically took notes: 'College of Arms, thrown out of. Half-wit with sticking-out teeth. Wife bit of a goer. Wife's lover paid for everything. Tongan boyfriend. Pushed her. Mother was widow of a Hambro. Bill Dearing was a sheep-shearer. Brought up Mickey Dearing. Mother v. pretty. Uncle was Lord Buler.' When I reread it, it didn't make much sense. 'Not a person you could trust. Mischief-maker.' Did this refer to Dick, his ex-wife or the ex-wife's lover? Nancy had spoken so quickly I hadn't understood half of what she had said and I didn't feel I could call her back.

Nevertheless, I rang Emily and started to read out my notes. She, however, had already lost interest in Dick. It is not Larissa she should be careful of. One of Emily's sisters had just told her that Miranda had been Dick's mistress for eight years, long before she met the Spaniard. I am absolutely astounded.

March

Sunday, 1 March

Sussex. Yesterday morning when I arrived here Joseph was missing. Mrs Douthwaite, who'd been with him in the kitchen only a few minutes earlier, was desperate. Mr D went off in the car with me to look for him. He was going to drive through the village, but by some instinct I told him to go in the other direction. Almost at once we met Joseph coming up the road in the red jumper with animals on that I'd bought him for his birthday. He said he had been following Lucy on her pony.

Later in the day Joseph asks me, 'Would you rather have children or not have children? If you have children you're poor, because they're always nagging you to buy them things.'

Later he talks about the Mowcow, an animal that had appeared in one of Lucy's nightmares.

'Did Lucy see the Mowcow with the human eye?'

'She *thought* she saw it in a dream,' I reply.

'In a dream you really see things,' my son says.

We drive up on to the Downs and see a lot of people on horses. A hunt's going on. We walk towards the sea and then hang about with other spectators, some in parked cars, some with dogs. Lucy says, 'I wonder if they're "antis".'

Nothing happens and we start walking back. Suddenly there's a movement in the valley below us. We see the whole hunt galloping across the valley to a coppice where the hounds stream through the trees. The horses and riders, some in red coats, look wonderful.

Joseph says, 'How beautiful!'

Lucy says, 'Hunting's been going on a very long time. It's a tradition. They were doing it in the same way a hundred years ago.'

We drive to the valley near the farm shop and meet Augusta carrying a milk-churn. Augusta's life, making bread, looking after her husband and children, hardly ever leaving the valley except to go to the town on errands and on holiday once a year, seems quite different from mine. In a way I envy its stability, but if I did it – and I am not domestically competent like she is – I would get bored.

As we're talking, I see Nicholas Mosley crossing the field by his cottage. I recognize his stooping walk. There's smoke coming from his chimney. I still haven't seen him since the Booker evening.

Augusta's asked me to talk on the telephone to a woman she knows who's just heard she has breast cancer and may have to have a mastectomy.

I ring her up. This woman says she was devastated when she was diagnosed last week. She rang the Bristol Cancer Help Centre and has already been down there for a consultation. The doctor – a woman, who'd worked there for years – was 'absolutely marvellous, very matter-of-fact', and explained to her what the different treatments that she'd been offered involved. Before that, Augusta's friend explained, she'd been completely bewildered by the choice of a mastectomy, lumpectomy with chemotherapy or chemotherapy on its own. The doctor at the centre gave her a 'holistic' model to follow and made her feel she could 'beat it'. She admitted that at first she'd been nervous that she'd be forced to eat just beans, and when she'd asked for sugar in her tea she'd been thrown to find they didn't have sugar. But as she wasn't staying overnight, this didn't really matter.

I said I'd never wanted to go to the centre as I hadn't wanted to be among terminally ill people. I found the idea of this frightening and I didn't want to realize how I might end up. (Perhaps I was saving it for later, in case I got a recurrence, but I did not say this.)

This evening Joseph complains, 'I won't be an angel. I'll just have a boring life. I'll be nothing when I die. I won't see anything with the human eye. I won't even be a soul on the telephone.' He continues, 'I wish Daddy was a dead-body person. Then I could see the dead bodies. I'd punch them in the nose and give them a nose-bleed. I'd stab them in the heart and take their heart out so they couldn't go to Heaven.'

Mrs Douthwaite showed the children a video of *The Omen*. Joseph is now talking all the time about Damian, the devil-child.

'I'd like to be a priest so my head would be blown off in the wind.'

Why on earth did Mrs D show them this video? She knows how susceptible Joseph is to anything macabre and how preoccupied he is with death.

Lucy doesn't seem bothered by it and at one moment starts imitating the devil-dog in the movie, panting heavily. Joseph finds this funny.

2 *March*
This morning in London I had to write a letter to Lucy's headmistress asking if she could leave early one afternoon next week to go to the dentist.

This afternoon Lucy brings back the letter undelivered. 'I didn't give your letter to Miss Calney as there were too many dodgy things in it.' She explains that she doesn't want Miss Calney to know that I'm about to divorce. She says if I don't tell her, Miss Calney will go on thinking Lucy's very stable because she comes from a stable background.

I have just talked to Jacob on the telephone. Last Friday he had another appointment with a psychiatrist, this time in a Portakabin at his local hospital. He could hear through the wall what the psychiatrist next door was saying to his patient, but not the patient's replies.

This is what he heard: 'Can you describe these feelings of anger you get before you strangle one of your victims?'

I exclaimed, 'My God! Shouldn't he be in Broadmoor? What does he look like?'

Jacob said he had seen the man in the waiting-room earlier and that he looked very disturbed. But so did most of the others in the waiting-room. He added that it was possible that the man was discussing a dream.

Jacob then talked about the effect of grief and loss on young children. I said that I was sure my son had been marked by the deaths of my two brothers, even though he had never met them. Jacob thought he had been affected by similar deaths in his own family. His mother had had a baby girl who had died, when she was already pregnant with Jacob. He had probably been affected by his mother's grief even in her womb.

3 March

Spanish class. For the first time Pedro, the teacher, talks to us about his three-year-old son.

Marie-Ange, with her long red hair, looks disappointed.

This time the teacher plays us a tape of an interview with a Mexican peasant, to improve our ear. The Englishwoman I call the Mayoress is horrified that the Mexican peasant family sometimes don't have enough food, and that the children don't always go to school.

The older Frenchwoman, the one I like who lived in Africa, can't stand the Mayoress. She hates her lack of seriousness and application. She whispers to me that there is no point in learning a language unless you keep to a logical system. She may not come back for the class next term. The Mayoress goes on cracking jokes regardless. She is rather thick-skinned.

Maureen telephoned from a hostel near Times Square. She did not manage to get work as a nanny in LA and left almost at once for New York. She is thinking of coming back to England and wondered if she could work for me again. I told her that Margie was getting on well and the job wasn't available at the moment.

4 March

I had a horrible dream about being in a ward with women each side of me who'd had breast operations. One, who had red hair, had started sprouting hair between her breasts.

Yesterday Annie took me to Holborn on the tube to buy a word processor. We ordered the same model as she has so she can help me if things go wrong. She thought that a word processor would make me work more efficiently. She said I should start writing properly again.

This morning a man with a Jewish cap on his head came round to install it, together with a printer. I offered him some grape juice, but he said Orthodox Jews aren't allowed it. I was reminded of Catholics being forbidden to eat meat on Friday, like I was as a child. My father's mother, who became a fanatic Catholic, was Jewish, but my father and my aunt maintained that she couldn't be because she was the illegitimate daughter of a dark-skinned English Catholic. Did they persuade themselves that this was true because they didn't want to have a Jewish mother?

I do not yet know how to use the word processor. Lucy, however, when she came home from school, immediately set it up and typed out and printed a poem she had written about our dog, Toby. She is sending it to her school magazine.

Drink with Mary Killen, the agony aunt, at the club last night. I take some excerpts from my diary about breast cancer. She is extremely helpful and tells me to put more of myself into it. She suggests ordering a bottle of champagne, so we do.

Mary, who's an Irish Protestant and the daughter of a doctor, says all the people she knows who are practising Catholics are happier than her other friends. A few minutes later she looks concerned and says she has nothing to do this evening. She rings up a woman called Lucinda on the bar telephone, but Lucinda's busy.

I suggest that Mary come with me to a drinks party that will be full of happy Catholics. My cousin Nancy will be there.

At seven we leave the club and leap into a taxi, Mary waving aside my statement that I have an underground ticket.

Mrs Evans (the hostess and Joseph's music teacher) greets us both in a very friendly way. She is delighted to see Mary, who is famous in some circles (i.e. *Spectator* readers). I'm introduced to a Spaniard, and he becomes very defensive about Franco. (I began the conversation by asking if he liked Almodovar's films.) He says, firmly, 'No', and claims that only a small percentage of the Spanish population, those who were political, had cared about censorship. I say Almodovar's films are partly a reaction against the strict Franco regime and that I saw pornographic cartoons in a nightclub in Palma soon after Franco died. The Spaniard then tries to argue that Franco wasn't extreme, but adds, illogically, that there's always a violent swing-back after repression.

A very Catholic-looking girl, with a pale face and no make-up, who could almost be a nun, has joined us and quietly agrees with me about Franco. Meanwhile Mary's getting on very well, surrounded by a group of people headed by a tall red-haired elderly man.

Mrs Evans then introduces me to a woman in charge of reviews on the Catholic newspaper the *Tablet*. I tell this woman about my experiences with Joseph and the Sacrament of Reconciliation. She sympathizes and says that certain people don't suit being in a group, and this is quite normal.

Nancy, Lulu's mother, then asks cheekily, 'What's happening with your friend Miranda? Lulu says she's living in London and her husband's commuting from Essex. That's always a bad sign. Latin women' – Nancy, being a quarter Peruvian, thinks of herself as Latin – 'never let their husbands out of their sight. What does she do in the evenings, for example?'

I get rather nervous and can't think what to say. What *does* Miranda do in the evenings? At last I blurt out, 'She does sewing.' I'd suddenly remembered Miranda told me that she has taken up tapestry. I am unnerved by Nancy's acuteness. She may be an awful gossip.

Mary is still talking to the tall red-haired man.

As we leave, Mary recounts how, as soon as they began talking, the man told her how difficult it was to combine his job with living in the country. Mary, of course, asked him what his job was and he gratefully replied that he was in the House of Lords.

She is now going to write a letter for her agony column saying, 'How do I quickly let strangers know I am in the House of Lords?' The reply is 'Say how difficult it is to combine your job with living in the country and they will naturally ask what your job is.'

After the party we went back to my house, though at first Mary had wanted to go round some local night-spots, such as Emily's club, the Globe. I'm not a member.

Mary asked if she could sleep on the sitting-room sofa. At midnight I went in and chatted to her. She said, 'Sorry if it's a bit babyish, but I like to go to sleep with someone talking to me.'

Mary appeared at breakfast in the same African wrap-around skirt she'd worn as a nightdress. She asked if I thought it was OK for work at the offices of *Harpers & Queen*. I said she should iron it. She said she couldn't be bothered. She explained that the editor liked her to wear a different skirt every day.

I then told her I had written to the editor of the *Spectator* asking if I could do Zenga Longmore's column, and showed her the letter. I said I vaguely wondered if she could help me as she is having lunch with the editor, Dominic Lawson, today, but she told me a long anecdote about how a friend of hers, a millionairess, had wanted to write an article for the *Spectator* on a memory-improving course she'd attended. When Mary had mentioned the article to Dominic, he had said, without seeing it, 'It's not for us.'

As we were talking, my son came in and said, 'Hello, Posy; I didn't know Mummy loved you as well.'

I realized that he must have often seen Mary at my ex-husband's flat. For some reason he thought she was Posy Simmonds, whom my ex-husband once interviewed here in our kitchen.

5 *March*

My therapist is very keen on the Cancer Help Centre in Bristol
and on any form of holistic medicine. When I told her about
talking to Augusta's friend, she gave me the telephone number
of a masseuse, a cranial osteopath and a healer. (They are all in
places such as Finchley Road, however, and the stress of getting
there in my present condition will surely cancel out the benefits?)
She also persuaded me to buy some comic postcards designed by
one of her other patients. I stupidly wrote out a cheque in
advance for these.

Last night I gave another dinner-party. I had arranged this very
carefully with the young blonde cook I had had before, for
twenty people. The day before one of the guests rang up and
said he had to sit with his mother, who is a recent widow, as his
sister-in-law couldn't do it as arranged. I asked if he could get a
babysitter, but he said no. He explained that his life had
completely changed since his father died last summer.

Julian then telephoned and said he couldn't come because he is
going to Majorca for a platonic week with a woman he says he
hates in order to visit the woman for whom he suffered
unrequited love for ten years and who mentally tortured him. I
am extremely annoyed about this.

I then received a call from someone else who couldn't come as
his new wife's father was having a surprise birthday party. This
seemed the most reasonable excuse so far.

That afternoon M, the writer, rang and said she had a hole in
her roof and a burst pipe and that plumbers would be there all
afternoon. I said surely it would be wonderful for her to leave
the scene of wreckage after that and come to my dinner. (I would
have jumped at the chance, but I am not home-loving as M is.)

At six Patrick, the painter, called to say his wife's mother had
had an eye operation in Cornwall. His wife, who'd cooked
pumpkin soup for me in December, was arriving in London on a
late train from Penzance and he was meeting her. I phoned M
again to persuade her to come, but she said she was in a state of

collapse now the plumbers had left. I told her she was over-
domesticated, and that it would be much better if she came over
to my house and had a bath. I asked if her husband could come
if she wouldn't. She said he hadn't returned from work, but
when he came he would want to look after her. I yelled in a
semi-joking way, 'I have no one to look after me!'

I quickly invited three gay men instead – Jacob, Duncan's
friend Simon Burt and Andrew, who used to edit *Gay News*. (We
had first met when I was twenty-one, when he had left a pair of
red stiletto shoes in my room at King Edward VII's Hospital for
Officers where I was having my tonsils out.)

Simon and Andrew arrived on the doorstep at the same time,
just as I was arranging some spectacular orange tulips in the
vase my friend Tessa, the potter, had given to me for Christmas.
Both men had brought bottles of wine. They had not met since
the heady days of Gay Liberation, when Andrew had dropped
out of his job as a *Times* journalist, stormed his father's St James's
club wearing women's clothes and written an article in the
Spectator about 'coming out'. He has now left the seventies
behind him and lives a quiet life painting and working part-time
as a courier in Europe. They talked about gay matters while I
went upstairs.

Then Paolo and Emily arrived. (I had reversed my decision not
to ever have her to dinner, and had invited her for Old Times'
Sake.) Emily was wearing a swirling skirt with gold bands that I
assumed was from Latin America, but she said she had bought it
for three pounds in Portobello Market. Paolo looked more
serious than usual. I couldn't be bothered to ask whether they
were really back together. Roger, the American I had met at the
wedding in January, and his wife, who'd written the book on
Russia, arrived. Roger began talking to Annie about prisons. (He
is writing an article on Wandsworth Prison and Annie is
interested in the design of prison buildings.) There was also
Vaneeta, Jacob, Giles (a museum curator) and Angela, a single
mother from Hammersmith who teaches English literature to
adults. Giles helped me count the guests before the meal, but we

got into a muddle about who was missing. Giles remembered
suddenly that it was Geraldine Cooke, who had telephoned him
earlier saying she was on a busy schedule and might not turn up
at all. Suddenly Geraldine did arrive, however, looking very
sprightly.

Meanwhile Simon was recounting how he had been mugged
at the north end of Portobello Road at 1 a.m. a few weeks ago.
He had just had a foot operation and was already limping when
three young men set on him. Casualty at St Charles' Hospital
told him that luckily he had a very thick skull.

When we sat down, Emily and I argued across Roger about
Catholicism. (I was annoyed that we had got on to that subject
so quickly.) Emily seemed to think foreign Catholics were more
repressed, but I said English ones were. I then lied, out of
excitement, to clinch the argument, and said I had lived in Spain
for five years when really I had left when I was three. Roger
thought that in many ways Islam was more accessible to an
ordinary person in his or her daily life. In mosques, people
walked about chatting, using them as meeting-places. He said he
was envious of Catholics and others who had a religion.

Annie was sitting next to Paolo, who knew Lucia, the
Guatemalan painter, and some of Lucia's women friends in
Rome. He warned Annie, 'They will find you very attractive
with your little-girl looks and pale English skin.' He thought he
was putting her off, but of course Annie found this very exciting.

Roger, when I told him I used to work at the North
Kensington Law Centre, suggested I should become a prison
visitor. Once Giles asked, 'Do you have a lavatory in your lovely
home?' and the cook, who was serving him tomato coulis, burst
out laughing.

When Geraldine Cooke rang up to thank me the next day she
told me that one guest had mistaken her for the cook. So as not
to embarrass him she had thought very quickly and said
graciously, 'I'm not the cook, but I wish I had been.'

Friday, 6 March

Joseph comes into my bed before seven and tells me, 'A boy with red hair called Buzz killed another boy.'

I ask, 'Did you see the dead body?'

He replies, 'Yes', and clings to me, taut with fear. Margie says he woke three times in the night.

At nine I ring up the local doctor, the one I first went to when I had the lump. He tells me to let Joseph sleep in my bed and dose him more heavily with Phenergan.

Cynthia is back from Cuba. She came round yesterday evening. I asked her some questions about the trip. She said that the main food for tourists in Cuba was 'cheese sandwich'. She seemed naïvely delighted by this. I couldn't get to grips with what it was really like, partly because she was determined to say nothing critical, and also perhaps because I was jealous I couldn't go myself and didn't ask enough questions.

She and Lucy did a French play in the kitchen, part of Lucy's homework. Cynthia wore Joseph's school cap and Lucy wore a French beret. Cynthia threw herself into it with great zest.

Later Lucy told me she needed a 'hippy' costume for another play they're doing at school. I gave her my old Paisley shirt. My brother had had one like it and we had worn them together when we smoked dope. I told Lucy I had had it when I was a hippy.

Lucy said, 'I didn't know people like you were hippies.'

Later. Hospital again. Chemotherapy.

In the waiting-room at Clinic 4 are a mother and daughter. The daughter's in baggy black trousers and a black and white checked top, has long permed hair and could be half West Indian. The mother has dyed, very blonde hair and a trendy black and white jacket. I like their zany clothes and the fact that they're together. If Lucy were a few years older she might come to the hospital with me.

Today another friend, Elizabeth, has offered to come with me to chemotherapy. She arrives in Clinic 4 as I'm waiting for the results of my blood count. In her twenties Elizabeth was a 'goer'

– open marriage, lots of affairs (one with my ex-husband, whom she started flirting with at her own wedding) – and wrote amusing and original articles in glossy magazines. Now she says she has agoraphobia, is very wrapped up in her children and won't go out much because she thinks she's overweight.

In Clinic 4 I see a new doctor who is young and very optimistic. He says it's lucky I found the lump when it was still small as my chances of recovery are much higher. It's unlikely that I'll find bigger lumps in my body later. Despite, or because of, his enthusiasm, he forgets to write a prescription for the folinic acid and Ondansetron, so Elizabeth is sent upstairs to get it before I have my injection.

When I get to the oncology ward, there's a completely bald woman of my age or younger in one of the beds being sick. I get into the end bed near the wall, as far away from her as possible, next to the Indian man who always seems to be in there at the same time as me. He smiles at me and I feel ashamed that I've avoided him before.

While I'm waiting, Elizabeth returns. What I like about her is that she is completely honest. I find her relaxed attitude to love and sex refreshing because of its lack of hypocrisy. She assumes that most people will fall in love and want to have affairs, that this is part of the human condition. She is still with the man she married in her twenties, however: because she and her husband have never wanted to divorce, she hasn't had to take any of her love affairs to its logical conclusion.

Elizabeth sits beside me and chats about London social life. In spite of saying that she never goes out, she seems to know a surprising amount about it. Last week she was at a dinner where a man who hangs about 'the French pub' arrived and casually revealed that earlier in the evening the young woman who had been coming with him had been stabbed by 'a golden-haired rent boy'. Another guest took umbrage at the remark about the rent boy and accused the speaker of 'jumping to conclusions'. Meanwhile the woman who had been stabbed was presumably lying in hospital on her own.

Saturday, 7 March
I couldn't bear spending another weekend in London on my own
after chemotherapy, so I invited myself to stay in Suffolk with
Margaret, my friend who's a sculptor and rather highly strung.
When I first heard I'd got breast cancer I couldn't bear to talk to
Margaret. She always wanted to have very long conversations
and I didn't have the emotional energy. Also, I think her anxiety
communicated itself to me. For months I have felt very ashamed
of not wanting to talk to her as she is an old friend. Now I have
accepted her standing offer of hospitality.

I travel alone by train, armed with all my pills and a bottle of
Evian water. I go to bed early, in a deep, comfortable bed with
snow-white sheets. Margaret has put a vase of spring flowers on
the dressing-table. Out of the window I can see the church clock
and the graveyard, both in sand-coloured stone. It's very
beautiful here.

Sunday, 8 March
Eleven years ago Mike, Margaret's husband, had a car accident
and he still can't walk properly because of it. At first the doctors
thought his brain would also be permanently affected. I
remember going to visit him in hospital in London. He was
bravely making jokes, but several of the other patients in his
ward seemed to have lost their minds. One man was being
taught to recognize each suit of a pack of cards. He had to
relearn everything he had ever known. Mike made a determined
recovery, deliberately setting himself challenges, such as person-
ally covering a war in Africa for his magazine instead of sending
someone else.

Before lunch I open the newspaper and tell Mike, who's a
tease, that Bertie, a Canadian man he often makes fun of, has just
written a book that has got a very good review. I stupidly let slip
that I've been invited to Bertie's book-launching party next week.
Mike asks when it is, but I refuse to reveal the day, saying if I do,
he must also take *me* to a literary party.

He then declares that he'll make sure Bertie's book doesn't get reviewed in his magazine. I am shocked by this and say, 'You see, you don't wish him well. Why should you go to his launch-party?'

During lunch – delicious roast lamb, rocket and radicchio salad from the garden – Margaret is summoned by 82-year-old Mr Leary, the old man next door, whose dog's very ill. The dog, a black Labrador, is blundering about as though it's had a small stroke. Margaret and Mike rush to take the dog to the vet. I watch them out of the window and see them guide the poor dog towards the car.

While they're away, I cut out an article from yesterday's *Independent* about a Greek orthodox funeral. Since I've been ill I've become more interested in religion and death. 'An open coffin reminds us of the truth that the world is monstrous . . . The prevailing culture has reduced death to a non-event . . . it is not death which is thus dehumanised. It is life . . . Life becomes trivial in its attempt to deny the existence of mortality. It becomes a lie . . . '

I find this article, which explains that the reasons for having an open coffin are to acknowledge the awfulness of death and mourn properly in front of the dead person, instead of suppressing one's feelings or doing it later, convincing. At the same time I don't think I, or many other English people, would be able to grieve in public. I also think it won't make much sense to a person who doesn't believe in the after-life.

Evening. I am in bed again, still at Margaret's. I am trying to concentrate on other things, such as reading and writing my diary, to avoid feeling sick. I have brought two of the joints that Annie rolled for me in a little cardboard box. Margaret rolled another one for me as well. I smoked one last night, but I think it made me feel sicker than the chemotherapy drugs.

I wake up in the night and read a book I've found here – *Never Mind*, by Teddy St Aubyn. It is a new novel, about privileged decadent people in the south of France. It is well written and the author is younger than I am.

Monday, 9 March
Back to London on a slow train.

Margaret has given me a special net bag in which I can carry my water bottles over my shoulder. I drink water all the way back, sitting next to the train lavatory on purpose. Every so often waves of sickness come over me.

There's a review in yesterday's paper of some memoirs of the sixties by Katie Campbell, a Canadian poet I met last year at a poetry reading: 'The rambling, intelligent, witty reminiscences of a 33-year-old female narrator chart a lifetime's search for emotional, sexual and mental stability.'

Why can't I get my own book on the sixties published?

There is also a review of Teddy St Aubyn's novel, the one I've just read. He used to be a junky, or was it a cocaine addict? If he can pull it off, why can't I? I am not a junky, for Heaven's sake.

10 March

Dear Elisa

Thank you for your letter. I enjoyed your diary, but cannot see it finding a place in the *Literary Review*. We are squeezed to death, and can only put in the occasional non-review pieces; I don't think it would stand up as a regular feature and as a one-off it would be too puzzling . . .

Yours
Bron

I am now consumed with anxiety about Margie. I think she is at the end of her tether. She is constantly late and is always talking about her emotional life. My ex-husband thinks that she wants to be like a character out of *Neighbours*. I asked Lucy why the people on *Neighbours* had so many problems and she said if they didn't, there wouldn't be a series.

An unpleasant thing happened today. I was driving back from Julian's flat, where I'd been for half an hour, when I saw Athena, sitting behind the wheel of her car very near my house, smiling. I haven't heard from her since she never replied to my call about

going to see Mr Goat's play several months ago. I am extremely
hurt that she did not call and ask how I was.

11 *March*

I saw James L and his wife last night at Vaneeta's. James didn't
refer to my letter to the *Telegraph* attacking his article about
chemotherapy.

Vaneeta whispered to me that she'd mentioned it to him when
he first arrived. She had said, 'Elisa enjoyed writing that letter.'
James had replied, 'I know.' She said he didn't seem annoyed.
He obviously had the sense to see it wasn't meant as a personal
attack on him. I had written it to stop myself from drowning.

12 *March*

Various dramatic events. I saw R at a party. Margie crashed the
car.

We'd been to the Royal College of Art, where Lucy had had a
picture in an annual schools' exhibition. We'd seen Joseph's old
headmistress there, the one he doesn't like and who dislikes us.
Leaving the children with my ex-husband, I went home. At six I
began waiting anxiously for Margie, who was to come and get
my car, collect Joseph from my ex-husband's flat and take him to
a karate class. (My therapist has suggested he do karate, to
channel his aggression.)

I was annoyed with Margie for always being late and when
she finally arrived, I mildly ticked her off. I then rang my ex-
husband and told him to go with her to the karate lesson as I
was afraid she would drive erratically trying to hurry. She
returned to my house after a few minutes, however, saying she'd
crashed the car. It turned out my car wasn't damaged, nor was
she; only the car she'd banged into had suffered. She started
crying and saying she couldn't cope with the disturbed nights. I
said, 'But it's only three nights. If you were a young mother
you'd be up seven nights a week.'

She said vehemently that she would never have children.

I called my ex-husband and said he would have to bring Lucy

back himself as I couldn't send Margie out again.

Just as Lucy arrived, Duncan turned up to take me to the party and I rushed out in an escapist manner, away from my domestic problems. I was wearing a very short skirt and my New York tights. Duncan said he'd never seen me in such a short skirt.

The party was in a gallery near Cork Street. We went in just behind R's ex-wife. I was told to put my coat on the staircase and when I came back, Duncan was talking to her. I did not join them, but Duncan handed me a glass of champagne. I poured him some orange juice and went off to talk to a writer called Artemis.

Then I went to the other end of the room and joined Simon Burt and a friendly American girl. She worked in publishing and gave me the name of a young agent who might take me on. I wrote it down carefully.

Then a cousin of mine and Lulu's, approached me and announced that Lulu is going to have a baby. She has never been pregnant before and is forty. I was so stunned I couldn't take it in. The cousin, who lives near me, told me to ask her for help any time I needed it during the period of my treatment. She said I could bring my children round to be looked after. This was very kind of her, though I knew I would not be able to take up her offer as Joseph is paralytically jealous of small children and hers are much younger than mine.

She asked me what I'd done with my latest book, the sixties one, and I said I had given it to an agent called Faith.

I then saw that R, who I once thought was the love of my life, had come in and was wearing a dark-green jumper and was very thin. He looked to me as he'd looked the first time I'd met him, when I had fallen in love with him, frail and vulnerable, as well as very handsome. He went to the far end of the room. His ex-wife immediately went over, put a proprietorial hand on his shoulder and went away again. I did not approach him and he did not approach me.

I then talked to the publisher whom I had sat next to at the wedding in January. I apologized for criticizing him and his wife

for looking bored with each other at the table. (Duncan had said
that after my remark the wife had got up, looking green.) He
explained that he and his wife were tense at the wedding
because they had given up smoking the day before.

I joined Larissa, who was talking to a white-haired man about
human rights. He had got the OBE and lived in Geneva. Sarah
seemed impressed by him. He said that the US government was
now not going to give aid to countries with bad human rights
records. I could not butt in to this conversation; it was too high-
powered and I wasn't in the mood to concentrate, so I went
away.

Duncan wanted to leave. I said maybe I hadn't 'worked' the
room, but I meant I hadn't talked to R, who was still standing in
the same position he had been in all evening, with different
women coming up to him every so often. I decided I did not
really want to talk to him while other people were there, so I
agreed to go off with Duncan, Simon and the American girl. We
piled into Duncan's car and drove to Hanover Square to a
nightclub run by black men.

When I got home I found a bit of paper on my bed, neatly
printed from the word processor, in capitals:

DIARY 1992

MARCH 12

MARGIE CRASHED THE CAR. I SHALL NEVER FOR-
GET THE WORDS SHE USED ON THE PHONE. (I
HEARD AS I WAS GOING DOWNSTAIRS. I RAN BACK
UPSTAIRS THE MOMENT I HEARD THEM IN SHOCK.)
THE WORDS WERE 'I'M A FAILER. I'M QUITTING MY
JOB.' I HOPE SHE DOESN'T BECAUSE I LIKE HER.
WE'LL JUST HAVE TO WAIT AND SEE. I WILL GET
BACK TO YOU WHEN I KNOW. ANYWAY, THE GOOD
THING THAT HAPPENED WAS THAT MY PICTURE
WAS IN A EXSIBITION, AND MUMMY DID NOT
DRESS BADLY (BUT RATHER WELL). JOE WAS
SENSIBLE (NOW I KNOW I CAN TRUST HIM) WHICH

IS BRILL. MRS PERCIVAL WAS THERE. I THINK JOE
WAS SURPRISED MORE THAN SCARED. JOE (I
THINK) QUITE ENJOYED IT. THERE WAS CAPRI SUN
AND CHOCOLATE AND CRISPS. GOODBYE.

I was very delighted by my daughter's pithy summary of
events – I didn't know she was also writing a diary – but
alarmed by the content.

I am now demented with worry about Margie leaving. I
should have told Maureen she could have her job back when she
phoned from New York a few days ago. Now I don't even know
the number of the hostel in Times Square where she is staying.

Midnight. I have just rung Bill in New York. Perhaps he can find
out the number of Maureen's hostel by going there. It's very near
where he lives.

I asked how the play was going and he said it had had a
couple of good reviews. I also asked courteously about his
health, but did not want to know the answer as I fear he cannot
get better.

13 March
Chemotherapy. I was at the hospital by nine and had the blood
count. The gaunt Indian man was already there before me,
waiting.

Elizabeth was to join me. She had asked if I could guarantee
that she wouldn't see anything awful at the hospital, such as a
person with their face severely altered under plastic surgery. I
thought this was unlikely.

While I was still waiting, a woman came in and said that a
man was walking all over the hospital with blood pouring from
his foot. Elizabeth then arrived looking pale, saying there was a
trail of blood up the escalator and all over the first floor. We had
to walk past it a few minutes later on our way to Oncology.

This time in the chemotherapy ward I had the window bed.
No one else was in there. The doctor upstairs in Clinic 4 had

done something wrong, so my prescription had to be sent up again to be signed before I could have my injection. In the meantime I told Elizabeth the whole story of how I had fallen in love with R two years earlier and how, after leaving all his things in my house for eight months, he now refused to meet me or talk to me normally.

She said when she was young she had once had an affair with a famous pop singer in which she had behaved very emotionally. She had finally written him a calm letter saying she simply wanted to meet him for a drink. He had immediately responded. I said that R would not respond to such a letter and would instantly interpret it as an advance.

A man who was very sorry for himself then moved into the next bed. He was unshaven and said he had lost four and a half stone since his treatment in November. He complained that he still hadn't received his clothing allowance. I couldn't stand his self-pity, so I got up and went into the waiting-room.

In there was the bald punk girl with the baby I'd previously avoided, the girl with very white make-up and heavily blackened eyes. She had the baby with her as usual. She had it out of its buggy and was trying to get it to walk, but it couldn't. I noticed with relief that she had a French accent, so she wasn't a punk from south London after all. Why did this make me feel relieved? I began talking to her. The baby – a boy – was eleven months, she said, and she'd had something wrong with her uterus after his birth. Sometimes she has to be on a drip and stay in hospital overnight. Even on those occasions she kept the baby with her. She said he was no trouble.

I realized that I'd steered clear of her and the other patients, who, like me, were having chemotherapy. I'd deliberately had no contact with them because I'd felt they were contaminated. I'd also felt contaminated.

While I was having my injection, Bridie told me that the girl is from Brittany. I now find her attachment to her baby very sweet.

Saturday, 14 March
I had an emergency session yesterday with my therapist as she is going on holiday to Cyprus. By the time I got there I was on the verge of collapse.

The therapist was dressed all in green to match her eyes. She didn't seem to recognize that I was in terrible distress and seemed very tearful herself. (Maybe her own love affair has gone wrong?) She talked a great deal about alcoholics and how they manipulate you. She had lived for years with an alcoholic husband and her brother is alcoholic as well. She said again how important it was to be able to acknowledge my anger about my mother being drunk for much of my childhood. I would be less likely to get cancer again if I didn't hold these things back. This may or may not be true.

Midday. The Famous Writer and his wife have gone on holiday. I arrived back from the hospital yesterday to find Maria hoovering and Paquita cooking bean-curd stew.

Maria said excitedly that she had just passed 'Mr A's house'. (She seemed to be calling the Famous Writer by his wife's Christian name.) She said that her friend Francesca, who has worked for them as a housekeeper for seventeen years, was helping them carry suitcases out of the house as she passed.

Annie, who rang up this morning, is worried that the Famous Writer and his wife, ardent Labour supporters, will miss doing their bit for Labour just before the election. Today Annie is going to work on a Labour Party stall down at Kensington Library.

Teatime. I now find the smell of Paquita's cooking absolutely nauseating, as I associate it with chemotherapy and being ill. I can't eat the bean-curd stew. She has brought me some fresh ginger root from the health-food shop and advised me to make ginger tea. The idea of this revolts me. Also, I hate the puritanical overtones of health food. In another century Paquita would probably be a nun flagellating herself in a cell.

Annie came in and rolled joints for me again tonight. She had an unnerving experience outside the Library. A local mother, whose daughter had been at the same primary school as Annie's son, attacked her for campaigning for the Labour Party when she is sending her son to a private school. She called her a hypocrite and said, 'My daughter has to go with the dregs to Holland Park Comprehensive.' She is from Eastern Europe. Instead of defending herself, Annie turned and ran home.

As the evening wore on, Annie started soothingly telling me about her childhood. At first it had been idyllic, with just her and her mother. Her mother had warmed her little vest every morning on the radiator before she put it on. When she was six her baby brother was born. Her mother was then too busy to attend to her and she was looked after by a German au pair. She said it took her years to get over the shock, though she's now very close to her brother.

15 March
In the minicab on the way to Tessa's house in Brixton the African driver asks where I'm going and I reply, 'To the house of my best friend.'

He asks, 'What do you mean?'

I explain that Tessa is my oldest friend, and I am going to a seventy-fifth birthday party for her aunt.

The driver claimed that if someone lived a long time, she'd found the meaning of happiness. I said I didn't agree. My mother was seventy-six and she wasn't a happy person. The cab-driver said that *he* had found the secret of happiness, which was to promise nothing, and not to take on too many responsibilities. Life was dynamic and you couldn't anticipate the changes that would occur.

When we arrived he pointed out the balloons we could see through a window on the first floor and said that the party had already begun. I did not disillusion him by telling him that the first-floor flat belonged to someone else and that the party wasn't till tomorrow.

Tessa had lit a fire in the sitting-room. A framed photograph of her mother as a young woman was on the wall. Her brother Angus – tall, handsome and skinny, with a bush of iron-grey hair – was there, wearing his usual denim jeans. When I came in, he exclaimed, 'My God, you look well.'

I was wearing red tights with white hearts on them that I'd also bought in New York. I stuck my leg up in the air to give him and Andrew, another brother, who works in Poland and had come over for the party, a full view of the tights.

I asked Andrew about politics in Poland. He said that now that lower-rank Solidarity people were in charge, their attitude was: 'Teraz kurwa my' (literally 'Now, shit, us!' or 'Now it's our turn'). He said they would put almost anyone in, just to get power.

Tessa had cooked salmon she'd bought in a local Brixton market. Andrew had brought caviare from Warsaw. Tessa's friend Barbara, a nurse, then arrived from up the road. She had never tasted caviare before.

At the end of the meal I produced two joints that Annie had rolled for me last weekend. It seemed more sociable to smoke them in company.

After supper Angus asked how my writing was going. He had encouraged me since I was very young. I explained that I had just given a manuscript to a woman called Faith, recommended by his ex-wife, Stephanie, who was trying to help me get published. He said how much he liked Serpent's Tail as a publisher. He then left to stay with his girlfriend.

Sunday
Still in Brixton, where I spent the night. I took a sleeping pill about 1 a.m. I should have taken it earlier. Tessa's bedroom, where I slept, faces the road and seems very cold. But we had the gas fire on earlier in the evening, and I had an electric blanket and a duvet, eiderdown and my coat to cover me. I explained to Tessa that I have unnatural chills due to chemotherapy.

She kindly brought me breakfast in bed – toast, boiled eggs

and Rice Krispies. The Krispies made me feel sick.

I feel very vulnerable and when she's gone out, I start crying. I'm so worried about Margie leaving. How can I look after the children with all the hospital appointments?

Tessa comes in with a brochure on the Greek island she wants me to go to with her in June when I've finished my treatment. She says I should let my ex-husband look after the children so I can go. She doesn't mention I've been crying. We decide between two community centres on the island Skyros. Tessa reads out in the brochure that women outnumber men by two to one. This puts me off a bit, but on the other hand it's more of a challenge.

It's pouring with rain. Everything seems very bleak. I can't believe that we will ever get to the Greek island.

At eleven Tessa goes out to clean her car. Meanwhile Andrew is pottering about next door. I peep into the sitting-room and see his feet sticking out of the put-you-up bed.

I finally get up properly at twelve. It's still pouring with rain. Just as the three of us go out of the front door, two girls pass on horses. One is a beautiful grey Arab. Andrew, who's lived abroad since his teens, exclaims admiringly, 'Only in England!'

When we arrive at the Polish club in Kensington, Aunt Sophie and her family are gathered. I sit down beside Sophie, who looks bewildered. I'm very fond of her. I've known her since I was a teenager. Once, just before my grandmother died, I wrote her a letter about my grandmother going blind. I described how I had walked with my grandmother in her garden on an autumn day, and how, in the flower-beds she had looked after for sixty years, my grandmother could only make out the colour yellow. In her memory, however, she could still see all the flowers that she had originally planted. Sophie wrote back saying she liked the way I had written about my grandmother and that she hoped I would become a writer.

We sit down to lunch, and bortsch is served. The enormous, long table is full of relations – cousins, children, nephews and nieces, in-laws, grandchildren. At the high point of the banquet, when the birthday cake is brought in, the Poles take their glasses and start singing 'Stolat! Stolat!' – the equivalent of 'May she live a hundred years!' Suddenly I feel very alien, being in the company of people whose language I don't speak. At the same time I consider myself privileged to be included in this family gathering.

Then I realize that, by splitting up with my husband, I've burnt my boats, I've excluded myself from ever taking part in such 'normal' family get-togethers. I'm on my own.

Evening. I'm back in my own bed. Things are disintegrating. I feel as though I can't cope with anything. I ring up Vivian and suddenly I start to cry silently. There's a long silence as I hang on to the phone.

Vivian asks, 'Where are you? Are you downstairs?'

'No . . . I'm lying down.'

She asks me to think why I'm so distressed. I explain that the family birthday party made me realize finally that I'm no longer married. Months ago, before I got breast cancer, I'd told her, 'I'm afraid if I divorce I'll never marry again, I'll just have a series of crazy affairs.'

I say now that last week I saw the man I used to be in love with.

Vivian asks, 'Not that man who looks like your brother? You always get upset when you see him.'

She points out that she also often feels like this. Until recently, she'd been living entirely on her own, for a long time. When I put the telephone down I realize that Vivian may never marry and, unlike me, may never have children.

16 March

Lucy shows me a dream she's typed out on the word processor, about breast cancer and me and her pony Spinet in a circus. She wants me to photocopy it. She says, 'Please show that to your psychiatrist.'

I now have a terrible aversion to that room at the hospital where we have chemotherapy. It is quite dreadful.

I told Duncan this in the health club today. I said I'd had an aversion to the other patients in there. He said it was natural if you were ill to veer towards people who were healthy. I realized this was another reason why I am attracted to Duncan (and also to Hal, in a different way). They're both robust.

We swam in the pool, but didn't stay in as long as usual. I happily went naked into the shower in the changing-room. A Japanese woman was in there and for some reason this made me feel less inhibited. Another woman with fluffy blonde hair was parading in front of a mirror in a tight vest, admiring her waist and bottom half.

We then went to Duncan's flat for tea. He's waiting to hear if he can interview Albert Finney for *Woman's Journal* before he goes to France in a week. (He's going to stay at his parents' house in St Tropez for several weeks and write. What will I do without him?)

I have rung Bill in New York several nights running, at 2 and 3 a.m., leaving messages on his answerphone. I want to find out if he's traced Maureen at the hostel near Times Square.

Later. I finally get through to Bill. The receptionists at the hostel were all back-packers and transients and didn't know Maureen. I then took the plunge and asked Bill, 'How will I know if you've died?'

Bill did not seem thrown by the question. He simply gave me the telephone number of his neighbours whom we'd met in the café the evening I saw Bill's play.

I am extremely worried about getting a new nanny. I have started praying in the night, saying the Hail Mary and Our Father.

Tuesday, 17 March
This morning I got a call from Maureen from Notting Hill Gate, saying she was in London and wanted her job back. I told her to come over in half an hour and then re-employed her on the spot. She's starting on Thursday. She's lost a lot of weight as she didn't eat much in America.

Margie has already applied to the agency to find her a new job.

18 March

Joseph is again sleeping in bed with me. He seems pleased about this. This morning he woke me at 5.30 with a sharp cry. He said that Lucy was being cruel to him in a dream. He snuggled up to me with his taut little body. He talked again about past nightmares and asked which was the worst one – Lucy's about the Mowcow or mine about the child in a wheelchair. As I tell him that the nightmares aren't real, dreams aren't real, I wonder if they *are* real, in the influence that they and the subconscious have on our daily lives. I think of Ben Okri's novel *The Famished Road*, about the child who lives half in a spirit world.

At around 7.30 I go to sleep for half an hour and have the following dream. Or it could be a pure memory. I'm not sure.

I am being lifted high in the air by my father, higher and higher. It's a bit frightening but exhilarating. I feel safe. Then I'm climbing down a huge red staircase pulling a doll's pushchair with me, like the one Lucy used to have. I am going very slowly. I get to the bottom and my father is there waiting for me. I step on to the grass in my red sandals. One of my feet in its red sandal goes into deep grass and gets covered with mud and I start crying uncontrollably. My father is concerned.

Then Lucy wakes me up carrying a tray with a bowl of muesli, a banana and a cup of tea.

Later Julian came to take me out to dinner in Battersea. A woman friend of his had invited us. This time I didn't like Julian's smart car so much; I found it rather irritating. Is its luxuriousness a symbol of Julian's narcissism?

The hostess had two dogs like rugs on her sitting-room floor; I think they were Tibetan terriers. I did not feel well. In fact, I felt extremely ill and sick throughout the dinner and realized I shouldn't have gone out.

19 *March*

I wake very early, long before seven. I didn't go to sleep till after one. I feel dreadful as I have my period. (I do not seem to be having the menopause yet.) I was going down to Sussex for a day to sort out some things, but I can't. Instead I have a long conversation on the telephone with Paula, the girl who does the garden there, about flowers.

I go back to sleep about 9.30 and again for two hours at two. Joseph has a friend for tea, a boy called Jonathan.

At six Maureen arrives to start the job again. She has been staying for two nights in a hostel up the road. The children were delighted to see her. She said she had missed them.

20 *March*

Last night Duncan took me to Joan Wyndham's party to launch the publication of her third volume of diaries, *Anything Once*. Joan, who's now in her sixties, is a natural diarist, honest, funny and spontaneous.

When we arrive at the party, I start talking to a tall American widow I've met once before. She tells me how much fun she had in Boston as a young woman, dating lots of young men, but not sleeping with them. In her children's generation, she says – the sixties and seventies – her daughters had to find one young man to protect them from the others.

Two older men, Michael and Christopher, who go to many London parties, were both there. Michael said I looked very well and asked, 'Is this your new image?' I wasn't sure what he meant. I said, 'When I first met you I was a confused young woman.' (I was twenty-eight, and it was the year I met my husband.) He said, 'You were a scrubber.' I said, mildly amused at the inaccuracy of this, 'No I wasn't.'

My ex-husband was also at the party; so was Mary Killen. She told me, 'I like your outie.' (She meant the navy and white jumper I'd bought the week before.) My ex-husband said, 'Mary often abbreviates words.' She and he were going to some posh dinner afterwards, but he wouldn't say where.

I went downstairs to the kitchen, where food was being served, and talked briefly to a flamboyant blonde Russian woman and her dark boyfriend from St Petersburg. Duncan then came in and I introduced them.

Suddenly I smelt the smell. It could have been a floor cleaner. It reminded me of the oncology ward at the hospital and I was nearly sick. As I stood there reeling and nauseated, two older women sitting at the kitchen table admired the Andrew Logan ring I was wearing, made of coloured glass.

I went back upstairs to get away from the smell and talked to Cynthia, who seemed surprised I was there. I did not feel at all well. I leaned against the wall and then had to sit down. I had wanted to talk to a publisher I knew was in the room, in case he might publish me in the future, but suddenly it all seemed too difficult.

Duncan brought me home and made some delicious salad. We also ate sweetcorn. I told him about Julian taking me out and not seducing me, but instead talking about sex.

Duncan laughed and said, 'Oh so *that's* why you've been complaining about Julian recently.'

I am on the cross-Channel ferry with Andy Kershaw, his girlfriend, Juliette, and their friend Tony, whom they met in Korea. We are on our way to Hal's fiftieth birthday party, which is tomorrow. I am writing my diary. The others are in the self-service restaurant.

I did not go to sleep till three after Joan Wyndham's party. I woke around seven and almost decided not to go to Paris. I was still feeling extremely sick.

I then phoned the minicab service, however, and arranged for a cab to come at nine to take me to Andy's flat in Crouch End.

The minicab arrived before I was ready. At the wheel was a driver I'd had before, from Newcastle. He told me about a gall-bladder operation he'd waited seven years to have on the NHS, then a different doctor told him it wasn't necessary.

When we reached Andy Kershaw's street, I had got the house

number wrong and we had to phone home to ask Maureen to look in my address book. When I finally rang the right bell, no one was ready. Andy was in his underpants in the kitchen – he has a very good figure – and another young man came out of the bathroom looking unfriendly. (He had a hangover.) Juliette offered me tea, but then forgot to give it to me.

We did not set off for Dover till about eleven. Andy flew at Juliette for getting his car in a wheel-lock, which he said had never happened in the three years since he'd had it. She blushed, but managed to release the wheel immediately.

Tony, a thin man with an elfin face, one red and blue ear-ring and lively, mischievous eyes, greeted us in his basement flat in Pimlico, accompanied by three adorable black kittens Andy and Juliette had given him for his birthday. (He works as a telephonist on a night-shift at Whitehall. People ring at all hours, sometimes drunks demanding to speak to John Major.) Tony proudly showed us his new five-part cat food dish that allows you to leave your cats for up to five days. Each day a different section is revealed and it is all kept cool by ice underneath.

As he drove towards Dover, I told Andy about Mary Killen's book, *The Tatler Book of Alternative Etiquette*, a collection of her problem letters and answers. When I told him about a letter by a man who couldn't dance and was afraid that this would make other people think he was hopeless in bed, he roared with laughter. He had bought Hal the latest copy of the *Oldie*.

The boat was much more luxurious than the Newhaven ferry I was used to. We rushed up to the self-service restaurant at once. I had a prawn sandwich. Tony had a fry-up; he smoked roll-ups endlessly, using tobacco from an old tin with a picture of the sun and the moon on the front.

I still felt sick from chemotherapy. In the car going to Paris Juliette and I sat in the back. She's very pretty, with china-blue eyes and thick black hair. I nibbled digestive biscuits that she offered me and drank from a bottle of water. Halfway to Paris Andy put on loud reggae music. One singer kept repeating the word 'Fulfilment'. Then Andy turned the music down because

Juliette was asleep. I wished Hal would show such consideration to me. (Once, years ago, he had bought a new cake of soap when I came to Paris for the weekend because I hated the smell of his Wright's Coal Tar.) Throughout the trip I felt I was in the company of extremely pleasant, friendly and straightforward people.

That evening in Montmartre the four of us ended up in a Caribbean restaurant with Hal and his wife, Polly (Hal had arrived back from Africa that afternoon. There had been some doubt about whether he would arrive in time for his own party.)

During the meal Hal grabbed me, put his hand on my leg and jammed his thigh against mine. Tony observed, 'He almost goes too far, but he just gets away with it.'

His wife sat on his other side looking a bit sad and occasionally making witty and sarcastic remarks that she didn't seem to remember later. At one moment she stroked his face. She hadn't seen him since he went to Africa two months earlier. She told me he had only rung her to give orders, not to ask how she was.

After the meal we went to a bar. It was full of smoke and people in black leather. It reminded me of a bar on the rue St-Jacques that I had frequented almost twenty years earlier when I lived in Paris. Now I was older and didn't like those crowded bars. I was also exhausted after the trip, because of recently having had chemotherapy.

We stood outside and Andy and Tony went and bought beers for everyone. Hal leaned against me, pulling at my black leggings. He said into my ear that he loved me. His wife was standing on his other side. He loved her too of course. I knew that, but I didn't care. Once she'd asked me if I'd marry Hal if he were free. I had replied, 'Certainly not, he'd drive me mad.'

At 1 a.m. I walked alone back to the hotel where I was staying with Andy and Juliette and Tony. A group of youths passed me. One said in French, 'I don't like women who hold their handbags like that!' I saw myself as a middle-aged woman and thought longingly of how I had lived happily in Paris as a young woman, going around on the back of Hal's motor bike, drinking in bars, in those days when I was young and free.

21 *March*

I slept late in the hotel and was woken by Polly phoning me. She wanted me to go with her to buy a birthday cake for Hal in the north-east of Paris. On the metro we passed the canal where Hal had once taken me on his motor bike. He had given two little African girls rides on it up and down beside the canal.

As we got near the cake-shop we kept seeing people with cakes in large boxes. Many were Africans, in beautiful long robes. One little black boy in a green shirt went crying up the street in a temper. His father seemed amused and went on walking in the other direction.

The bakery was in an enormous room and the cakes were displayed in open fridges. We chose one decorated with cherries and chocolate. I worked out that it could feed forty people. I paid for the cake as my present to Hal. Polly already owed me money. I had lent it to her a year before, perhaps out of guilt that I was having an affair with her husband. Polly then wanted to buy a tart as well. We picked one with different red berries.

Polly and I then went into a café full of French workers with pale faces and ate salad. Polly was talking about a short story she'd written, containing different levels of deceit. She said in the story she'd tried to examine how much women were prepared to tell each other and how much they kept things back. She had slept once with a good friend's boyfriend, for instance, but had never told her. I did not want to talk about sleeping with her husband as I found it embarrassing; also, I thought if it hadn't been me it would have been someone else. I knew that Polly liked me more than some of the other women Hal had been interested in and I also liked her. Apropos the story, I said there was one thing I did disapprove of, and that was a man whose wife was pregnant or had small children, as then she was completely vulnerable.

We carried the tart and cake back on the metro. Just as I was coming down the steps outside Hal's building, Hal appeared and made signals to me. He said I shouldn't have let the door close as he hadn't got his key, but perhaps this was the time for him to make love to me in the hotel.

This encounter made me very happy.

When I woke up, Andy, Juliette and Tony were back. Juliette had put on a skirt and clumpy shoes and make-up for the party. I put on my red tights with white hearts and a skirt.

In Polly's kitchen were the first guests, a Maltese woman with a new baby dressed all in pink, and Rick, who worked at a news agency in London.

A witty woman from Durham then arrived and reminded me of how last year she, myself, two Canadians and a young American I'd met at Jim Haynes's had been to a party in an Irish pub near the rue de Rivoli and ended up at the Hôtel Meurice having brandies at ninety francs each. I reminded her of how, except for four glamorous Italians, the hotel had been almost empty because of the Gulf War.

We went into the main room, where a musician, hired by Polly for the evening, was playing a guitar. He looked like Harold Pinter, but his hair was much wilder and woollier. Polly said he was 'a Jew from Algeria'.

I had to sit on the sofa for most of the party, yet managed to talk to a good many people, including an African woman whom Hal calls 'The Chameleon'. I asked after her two little girls, who had once done drawings for my children.

Hal came up and told me that Rick had said I was by far the best-looking woman in the room and that my legs were fabulous. Naturally I was very pleased about this.

A Zambian painter then told me that he could sell a painting for two thousand dollars. He seemed conceited, egoistic and insecure. Nevertheless, he chivalrously fetched me a glass of champagne.

At midnight Polly came in bearing the cake we'd bought earlier. She'd put fifty candles on it. I stood behind Hal and she stood in front of him. I told him assertively, 'I bought the cake.' (I didn't want him to think I hadn't brought a present, though he had never bought me a present on any of my birthdays.)

He made a short speech in which he said he wished he could live till he was a hundred and fifty. As I stood there I thought that Polly, myself and his mother, whose smiling face was in a photograph frame looking at us, were probably the three most important women in his life.

A beautiful Indian woman then started toasting everyone and making long speeches. Juliette whispered, 'She might as well toast my mother while she's about it.'

I sat down again and Rick asked me to dance. I took my shoes off as I was taller than him. As soon as we began dancing we were interrupted by Hal, who was very jealous and tried to grab me away.

Monday, 23 March

Back in London. Joseph: 'You know those insects with pincers? Mrs Douthwaite's one.' He has now become fascinated by insects, particularly spiders. At the weekend my ex-husband bought him a book on spiders. My son pores over the book with me at every possible opportunity. He points out the Chilean red-leg tarantulas, orange with black stripes.

'They look like Margie, don't they?'

Margie has now left for her new job, looking after a toddler in Soho, where the mother works in films. Margie has to drive it about London to swimming lessons and to the park. I felt obliged to tell the mother that Margie had crashed my car twice. She employed her anyway.

I ask Joseph, 'Would you rather be an adult than a child?'

'No, because I'd more likely die. Or I'd lose all my money.'

25 March

Last night when I returned from a meeting with Joseph's teacher and his therapist, Joseph had a temperature. He did not go to school today.

Duncan has gone to St Tropez for several weeks. I miss him terribly.

I spend most of the day writing a story based on a trip to Spain I'd been on with JB two years ago.

At five JB came round. We went to bed – the children were at the doctor's – then JB started whining about having nothing to do. I had told him on the telephone that I had arranged a haircut for me and Joseph at six so I said, 'That's your responsibility, not mine.'

He also complained about his insomnia.

Later my ex-husband and Nick, my friend who'd had Hodgkin's disease, appeared at the front door at the same time. I asked my ex-husband, 'When's your book coming out?'

He replied, 'May 26th. I hope you can arrange some publicity for it.' He winked at Nick, who smiled.

I said to Nick, 'Stop allying yourself with the other male.'

My ex-husband then left promptly.

Nick and I started eating left-overs and Daisy, the woman who was going to cut Joseph's and my hair, arrived, fifteen minutes late. Joseph was very rude to her. He pulled his trousers down and spat. Daisy was equal to this. She said she had a stepson the same age. I explained that Joseph is terrified of having his hair cut.

Nick and I then went out to see a film called *Black Robe* about a young Jesuit trying to convert the Huron Indians in Canada. Several Indians were massacred by another tribe when they went to help the priest.

Afterwards Nick commented that the priest had turned out to be the kiss of death for many that met him.

27 March

Sussex. I arrive here for the Easter holidays to find that Herbert, the large black retriever who has bitten Toby twice – each time he had to go to the vet – is on the loose again.

I have composed a letter to the Fanshaws. I am quite proud of it:

Dear Mr and Mrs Fanshaw

I am writing to you again about your dog, Herbert.

I have now been intimidated by your dog from taking my
dog, Toby, and my children for a walk along the road outside
my house or, indeed, along any of the roads where I might
find Herbert loose. He has been seen several times recently by
people in the village, and by myself yesterday at 11 a.m., on
the road without a lead. Not only that; he has been seen inside
my own gateway several times, unsupervised by you.

I have been to the Citizens Advice Bureau and found out
my position *vis-à-vis* the Dangerous Dogs Act of March 1991. I
shall have no hesitation in going to court if you continue to
take Herbert on the road without a lead or allow him to roam
the village unsupervised or to come into my driveway.

The fact that I am not here all the time is irrelevant. I have
talked to the Leslies, whose Jack Russell was attacked by
Herbert outside the post office recently when being looked
after by Mrs Franks, the doctor's wife. According to them, this
dog had to go to the vet as Herbert 'took a hole out of his
back'. Mr Hiller, the taxi-driver, also saw this attack and said
Herbert 'shook their dog like a rat'.

I have pointed out before that a dog of Herbert's size could
easily kill a small dog.

I find it extraordinary that you, who are always so ready to
take petitions round the village about other matters, are
prepared to take the risk of your dog attacking smaller dogs.
The fact that I am now afraid to go on the public road for fear
of meeting your dog, simply because you refuse to put him on
a lead, is an infringement of civil liberties and any sane person
would realize this.

Yours sincerely

I deliberately did not put in that I had breast cancer as I thought it
was 'playing dirty'. I do not want sympathy from the Fanshaws.

I had already written two letters to Herbert's owners in the last
couple of years, asking politely if they would keep their dog on a

lead. They had not complied with my request.

Herbert has also attacked another dog in the neighbourhood, a dog called Belcher belonging to a bachelor known as 'Mr Fixit'. Now Mr Fixit doesn't dare walk along the road with Belcher except after dark.

I telephoned Mr Fixit, hoping we could exert concerted pressure, but he does not want to risk an out-and-out confrontation with Mrs Fanshaw. She tends to lose her temper with anyone who disagrees with her. She had an argument at a local Parish Council meeting with someone who didn't want the new thirty mile an hour limit and also fell out with Mr Hiller, who said he didn't mind about the extra cars congregating outside his house if a local nursery school was started. (Mrs Fanshaw was against the nursery school.) Mr Hiller is a well-balanced man who has lived in the area since he was a child, unlike most people in the village.

28 March
A woman called Rosemary has been convicted of taking millions of pounds from a charity – £2.7 million from the National Hospital Development Foundation – and has been jailed for four years. Among the expenditure listed in court was 'Servants, £134,219'. The servants included a chauffeur, a chef, a butler, a bodyguard and two secretaries. The money she spent on champagne amounted to £14,000. In one week she bought twenty cases of 1982 Dom Pérignon. A friend's birthday treat consisted of a bath filled with two hundred and forty bottles of champagne. She spent £214,265 on a penthouse flat overlooking the Thames.

The journalist reported that, according to the doctor who examined her: 'Her outwardly personable and well-adjusted characteristics hid a deep-rooted, impenetrable insecurity, im-maturity and lack of self-esteem. Inwardly she felt lonely and gauche and thought of herself as unattractive and craved attention. Her insecurity bordered on hysteria.'

Mrs Douthwaite is absolutely disgusted by the whole thing.

She said she could have felt deeply insecure while queuing for rations heavily pregnant in Peckham Rye during the war. And what about Mr Douthwaite feeling insecure during four years in submarines?

Pete and Sarah are about to arrive for the weekend with their two children. They have never been here before. Sarah is vegetarian, so I asked Paquita to cook an extra amount of bean-curd stew. I brought it down yesterday and put it in the freezer. Everything cooked by Paquita now reminds me of having chemotherapy. The smell of the brown paste, miso, that she uses instead of salt, for instance, now reminds me of being ill. The fridge here is full of disgusting old bits of ginger root, which look like huge warts. Paquita keeps urging me to eat ginger. I have bought some lumps of sugared ginger from the health-food shop. They're supposed to stop you feeling sick. I am trying them instead of dope.

Pete and his family have now turned up. They are very generous and have brought enormous amounts of food you can't get in the village, such as olives in herbs and smelly French cheese and Italian bread. Sarah, however, does not like bean curd or bean stew. What am I going to do with it? I'd already taken it out of the freezer. I simply can't eat it. It reminds me too much of chemotherapy.

I have discovered that Sarah is my age. I thought she was younger. She had her children very late. She was extremely left-wing at Cambridge and I think met Pete in a left-wing group in London. She used to be a health worker. I like her tremendously and admire her delicacy.

I asked the Skidelskys to tea as Pete wanted to meet them.

Robert didn't come, because he was working hard on the second volume of the life of Maynard Keynes. Augusta came with her son Edward, who's at Oxford. Pete had fallen asleep upstairs, exhausted from reading too many manuscripts from aspiring authors.

Edward and I argued about the novel *Lolita*, which I had first

read when I was thirteen. I asked, 'Were there two Quiltys?'
Edward said he didn't think there were two Quiltys, just one,
who chased the main character, Humbert Humbert. He said he
thought that Lolita was a fantasy of Humbert Humbert and that
he found the descriptions of Lolita pornographic, with her cheeks
like apples and so on. I said I found Nabokov's portrait of her
romantic and I thought that the book was a superb evocation of
illicit love. No one else at the table seemed familiar with the
novel.

Pete came downstairs just in time to hear Augusta telling us
how she has become a prison visitor. She particularly likes a
young man called Mick, who's just left prison and has absconded
from his hostel in London. She said Mick had 'drawn all the
short straws in life'. She said at first she'd had reservations about
becoming a prisoner visitor as she thought it was like being Lady
Bountiful. She then discovered that certain prisoners, who had no
one to visit them, specifically asked for visitors, so she'd thought,
why not?

After tea Joseph threw a stone at a pane of the tiny new
greenhouse and broke it. I was too tired to punish him. Later
when I shouted an order at my daughter I saw Pete smiling. I
realized he had not seen me with my children before, only at
London publishing parties and in his own house as a single
person.

29 March
I am still monitoring the dog Herbert's movements very
carefully. On the road last night I saw Mr Fanshaw with Herbert
on a lead. This morning, however, when I was driving with Pete
and Sarah and our children to the Downs, I saw Herbert on the
road with Mr Fanshaw again, this time *without* a lead. I quickly
made a note of the time on a bit of paper and put it in my
handbag. Pete made a joke about dog vigilantes.

Pete and Sarah seemed to enjoy our walk. Pete wore a French
beret and looked very foreign. I realized that English country life

is alien to him. He was brought up in New York and Paris and
has a house in France. His five-year-old daughter already speaks
fluent French.

30 March

I ring up the local policeman and explain that it's impossible for
me to walk my dog on the road for fear it is attacked.

At 12.30 PC Travers arrives. Unfortunately, he has just met the
Fanshaws outside their house with Herbert, this time *on* a lead.
He tells me, 'They seem very reasonable people.'

I say, 'Well, they would be, to you.'

I am still wearing a dressing-gown at 12.30, which may make
me seem dissolute and unhinged, so I tell him I have been in
hospital.

I admit that Toby has not been bitten for two years, but this is
because I have consistently kept him off the road after the first
two successful attacks by Herbert, and after two further
attempted attacks. The policeman says I should have reported
the attacks at the time. 'Does this mean I must let Toby be bitten
again before I can make the Fanshaws put their dog on a lead?' I
ask. The policeman replies that he can't make them put him on a
lead *outside* the village. I can't think why not. Most other people
keep their dogs on leads on public roads.

At teatime Toby was found under the car fiddling with a baby
bird. It was dead. Then he swallowed the bird whole. That
evening Lucy said she was disgusted and couldn't bear to have
him sleeping on her bed as he does normally. I teased her by
saying the bird's beak might pop out of Toby's mouth. I then
heard her leaving a message on her father's answerphone about
the bird, saying she was horrified by what Toby had done. She
started crying about it on the sofa. I felt guilty that I had teased
her.

Before this Lucy and I went to lunch at my mother's. My
mother has now arranged her photographs all round the sitting-
room, many hung up on the wall in frames. The room is like a

mini museum. One photograph, which my ex-husband took, is of Joseph sitting on a boat in Scotland. There's another of him as a toddler, peeping from behind a curtain. There are fifteen photographs of her basset hound. The photos of this dog outnumber those of my children. She also has two old snaps of herself, one as a child on a Shetland pony and the other of herself at a local meet in my grandmother's village, riding side-saddle.

Near the fireplace is a framed photograph of a very handsome man. When I ask who it is, my mother says it's my father's relation who broke the land speed record.

April

1 April

I'm going to a plant sale with Mrs Mortimer and Augusta, and arrive at Mrs Mortimer's house under the Downs. I notice how hunched her back is, the result of osteoporosis. She doesn't talk about it much. I gather there is no cure. I gave her the name of an osteopath in the local town, but she didn't go; she didn't think it would make much difference.

Someone left four orchids outside her front door this morning. But Mrs Mortimer says the two-inch-long vases they're in come out of graves and she's rattled by this present.

Soon Augusta appears, excited because Mick, the young prisoner who absconded from the hostel he was sent to after leaving prison, is at her house now. She has invited him to stay.

When we get to the plant sale, several of my parents' friends from my childhood are there.

I introduce Augusta to Susan, who was at school with my mother, but has become a friend of mine. Augusta asks, 'Did you have a daughter called Patricia?' It turns out she meant Priscilla and that Augusta used to stay with Susan in the holidays and was a friend of her middle daughter. Susan says, 'You were one of my favourite girls.'

Eleanor, a leggy blonde, now in her sixties, who was friendly with my father, asks Mrs Mortimer how she is.

Mrs Mortimer says sharply, 'Don't ask what's wrong with my back.'

I buy a peony and two clematis, a jar of apricot jam and a jar of marmalade. A man I met in Sussex in January, who, like me, is having chemotherapy, is also there, behind a stall selling pansies.

We shyly ask after each other's health. Cancer is all we have in common.

Later I take Lucy into the local town to have her hair cut by a hairdresser Susan recommended. (Thank God no more of mine has fallen out.) In a chart in front of us Lucy's hair is 'honey blonde'. The girl who cuts it keeps saying how pretty she is. She combs out all the tangles and tries to make Lucy take a pride in the newly combed hair. I wish she would wear it loose, but she always pulls it back into a pony-tail. I, who as a child longed to be blonde – my mother was always going on about how attractive blonde children were – now have a blonde daughter.

On the way back I told Lucy that I was now divorced. She said she didn't mind. She liked going to her father's flat and she liked seeing more of her cousins. I have not yet told Joseph.

2 *April*

I took Lucy to ride in the local park about two miles away. I accompanied her there on a bike. I was glad I had summoned up the energy to do this. From the bike I could see the yellow celandines – after snowdrops, the first real wild flowers of the spring – on the side of the road. Lucy cantered a few times. She then scraped her leg on a gate as the pony went through too quickly and her stirrup came off.

We arrived home at about five and Lucy attended to the pony. I rushed to the local farm shop in the car to get some provisions, then took the dog for a walk in the nearby valley. I had a sudden desire to see Nicholas Mosley again. I looked through the window of his cottage and saw his spectacle case and the open lid of the typewriter, but he wasn't there. I felt nothing but affection for him.

I loved walking in the valley which was so peaceful. It seems monstrous that I must have chemotherapy again tomorrow.

3 *April.*

London. Chemotherapy later this morning.

I arrived here last night. JB was supposed to come at eight to go to a film. As usual, he rang and said he'd be late and would meet me at the cinema instead. We were planning to see *Fried Green Tomatoes at the Whistle Stop Café*. Fifteen minutes later he still wasn't there.

He then turned up on his bicycle. I said I was sick of waiting so long. We had missed the movie, so we went to the latest Almodovar film, *High Heels*, at another cinema nearby. I handed over the money for my ticket. JB said, 'You wouldn't believe how hard times are.' I said, 'The times you've taken me out in the two years since we met I can count on the fingers of one hand.' (He had once bought me an enormous bunch of flowers and taken me to a play. He had also taken me and some friends to a restaurant.)

Evening. I am so sick of chemotherapy.

The doctor I saw in Clinic 4 today after my blood test prescribed the anti-sickness drug that made me manic, though it was written on my notes not to give it to me. Luckily I recognized its name – Dexamethasone – as it was being offered to me to swallow by Nurse Blair in the chemotherapy ward before my injection. I asked her, 'What's that?' I then explained I had been told not to take it. We had to wait for a long time till someone got the prescription for the right anti-sickness drug from upstairs. I was not as indignant about this as I might have been.

Saturday, 4 April
Lucy rings me from her father's and decisively asks me to put ten pounds on a horse in the Grand National called Auntie Dot. I persuade her to let me put just five pounds on.

I then have lunch with Edward near Portobello Road. He has had bad flu. We discuss going to see a big exhibition together in Granada, which covers centuries of Moors, Jews and Christians in Spain, but it turns out that neither of us can get away this summer. He's going to Italy and I'm going on the Greek holiday with Tessa, though it still seems unreal to me.

After buying some asparagus and a tonic for Edward I go home and watch the Grand National on my own. None of my horses or Lucy's horse comes in. Just before the race, however, I have an intuition about the winner, Party Politics. The trainer is Nick Somebody, who, the commentator keeps repeating, is 'a very popular trainer and a very nice man'. I like the cosiness of the racing world. My grandmother had racehorses and I used to go racing with her.

Annie has a mysterious rash after going on holiday with her family to Holland. She has invited me to supper tonight. I go round with the asparagus to find she's retired to bed, which is very unlike her.

I ring Duncan in St Tropez, to find that he also has a mysterious rash. He got the first spots while driving to the ferry out of London nearly two weeks ago. He says it's pouring with rain. It has been raining ever since he arrived and the interview he hoped to do with Mick Hucknall, the lead singer of Simply Red, in Marseilles, has fallen through. His friend Natale has not come from Sicily as he had hoped.

Duncan advises me to ring Jenny Naipaul about doing a column in the *Spectator*. He says she's very nice and I can 'have a chat' with her. He is doing a 'Heroes and Villains' piece for the *Independent Magazine*. His hero is Michael Jackson. Duncan said he's doing the piece as 'a post-modernist imitation of Barthes. 'Tongue in cheek, of course.'

7.30. Annie's wearing a nightdress with a white T-shirt over it as she's still got the rash. Her husband has lost the asparagus I brought them this afternoon. He looks all over the house for it. Eventually it turns up in the wine-rack, beside some eggs.

I find the domestic atmosphere at Annie's very soothing. Gina, who writes a column about her teenage daughter in the *Guardian*, is there and starts talking about the new sex education class for eleven-year-olds in the school where she teaches. Rita, the local mother who gives the class, seems to love it and Gina and some of the other teachers wonder if she's 'getting enough of it' at home. Last week she took her class to the local swimming-pool and made a boy go and buy condoms out of the machine, saying, 'Go on,

Daniel, I know you're longing to.' She did demonstrations in class
with red and blue condoms, saying, 'You put it on a stiff willy.'

Gina said most of the children had bemused expressions as Rita
then made them repeat after her, 'Int-ra-ut-er-ine de-vice.' Gina
points out, 'The're not allowed to learn tables by heart, but they're
told to learn that.' She has volunteered to give a class on hygiene.
So far she's managed to say the word 'bottom' without being
paralysed with embarrassment.

Annie is still campaigning for the Labour Party. Yesterday she
bumped into the Famous Writer and they discussed how
wonderful it would be if Labour got in. The Famous Writer's face
took on a dark and aggressive expression and he said, 'This is only
the beginning of the struggle. We must get rid of Trident.'

Annie said she was overwhelmed by his intensity and felt
compelled to agree.

Sunday, 5 April

The Famous Writer's wife was very friendly to me outside the
Catholic church, asking after my health. After Mass I saw her
talking to a man who looks like Rowan Atkinson.

Before lunch Emily rang up, saying that Paolo is threatening to
return to Italy. He claims he needs some breathing space in which
to think about his marriage. Emily admitted that the vet still won't
see her on Saturday nights and she is worried he's secretly seeing
someone else. But the therapist Emily is now going to – Paolo
arranged it last week, saying he would pay for her to go to one for
three months – told her this is extremely unlikely. The therapist
said the vet wasn't emotionally equipped to have an affair with
anybody else, he thought he sounded too disturbed.

I think the vet sounds amusing, however, and it's no wonder
Emily likes him, especially since Ben is still preoccupied with the
young black model. The vet makes daily chores more fun, like
when he does his shopping at Marks & Spencer. In the check-out
queue when the vet had a full trolley, there was a man behind him
with only two milk cartons. The vet said cheekily, 'Is that all
you've got? You'll have to wait a long time, then, won't you?'

When he sees someone buying grated cheese he stands in front of the cheese counter going, 'Tut-tut!' Emily related these anecdotes with a mixture of pleasure at the vet's boyishness and worry that he might be out of control.

When she rang off, I telephoned Lulu, who has two friends who had affairs with vets. She says they are like sex-machines, extremely promiscuous. It must be looking at animals' balls all day. I will not tell Emily this.

Afternoon. I have just been to lunch with Vivian. Her niece Hetty was there. It felt odd being with a girl the same age as my daughter when my daughter's somewhere else (with her father in the country).

We played Scrabble. I gave Hetty her last word, which scored eighteen points and won her the game. It was 'soma'.

As I was leaving, an American neighbour came in to borrow a screwdriver. Vivian offered her some herbal tea and she sat down. It emerged that she had just had radical breast surgery – both of her breasts cut off in a clinic in California. She had been getting lumps for the last five years and twice they had been malignant. Each time she had had radiotherapy. She said she could no longer stand the tension when she got a new lump; also, she had always had very small breasts, so they didn't think it mattered if they weren't there. To do the operation, they had to graft some skin from her back. (The idea of this made me wince.)

She looked very thin and white and fragile. I said it must have been traumatic having that kind of surgery. Apparently her mother-in-law and some other members of her family had tried to stop her, saying she'd regret it. So far she hasn't. She's relieved.

Later I wondered if it wasn't simpler just to have the breast, or breasts, straight off, as this woman and Mrs Slater, Tiggy's friend in Hobe Sound, had done, though my surgeon had said in October, 'If a doctor tells you nowadays to have a breast off, walk straight out of his surgery.'

Mrs Slater, however, has lived into her eighties without any recurrence, and without chemotherapy or radiotherapy either.

When I left Vivian's, it had turned into a lovely spring day. The cherry blossom was coming out everywhere and the parks were full of daffodils. With a burst of energy I drove to Waterstone's and bought some tapes for the car, to improve my Spanish.

At night I dream about Vivian and me and some other people in a big auction room. It's dark. I'm waiting for Vivian to take me to a party.

The crucial thing about this dream is that I am then examined by a doctor and my throat is jammed up. I am unable to speak. Vivian will help me speak.

6 April
I rang Vivian to tell her about the dream. I want her to know how grateful I am for helping me, in real life.

Jason Donovan has been awarded £206,000 because *The Face* alleged that he was gay. Duncan, who's just rung, from France, says this may put the magazine out of business.

Duncan's rash is a mild form of eczema. He's returning early to England for Easter as it's still raining in St Tropez. Also, his friend Natale is about to arrive in London from Sicily with a group of fellow students. I'm so pleased Duncan's coming back.

Later Lulu telephoned up from a wine bar in Crouch End where she and her boyfriend had just met Andy Kershaw. Andy then came on the line and said he'd arranged with the *Guardian* to interview Jim Haynes in Paris. He invited me to drive to Paris with him and Juliette the weekend of the interview (3 May), 'crash out' there all day Sunday and go to Jim Haynes's party that evening.

I explained I couldn't do something so strenuous as I would have just got back from the hospital after chemotherapy. I felt a bit wet. Andy said I should fly and meet them there. I liked being asked, so I didn't definitely say no, though I still thought it unlikely I would make it.

7 *April*

Annie's rash turns out to be an allergy to a new three-hundred-pound mattress her husband's just bought. I have suggested advertising the mattress in *Exchange & Mart*.

This morning I received a letter from the literary agent called Faith.

> Thank you for sending us the manuscript of your novel 'The Merry Meadow' and other samples of your work.
>
> We have now received our reader's report and although she enjoyed reading the material, and was complimentary about your articles and your fictional distillation of childhood memories, she feels she cannot express confidence about the possibility of placing any of it with a publisher. The first question all publishers ask these days is 'Who is going to buy the book?' and if they don't think the market will be substantial enough, they won't make an offer, even a paltry one.
>
> You will, I hope, understand that as we are a very small agency, we can only afford to take on projects that we can be fairly sure of placing. The recession has forced cautiousness upon us.
>
> I am so sorry not to be more helpful, and I do wish you every success with your work. As you are already 'in' with Serpent's Tail, might you consider approaching them direct?

I rang Stephanie, Tessa's former sister-in-law, who had originally suggested Faith, and told her. She was sorry.

I do not know now if I will ever get 'The Merry Meadow' published. Duncan prefers my book on the sixties. He says everyone writes about their childhoods.

There was a bomb in Golden Square yesterday, near the offices of Jay Cox, yet another woman who wouldn't be my literary agent.

This afternoon I went to my therapist. I was five minutes early. She was having an animated conversation with another patient in

Russian, which was annoying. When I went into her room, she began sounding off about an incident with her gardener, also Russian, who had gone round London saying she owed him four thousand pounds.

For some reason I began talking about Patrick M, the writer I had seen with Merrill in New York. My therapist said, 'Go for a man like that.' I explained that he lived in New York and had just remarried.

The therapist said I had entered my own marriage as a 'damaged' personality. It would take some time to recover. I probably expected to be made unhappy from intimacy as my mother had not been 'there' for me. She told me to close my eyes and think of depressions I'd had related to my childhood.

I described the constant feeling of unreality and waste. I added that my father had had a strict regard for truth. The therapist wondered why he hadn't then been able to confront my mother with reality. He must have given up. She promised to talk about my father in another session.

When I returned home, Tim, Jill's ex-husband, rang and said he was thinking of making a film about her.

8 April
Back in Sussex as it's still the school holidays.

Joseph said yesterday, 'I'd like to be fat and jolly and famous.'

I've assured him he's handsome and that I like the way he looks. His drawings are getting better and better. His flicking books, one image succeeding another, like an animated cartoon, are very good indeed.

Vivian phoned at six from a call-box in Notting Hill Gate. I told her that Tim wanted to make a film about Jill. She asked, 'How well do you know Tim?'

I said, surprising myself, 'I know him very well.' I added that Tim was intelligent and sensitive, and that Jill had been very fond of him. Then I had terrible feelings of grief, as I usually do when I think about Jill.

Joseph came in and said, 'When I die I don't want to be a dead body laid out like this.'

He then lay spread-eagled on the bed with a fixed smile on his face.

I asked 'Have you seen something like that on television?'

He said, 'Someone brought a dead body into school.'

'They wouldn't be allowed to.'

Thursday, 9 April
Joseph sleeps in my bed all night. He says, 'Mummy, I love you.'

Lucy's first cousin Effie, aged thirteen, is here and is sleeping on a mattress in Lucy's room. Lucy's very fond of her. At least my divorce means that Lucy's closer to her cousins.

Later. Am writing this on the train from Sussex to Victoria. I have to go up again for chemotherapy.

I have discovered that mint-flavour chewing-gum, Wrigley's or Orbit, is the most effective anti-sickness remedy I've tried so far. I found the sugared ginger too sickly, and I don't really like ginger. As for dope, I'm tired of all the paraphernalia attached to it and I'm not keen on inhaling the tobacco. Besides, it's sometimes made me sicker than the chemotherapy. I wish I'd realized about the chewing-gum earlier on in my treatment. I have just bought two more packets at the station to have ready for tomorrow.

Somewhere between Gatwick and East Croydon. I am now alone in the carriage, one of the only second-class old-fashioned six-seater compartments, with a sliding door. I normally avoid being alone in these compartments. A sinister slim man with dark glasses passes on his way to the lavatory. After Gatwick there's an announcement:

'Will Mr Franklin please come to the guard's van at the rear of the train?' I hope Mr Franklin is not the man with dark glasses.

At East Croydon there is another announcement: 'Would Mr Jeremy Franklin get off this train as his friend is looking for him on the platform.'

He is obviously not an escaped prisoner, unless 'friend' is a euphemism for 'police'.

In the *Independent* I read that a man called Sid Shore who runs a shop called Elvisly Yours in the East End has now opened a shop called Super in St Petersburg. I must tell Duncan. He can visit the shop when he goes there. He has now been told where to find cheap accommodation in St Petersburg.

Later. I arrived in London only just in time to vote. I got to my local polling station, the school where my Spanish class is, at a quarter to ten. Annie had been there for several hours earlier that day. It was just as well she'd left as she would have stood over me trying to get me to vote Labour. I was amazed at how many different parties there were. In the end I voted Green for lack of anything better.

When I arrived at my house, there was a message from Julian on my answerphone inviting me to an election party at my old friend Sally's. He said to turn up there if I got the message in time, so I went. Among the guests was an Indian maharaja, a film director and a woman who worked with Arab political prisoners in Cairo. She was the only person who had voted Labour. I thought Julian seemed worried that I found the film director attractive, but I forgot him immediately. I went home before Julian as I had to have chemotherapy the next day.

Friday, 10 April
London. Chemotherapy again. I'm very reluctant to go to the hospital. These chemotherapy appointments now seem less like part of my life, which in a way makes having them harder. The summer is approaching; I know that after this one I have only two more.

This morning I switched on the radio and was surprised to find that the Conservatives had won.

I then went out to get a taxi and unexpectedly met the mother of the head-banging child coming out of Annie's house carrying a table. We nodded politely to each other.

In the taxi I talked to the driver about the election. He had voted Conservative. He said the public didn't have much faith in Neil Kinnock and they were afraid their taxes would go up.

After the blood test in Clinic 4 I was going down to Oncology when I met Nurse Blair, who'd forgotten to bring my notes upstairs as she should have done. I had to go to Oncology with her and get them, then take them back to Clinic 4 where I'd just been. In the waiting-room there was now a family of lively young children, all blond, three little boys with crew-cuts. This was unusual as people don't normally bring children in there.

I felt very depressed. I nearly started crying. I think it was because Julian is going back to Japan today for several months. I have relied on him more than I realized. I'm also very fond of him.

Now, in the chemotherapy ward, I close my eyes and wait. At about 10.30 the volunteer who's a retired actress, the one who speaks fluent French, turns up. She says she was working all day yesterday for the Liberal Democrats in Greenwich. As a result she's suffering from vertigo. She was also awake intermittently all night listening to the Election results.

This time, probably because I don't have a friend with me, I talk to her properly and am glad she's here to divert me. She tells me that her father was a Navy doctor and went through two wars. I say that my father was in the Navy – he commanded destroyers for four years in the north Atlantic – and that my mother had worked decoding at Bletchley. She says she too had been involved with Intelligence. She adds that her father was in Malta during the Second World War and that the Maltese people had nearly starved. She went off to answer the ward telephone, but did not come back to me. Instead she talked to a young male patient in a bed at the other end of the ward.

At eleven o'clock Emily arrived. I was delighted to see her. She had brought some more Spanish tapes for me as she and Paolo have just been to Madrid in yet another attempt at reconciliation. They are also attempting a health cure. They are on a special diet without drink or rich foods. I suspect this is a compromise arranged by Paolo. He doesn't drink and Emily doesn't eat rich foods.

Bridie injected me today, talking soothingly as she always does. (To me she is a saint.) When I asked about her life, she said she had worked in the chemotherapy ward since the eighties. Then she asked Emily if she'd mind going off to get my drugs at the pharmacy, to save time.

While I was lying there on my own, two black women came in. The younger one was cheerful and outgoing. I heard her saying boisterously to the nurses, whom she seemed to know already, 'This is my mother!'

Then her mother left. She got on to the bed beside me and waved. We started chatting. She'd had throat cancer two years earlier and had been treated at the hospital. Eight months ago she'd gone to one of the doctors here because of a 'complaint'. The woman doctor whom she saw said she would get her a further appointment immediately, for it to be investigated. She then heard nothing. Months later she went to her GP and he sent her straight back to the hospital. Now she has a big lump on her neck. She showed it to me. It was horribly visible. She has cancer again.

She said, 'I think we're given this suffering so we can understand the suffering of Jesus. Everyone must bear a cross. Do you agree with me?'

I couldn't really agree because I thought she should have gone to the doctor earlier. Why on earth didn't she telephone and ask about her appointment? She was either too passive, or too trusting. At the same time I respected her clear religious faith.

When I got home I thought of this young black woman, who seemed so full of life and trust and was so good-natured, for a long time. I keep thinking of her.

Saturday, 11 April
I woke abruptly at 1.30 a.m. with a terrible pain in my stomach. Was it the effects of chemotherapy?

At lunchtime I went to meet Simon Burt at my local bookshop

near Portobello Road. It was very sunny and all the nearby cafés were full. Simon suggested going to the London Lighthouse. I was apprehensive about going there as I imagined it would be awful seeing people dying of AIDS.

The building is very attractive and light, however, with a tremendous feeling of space. We stepped through a French window into a garden where people were sitting at café tables. Simon said the garden had been designed and donated by Crabtree & Evelyn. He bought me an Aqua Libra and we sat outside at a table. Simon gave me the name of an agent at Curtis Brown who was looking for new authors. He mentioned that Richard, whom we had both known, but I had not seen since the seventies, had died of AIDS. Richard, a friend of my friend Andrew, was flamboyant. Simon said he went back to die at a hospice in Coventry, where his parents live. I told Simon how once in the heady days of Gay Liberation Richard, Andrew and some others had hired horses on a beach in Norfolk and the horses had bolted. Richard, dressed in his usual outlandish and effeminate costume, wasn't at all frightened, but had urged his horse on faster and faster along the sands, yelling with excitement.

In front of us at a table a woman in a black lacy bra and black skirt was sunbathing. I asked Simon if he knew her and he said, 'No, I'm glad I don't.'

A little girl and her mother then came and sat down at a table. There were also several men with shaved heads looking very ill.

As I left I had a look at the noticeboard in the hall. There was one plaintive request: 'Will the person who has taken my son's Walkman please return it to the main desk? We are on Family Benefit.'

Simon said there had been problems with drug addicts who'd got AIDS through drug abuse; like all addicts, they had no morals and stealing went on.

13 April
Visit to my therapist. I meant to talk about cancer, but she was late as usual and overexcited. There'd been another fiasco at Victoria

Station and her train had stopped just outside the station for several minutes. Eventually she got so fed up she got out and walked up the line. Isn't this a bit unstable? I am rather worried. Also the postcards designed by one of her patients, for which I wrote a cheque over a month ago, have still not arrived.

14 April

Sussex. I arrived here at seven yesterday evening.

At night I'm tortured by lust and think about Hal and even R. At six Joseph comes in and lies beside me in bed, talking about his various preoccupations. '*Charlie and the Chocolate Factory* is just a lot of people blathering like in *Neighbours* and *Home and Away*'. He then bursts out laughing at the slurping noise the water makes when I drink from the Evian bottle. I let him have it and he spills it in bed and over his pyjama top.

Mrs Douthwaite arrived at 10.30. She has seen a religious programme on TV in which the vicar's daughter who'd been raped in the Ealing case said she had written to her transgressors in prison and forgiven them. Mrs D thought this was 'barmy'. Another woman, who'd been permanently injured in a mugging, was also on the programme. This woman said she would not forgive the man who had done it. He had left her in a terrible state, a cripple who couldn't even look after her grandchildren on her own. Also, he might do it again to someone else. When the vicar on the programme tried to argue with her, she said, 'Where was God for me that night?'

This reminded me of the young woman in the chemotherapy ward who'd got a huge lump on her neck and equated this with the suffering of Jesus. Her attitude might be considered 'barmy'. On the other hand, what was the point of being bitter after the event?

I'd asked Lucy to record a TV programme on breast cancer for me, but she pressed the wrong button and instead got a programme on hairy chimpanzees. In a way I'm relieved.

15 April

This morning Joseph comes in at seven and says in a sweet little voice, 'Mummy!' I tell him to come back later. When he returns he gives me a massage. Then he says, 'I hate Johnny Bigg's father. Why's he so bad-tempered? He's never been happy in his life.' Johnny Bigg is the man who recently built a *Dynasty*-style mansion near our house, pretending to the local council that it was going to be a farm cottage.

Joseph has drawn spiders all over one page of my diary, and also a fox, the character in the cartoon of *Robin Hood*. He says, 'Lucy's more normal than I am.' He adds, 'Normal means you don't care about anything.'

After breakfast he hits me and Maureen, shouting, 'Bitch!' He takes a big knife and holds it at his chest, saying he's going to stab himself. (This is because Maureen took a gun away from him as he was mean to Toby. Maureen's very calm about his holding the knife. She's not at all frightened.)

He comes to my room as I'm getting dressed and admits, 'I don't want you to die. I was afraid you were going to die when you went to hospital. I was upset. That's why I was aggressive with the children at school.'

'Poor little thing,' I say. 'It was bad luck for an eight-year-old boy that his mother went to hospital.'

He is now talking in a strange deep voice. He thinks this is more boyish. Yesterday he damaged the video machine by stamping on it. Mr Douthwaite has mended it.

16 April

Joseph comes into my room and says, 'I'd like to be a wolf in human form. Is that clear?'

Then: 'Which do you prefer, Peckham Rye or Six Mile Bottom?' Peckham Rye is where Mrs Douthwaite was brought up and Six Mile Bottom is where she and Mr Douthwaite once ran a village shop.

Yesterday Mrs Douthwaite was going on about violence and the modern child and how awful *Silence of the Lambs* was. She admitted she'd read the book, but did not seem to think this was in any way contradictory. (Maureen said later she'd heard the book was far more violent than the film.)

I went to the dentist to have a filling. I had to say, before I had an injection in the gum, that I was on chemotherapy treatment. In that cheerful setting – the dentist's room looks out on to the village green and I have never minded.going to the dentist – the fact that I'd had cancer seemed completely crazy. The dentist said comfortingly that his mother had had breast cancer last year and was now all right. He made it seem more like flu than something lethal.

When I returned home I found that Mr Bigg had come over to complain about Toby. Apparently Toby has been round to the mansion every day for the last ten days, after Mr Bigg's spaniel bitch, which is on heat. This morning at 6 a.m. Toby scratched all the putty off his kitchen door trying to get at her.

Mr Douthwaite is going to put wire along the garden wall to prevent Toby from jumping out.

Dinner with the Donaldsons in their bungalow up the road. I used to see them with my ex-husband. We met them in the eighties at a dinner of Lord Weidenfeld. Now I'm alone they still often invite me to meals and I invite them.

Today I get there early as asked. (They're both in their eighties and like to go to bed early.) Frankie immediately asks me about my health. She's having chemotherapy. She had a mastectomy twelve years ago and then had two types of drug treatment, but now she has five lumps in the other breast. She says she's decided not to do anything drastic as she's eighty-five. Jack, as he fetched us vodka and tonics, told us, 'You'd both be dead twenty years ago, and so would I.' He recovered from a heart attack a few years back.

Frankie says she doesn't feel sick after chemotherapy, but has terrible indigestion and feels very tired. She has told the doctors she only wants a mild treatment as she's very old and will have to die soon anyway. I agree out loud with her, but think inwardly

that my own situation is different. Frankie has had a full life. She is
a successful writer of biographies – I also love her autobiography,
Child of the Twenties, in which she describes her childhood as the
daughter of the playwright Freddy Lonsdale – and, after one
divorce, has had a long, happy marriage. She has three children
and several grandchildren.

I have had nothing published. I am divorced. I have two
children. The idea that I might get a recurrence and die in a few
years without achieving anything is awful.

Frankie realizes this. When we talk about my ex-husband's
novel coming out soon, she says, 'Now, I want *you* to have some
standing.'

One of her granddaughters has an article in *The Face*, on
Northern Ireland. It's on the sitting-room table. Frankie's proud of
her, but says she doesn't see how a person can write an article on
Northern Ireland after only one weekend there. She supposes this
is 'the modern thing'.

She tells me how she got to know Elizabeth Longford, years ago,
when they had gone on a train together to a reading of Weidenfeld
authors. Elizabeth's one of the genuinely *good* people she knows,
she adds. I would also say this of Frankie's husband, Jack, who
gave away half the money he inherited as a young man to fund a
pioneer health project in Peckham.

17 April. Good Friday

This morning I was in the car with Maureen going to the farm
shop when I saw Herbert with both his owners on the road
without a lead. I asked Maureen to slow down and shouted, 'Put
your dog on a lead!'

Mrs Fanshaw then yelled back, 'You can't talk! What about Mr
Bigg's door?'

The injustice of this – and her stupidity in not being able to
distinguish between Toby's testosterone and her dog ferociously
attacking Toby simply out of sadism – that I went berserk. I
screamed, 'Don't you know anything about sex, you fool?'

Maureen was embarrassed and started to edge the car forward while Mrs Fanshaw and I were still yelling insults at each other.

This afternoon I went with the children to see Molly's new puppies. (Molly is still working for my mother, thank goodness.)

Joseph took a great liking to one puppy, Flopsy, whose legs don't work very well. He rolled Flopsy over on his back, then put him inside his jacket. He asked if he could buy Flopsy, but admitted he'd want to return him when he was fully grown.

In the car going home Lucy said, 'Isn't it funny that Joseph likes the puppy that has something wrong with it?'

We stopped at a bookshop in Molly's local town. Joseph wanted another book about spiders, but there wasn't one. He decided he wanted to buy me an Easter egg. We went into Woolworths and I stupidly let them both buy bags of very unhealthy sweets. We were then late at the Catholic church, where I had suddenly insisted on taking them, probably out of nostalgia for my own childhood. (From the age of seven, until I left home at sixteen, I had gone there with my father every Sunday.)

Lucy was very rebellious about it and made a face at the Holy Communion stoup in the outer hall of the church. I lost my temper and slapped her across the face. Joseph became very excited and imitated me by slapping his own face several times. Inside the church Christ's Passion was being read out. I couldn't help thinking this was the most hideous church I had ever been in, and no wonder I had wanted to be Protestant as a child.

I made the children go up and kiss the cross with the other parishioners, and we left at Communion.

18 April

Joseph keeps imitating what happened at church. This morning he filled a glass a quarter full of red wine, broke off a piece of white bread and sang 'Hallelujah!' slapping himself across the face at the same time.

Last night Duncan and his friend Natale arrived, bringing the

ingredients for Pasta con le Sarde, a Sicilian Good Friday meal.
Natale had said he would cook it.

I suggested we all go to the local pub for a drink, which they
enjoyed. On the way Joseph asked Natale to teach him some
insults and swear-words in Italian.

After supper Natale told our fortunes from Sicilian tarot cards.
The cards had different symbols from those Duncan and I were
used to. One, which looked like a baseball bat, represented sex.
Coins symbolized money, and cups meant love.

Natale kept referring to 'a man in authority over you', who
appeared in both Duncan's and my cards. I suggested that this
figure, which was unfamiliar to me and Duncan, might represent
the Mafia and therefore be deeply embedded in the Sicilian
psyche. Duncan thought he might represent the Pope.

Natale told me I had been loved by a man but not loved enough
– was this my ex-husband? – that I had or would have a
relationship with another man, but there would be a problem
sleeping under the same roof – was this Hal? – and that I had been
emotionally close to a man who was now looking the other way
and that this was primarily a sexual attraction. Was this R?

Natale did not read in the cards that I was about to die,
fortunately, or if he did he didn't say so.

I was still exhausted from chemotherapy, but stayed up late
with the two men.

20 April

The children and I had been invited to an Easter Monday point-to-
point. Lee, the American, his wife, Sue, Anthony (another local
landowner) and his girlfriend (who'd had me to dinner in
Battersea with Julian), were having a picnic there. Duncan and
Natale had decided to go to Brighton for the day.

We arrived at Anthony's house at midday, then had to wait an
hour because his girlfriend's dogs, the ones that looked like rugs,
were lost. I didn't feel well and had to keep drinking more and
more water. Mrs Mortimer's granddaughter, who was with Lucy,
was wearing a T-shirt that changed from mauve to pink when it

got hot. Joseph kept blowing on it to make it change colour and this began to annoy her.

When we finally got to the races, I became very excited and rushed with the children to put bets on. (I tried to get to see the horses in the paddock, but discovered that I wasn't allowed there without a special badge.) We all placed bets and returned to the car. Lee had organized a wonderful picnic of chicken in herbs, potato salad, corn on the cob, champagne, strawberries and cheese. Joseph said, meaning to be complimentary, 'I just *love* junk food.' I explained to Lee, 'He means American food.'

I found it thrilling to see the horses running so close to us, only yards away from the rail where we were standing.

Later. Duncan and Natale arrived back from Brighton just after the Skidelskys had walked in for drinks. Robert took Duncan on to the lawn and said he knew Duncan wrote for the *Spectator* and wished that he, Robert, could write for it again, but he didn't know the present editor. He then talked to Mrs Mortimer, whom he already knew. By that time more people I'd invited had arrived. I introduced Duncan to someone who'd known April Ashley at the time of her sex change. Robert Skidelsky spent a long time talking to a man he'd recognized from the House of Lords.

Augusta's ex-prisoner was still staying with her. I remarked on the odd coincidence that Edward, her twenty-year-old son, had gone on a long trip to Eastern Europe at exactly the same time as this young man had turned up.

21 April
London. I went to the therapist. She was twenty minutes late. There was another hold-up at Victoria. This time the Russian receptionist was on the train with her, for some reason.

When I told her I was going to write a story about guilt – I'd discovered someone was doing an anthology on it – she said she wanted to do one as well. Isn't this a bit competitive? I talked about Joseph and how depressed I'd been around the pregnancy and birth. I said I sometimes feel angry with him because of this. The therapist said I should hold him a lot and attend to him.

At lunch later with Vivian we discussed a friend of hers who committed suicide two years ago. She had taken an overdose of pills, like my brother. Vivian said that the verdict of 'accidental death' was nearly always given if the person didn't leave a suicide note. I was surprised to hear this. I had always been uneasy about the verdict of 'accidental death' passed on my brother. It stripped him even of the dignity of making a choice. I also thought of it as another example of my mother's never facing the truth. I told Vivian, when she asked why my brother had done it, that it was for the same reason as her friend – depression. As we talked, I felt a terrible pain all over my body. I realized this was the first time I had properly discussed my brother's death with a friend.

I have now signed the decree absolute, which means I am properly divorced.

29 April

Joseph had a week's extra holiday, so on the spur of the moment I took him to Majorca.

My mother's now sold the house she had there, a converted farmhouse in a valley. She did it without consulting me or my children. Most of the contents were shipped to England, but so far no one has been allowed to unpack the cases, which are stacked in one room in her house.

One day on the beach where we used to go every summer as a family I tell Joseph that I'm now divorced. He flings himself on me, pretends to cry and begs, 'Please have mercy!'

Each day before breakfast in our two-roomed rented flat Joseph makes me look at the book on spiders that his father gave him. We examine the Chilean red-leg, the trapdoor spider, the funnel-web and several more. He makes me play a game in which we frighten each other by suddenly bringing up the picture of a spider close to the other's face.

My arm hurts, but I swim in the sea twice, to show myself that I

can. No one else is swimming at this time of year. Joseph also goes
in and out of the sea shrieking with excitement.

One evening I take him to meet my cousin Giles and his friend
Robert, who live together on the island. Giles and I talk about our
mutual ancestors who left Ireland in the 1860s and went to Peru to
make money out of exporting guano. One of them was my
grandmother's father.

Joseph chats with Robert about films he's seen. Afterwards he
says, 'I'd like to live on a desert island with those kind old
men.'

My Canadian friend Lyn, who's married to a Spaniard, invites
me and Victoria, who used to play with me as a child in Madrid,
for a drink one afternoon. I hadn't seen her since I was four.

Victoria, now a painter of flowers, is alert, amusing and busy.
She's been obsessively weeding her gravel all day and cooking for
her nineteen-year-old godson. We talk a bit about our childhood in
Madrid.

Victoria says my father was like 'a bull elephant' and was a
'breath of fresh air' in the diplomatic circles in Madrid where he
was naval attaché. Her mother, who's now in her eighties and still
very active, thought him 'absolutely hilarious'.

I explain that my father was just forty-one when he retired from
the Navy and I've only recently realized that this is usually when a
man is in his prime.

On our last evening I take Joseph to see my mother's old house in
the valley, where we went every summer. I explain to the blonde
English housekeeper that we used to own it and ask if we can see
the garden. She says yes, though the owners are away. Joseph and
I go round to the back, with a view of the mountains, and look at
the new swimming-pool, which is in a smart enclosure with
changing-rooms and a bar and fridge, and even a small cooker.
There are new big tubs of flowers everywhere. The garden is more
formal, but also cared for.

Joseph darts up the outside staircase, past the blue plumbago, to
what was my mother's bedroom. I follow him and we go into

every room in the house. There are some garish pictures, but the house looks much more cheerful and more comfortable than when my mother owned it.

The housekeeper doesn't hear us leave. I walk with Joseph into the heart of the valley. There are smells of wild roses and herbs.

Now that the house is sold I realize I loved this valley.

Afterwards in the car my son says, 'I'm heartbroken the house is sold. It's terrible for me. Two important parts of my life have disappeared: (a) you're not married and (b) the house is sold.' He adds, 'When I was five here I was all right and now I'm an unhappy, miserable, lost boy.'

30 April

Back in London. My therapist has a new punk haircut. I tell her it's amusing. She seems to like this. She hands back my three stories I gave her to read. She liked one I published in 1981, when my daughter was born, 'The Raw Food Eater', but she doesn't comment on my story about God.

I talk about Joseph and tell her a few of my dreams.

She says Joseph's reactions in Majorca are a sign of progress. When he says, 'I'm an unhappy, miserable, lost boy', at least he acknowledges this. Before, he had clammed up.

I ask her if she'll take Emily on as a patient. I say I think she's alcoholic. Do her eyes brighten up at this or am I imagining it?

When I get home I ring Emily and tell her. Surprisingly, she agrees to go. She has given up the therapist Paolo sent her to and wants nothing more to do with Paolo at the moment.

I have received a letter from the literary agent Simon suggested.

Dear Elisa

I took your novel home to read at Easter, so have managed to come back to you sooner than I thought.

I'm afraid I feel unable to make you an offer of representation with the full commitment and enthusiasm you deserve.

There are, of course, as many opinions as there are agents

and publishers, and I shall probably regret my decision . . .

I am sorry to disappoint you. Thank you for giving me the opportunity of reading your material and I wish you all the best in the future.

Best wishes

I was given a burst of adrenalin by this rejection. I quickly typed up some accounts of life in London and sent them to Jenny Naipaul, the woman at the *Spectator* whom Duncan suggested and whom everybody seems to like. I wrote: 'Surely the *Spectator* should have another woman columnist instead of three elderly men?' I used a pseudonym, as I thought the *Spectator* had already rejected me too many times. The name I chose was Hilda Morris.

Teatime. Lucy accuses Joseph and his friend Thomas of eating her tangerine sweets while she was out. Joseph says, 'Thomas begged me to.'

Lucy was talking in a very patronizing way to Joseph last night, to get him to let her play with his Game Boy. I saw her using 'feminine' wiles to manipulate his 'masculine' character.

Yesterday I collected her from school and when we got back to the house, I found I'd forgotten my keys. We rushed down towards Annie's house to wait there for Maureen and Joseph and met the Famous Writer's wife coming up the street. As she saw me she stumbled – in alarm? – and then raised her hand in greeting.

There has been terrible violence on the streets of Los Angeles. The white policemen who beat up a black motorist, which was recorded on video, have been acquitted by a white jury. I rang Liza to see if she was all right, but as usual the answerphone was on.

May

1 May

Today I was driven to the hospital by Miranda. As we neared the hospital, she touched me on the arm and told me how last weekend she had gone to the Scala opera house in Milan (with, I assumed, her Spanish lover). She said it was beautiful; there was a small light like a candle at the back of each box. She was probably giving me a signal that I could ask her about her affair, but for some reason I didn't want to. I couldn't relate to it. She made the whole experience sound like a romantic novel I had once read called *Chase the Moon*.

I was also worried about the conclusion. If Miranda got divorced, I did not think she would get on well on her own. I wanted to warn her that divorce was very difficult, but I have become so used to being a 'patient' with her that it is difficult for me to step into a role in which I give her advice.

When we arrived, I went upstairs as usual to have the blood count before chemotherapy and then discovered I had an appointment with the professor. I had to wait a long time for this. A woman called Vick said she had been waiting since 8.45 for the result of her blood count. It was now 10.30. She said she was starting a new job after lunch and didn't want her employers to know she had cancer. She asked me to tell the nurses in Oncology, if I got there before her, that she was coming and that she would be prepared to have her injection on a chair or sit on the floor if there was no bed.

Then I went in to see the professor. This time I decided to be more friendly. I said, 'Hi!' and he said, 'Hi!' He spent some time banging things out on a computer, which he could have done while I wasn't there. He said, 'I don't need to examine you, do I?'

and asked if I had any questions. I said, 'Am I more likely to get
skin cancer if I've had breast cancer?' and he said, 'No.' I told him
about the strange white patch on my back that hadn't got
sunburnt with the rest of me and he looked at it and said it
seemed all right. (I am sure it's connected with the effects of the
radiotherapy. Probably the rays have gone right through my
body.)

I asked if he'd been to the club in Notting Hill Gate again. I
thought that his eyes filled with tears while I was speaking to him.
I wasn't sure why.

Miranda and I went down to Oncology, where there was a
terrible delay. I began to get frightful stomach pains, particularly
after we were sent upstairs again to wait for pills at the pharmacy.
Miranda said it was nerves. I asked her to go and get me a copy of
the *Daily Sport*. I began laughing at some of the absurd sex
scandals in it. I thought I knew why men in wars, in physical
danger, read 'girlie' magazines. It was to distract them and give
them instant pleasure and adrenalin. Even reading about sex in
this absurd form gave me a sudden rush of energy.

When I eventually got on a bed in the chemotherapy ward,
however, my pains had got so bad that Rosie, the nurse, had to get
a doctor to see me. He examined me and said he could find
nothing wrong with my stomach and I could go ahead and have
the treatment. There were further delays as Nurse Blair has had
flu for two weeks and Bridie is the only other nurse authorized to
give injections.

While we were waiting, Miranda asked, 'Have you seen R?'

I explained I had seen him at a party, but we hadn't spoken to
each other. I continued, 'What the hell was he doing, leaving all
his stuff at my house for eight months? If he thought of me as a
friend why did he never see me afterwards? You don't treat a
friend like that. He can't have it both ways.'

Miranda said, 'It sounds as if he had it whatever way he liked.'

She thought there was some excuse for his erratic behaviour,
because he'd had a traumatic experience in South America when

he was lost in the jungle for several weeks. Also, he'd been in the middle of a divorce.

We then talked to the elderly actress who's a volunteer, about smell. She said one man couldn't bear the smell of the oncology ward to such an extent that he stuffed a handkerchief in his nose each time he came to have chemotherapy. I said I had suddenly smelt the smell at a party and was nearly sick.

This is my last treatment but one. Perhaps by getting these stomach pains I was finally allowing myself to admit how horrible the chemotherapy is. If I'd admitted it properly before I would have found it more difficult to go through with the whole course.

Last night, with terrible indigestion after some radishes, I dreamed that my mother and I are in America. I'm very angry with my mother and I confront her for being jealous. She admits it. I realize that for the first time I'm speaking the truth to her.

Saturday, 2 May
I was supposed to go to the conference on alcoholism that my therapist had recommended. The conference is in King's Cross at 9 a.m. My therapist will be speaking there and in a way this puts me off as it's too public.

4 May. May Day Bank Holiday
Sussex. I wake up this morning with a terrible pain all over my body. I feel lonely and that I will never have a mate. I also feel I'll never fall in love again with anybody like I did with R. It still hurts me.

I pull his book out of the bookcase and start reading it at random. One section, about a tribe in South America that lives to a great age, makes him seem sympathetic.

5 May
I wake up about three and don't sleep again till five. Like yesterday, I have dreadful pains all over my body, psychic pains. I talked to my ex-husband earlier this evening. This always makes me feel nervous and insecure.

Yesterday I was on my own in Sussex. In our village there was
maypole dancing. I walked up the road to it. First the May Queen
was transported in a horse and carriage with her attendants,
followed by a hay wagon with lots of little girls with garlands on
their heads and some little boys. The first child I recognized on the
hay wagon was Hilary's son, but he did not recognize me. I then
saw Michele, the woman who's helped Lucy so much with her
pony, heavily pregnant. (She is having a fourth child unexpectedly, aged forty.) Her eight-year-old daughter had rung me earlier
asking if I thought she could do maypole dancing without
rehearsing. I said yes. Now she was happily in the hay wagon
chatting to my neighbour's child. Both were wearing garlands on
their heads.

Michele asked me in a surprised voice, 'Where's Lucy?'

I said she was with my ex-husband. I found the question
unsettling, as it rubbed in the fact that I was divorced.

Hilary was darting around with a camera. She asked about my
treatment and I said vehemently, 'I'll never have it again.'

Hilary said, 'Oh, before, you didn't talk like that. I expect you
were keeping a stiff upper lip.' She added that too many people
did this.

I said I was disconcerted that a friend, Clare, had kept saying, in
the last few weeks, 'It wasn't *that* bad for you was it, Elisa?' Why
was it so important for Clare to think it wasn't that bad? I want to
say, 'Yes, it was. It was a nightmarish experience I will never have
again.'

I talked to Mrs Charlton, a lady in the village whom I've always
liked. The new vicar came and interrupted us. He said that young
couples nowadays were always booking weddings and then
cancelling them. I said I'd known a girl who'd kept the wedding
date but changed the young man only a few weeks before. (Lucy,
aged five, had been her bridesmaid.)

As she introduced me to the vicar Mrs Charlton said, 'She's the
other lot', meaning I was Catholic. The vicar did not understand
this.

*

Ten o'clock. I'm in the house on my own. Just seeing those red pills now makes me feel sick. I liked the way Mrs Charlton kissed me at the maypole dancing today. I remember when I first fell in love with R and lost a stone in weight, she was the only person who noticed. At a Christmas drinks party that winter she said, 'You're very thin, Elisa. Are you all right?'

I nearly said, 'I've fallen in love, Mrs Charlton. What shall I do?' But instead I held my tongue.

7 May
London. This morning Lucy tells me a secret. The girlfriend of the father of one of her best friends takes ecstasy.

Today when I was with Lucy in Marks & Spencer we saw Mrs Percival, Joseph's old headmistress, and one of Lucy's teachers, whom she likes. Mrs Percival stared unpleasantly at me and Lucy. I did not acknowledge her.

Spanish. (This term it is on a Thursday.) I have finally had a row with Marie-Ange, the Frenchwoman. It was very exciting.

She began arguing with me over some verbs, so finally I said, 'Oh, all right, have it your own way. The French are always right.'

Marie-Ange said, 'I do not like thees! I 'ave lived 'ere ten years. I do not like thees talk against ze French!'

I said, 'Marie-Ange, I have lived in Paris and have several French friends. You must not be so sensitive.'

The elderly man sitting between us, who retired from the British Council last year, looked extremely nervous. I then withdrew in a dignified way, but adrenalin was pumping round my body. She will not cross swords with me again.

8 May
Raymond's birthday. He would be forty-one.

Dream. I am in a field of cows, about to ride my daughter's piebald pony. Our way is barred by a bull, which suddenly becomes very aggressive. This bull is associated in my mind with my mother. It is my mother.

Then a funeral procession arrives, to bury a child. A black-haired woman openly weeps and mourns this dead child. In the dream I cannot see past this woman; I can't pass her grief.

Raymond's birthday is an important day for my mother. I hate it. I hate the feelings it arouses in me: pity for my mother, jealousy that she preferred my brother to me and rage about what happened.

I go again to chemotherapy with Miranda. It is my last one. Bridie gives me the injection. While I'm lying there afterwards, a cheerful blonde woman of about fifty comes in with a present of a tin of biscuits for us all. She tells me and the other patients that she had chemotherapy here a year ago and now she's OK. She chats to each of us in turn. She says she feels very well. I wonder whether I will ever have the courage to come to this ward again just to cheer people up. I want to convey to Bridie and the other nurses how grateful I am to them, how much I admire them, but do not know how to say this. Last time I came Miranda and I discussed what I should give the nurses as a thank-you present. She suggested Marks & Spencer gift vouchers. I have three in my handbag, in envelopes, ready to give them when I leave. I find giving presents embarrassing. Rosie's voucher was ten pounds less than the others, because she isn't in such a position of responsibility. Maybe I shouldn't have done this. Maybe I should have given them the same.

I don't know how to thank Miranda either. I can take her to a play or offer to pay the bill for recent damage to her car, but this doesn't seem enough.

When Nick broke his collarbone on the motor bike, he casually said he was going down to his sister's for a few days to recover. When Miranda had flu, she said she was going to her parents to get over it. I understood then how dependent I was on my friends, and told Miranda, 'I've got no proper family, except for my aunt and my American cousins.'

Miranda said modestly, refusing to take any credit for what she'd done for me, 'We've all realized that.'

9 May

Sussex. Today, instead of feeling elated it's all over, I'm extremely depressed. When I woke this morning in London I felt dreadful. I decided not to come to Sussex as I'd planned – the children were already there with my ex-husband – I felt so ill. At three, when I was supposed to leave for the station, I phoned to say I wasn't coming and Lucy started crying on the telephone, saying she couldn't go to the horse show the next day with just her father; she begged me to come down and go with her. I then started crying myself. (Meanwhile I started praying in desperation.)

I then forced myself to get up and dressed, and five minutes later Maureen drove me to the station.

It's now evening. I'm taking Dextrose sweets to give myself energy and to alleviate the unpleasant feelings after chemo-therapy.

Joseph, rooting in the bathroom cupboard, said, about the sweets, 'I'm not trying to find them to eat them. I wouldn't dream of it.'

He then got into the bath with me and asked, 'Which is more unhygienic, a gorilla, a wig, or a bad smell?'

10 May

Early morning. Last night at supper my ex-husband gave me crab paté, fish pie from a recipe of his sister-in-law's and delicious summer pudding from Marks & Spencer. He's always served very good meals.

I went to bed at about ten and was woken at eleven by a scrabbling sound. I thought it was a bird, but when I switched the light on, a mouse was running along the radiator. It looked like the mouse that had been in the larder here last week. It's grey, with rather a large head. As before, when it saw me, it did not run off, but looked at me.

I got up and it went behind the chest of drawers. I shouted to my ex-husband, 'There's a mouse!'

He came from where he was sleeping to help me. We called

Toby in. Toby got quite excited, but the mouse had disappeared.
My ex-husband said, 'Look after your mistress, Toby.'
  I kept Toby on my bed all night.

5.30 a.m. Dream. I'm in a foreign country waiting for something.
The food runs out. There's nothing left in the fridge. I'm with
some people in a flat in a garden; I think it's America.
  R arrives. We go to a town, perhaps a town in Czechoslovakia.
We're all seated at a table. I read something out of a book to R. I'm
aware I want him to have my attention. He *must* pay more
attention to me.
  We have to go home. It's getting late. By this time R's more
friendly to me, but he suggests walking home with a man, not me.
I think the man is my ex-husband and R is showing loyalty to
him. The women – now there are two women – decide to go on
the subway. I hesitantly follow them. We get on a train right away.
But it's absolutely horrible. The line we pass over has so many
cats and mice and rats they're almost touching our feet; there are
also entrails, like the insides of animals from butchers, hanging
everywhere. They're horrific. They're all symbols of death. We
arrive at a station and get off. Then I'm driving to Sussex in a car
along a motorway with a friend of Miranda. I tell her it's precisely
one hour from where we are to Sussex. Soon with relief I see the
familiar tunnel in our town. I'm home.
  Then I'm in a hospital ward where R's a patient. Vaneeta's in
the dream. We're reading a book. Vaneeta's talking about India.
R's very ill. I go and find a nurse. I want to prove to her he really
is ill. But the nurse won't come with me. I get back to the ward
and I'm afraid he's died, like my brothers.

11 May

Yesterday morning, Sunday, Lucy woke me up early with a tray.
There was only dry toast on it. She asked if I wanted tea or coffee.
I said tea. My ex-husband then brought me a cup of tea. I had also
asked Lucy for a boiled egg and honey. The tray reappeared with
these things on it, but without a knife. I then got up and dressed.

Lucy went ahead on her bike to the stables where the pony was. When I arrived, she was getting her ready. Lucy looked rather grown-up; she had her hair in a net.

We set off along the road, passing the pub, several houses and fields and finally the house where R had lived, as a lodger with a local family, when I first met him four years ago.

I stopped here and waited for Lucy. The house was for sale; there was a beautiful magnolia tree outside it. Lucy caught me up and we went on to the show.

We didn't see Michele at first, though Lucy recognized her car. Lucy entered her classes while I held Spinet. Lucy seemed very tense. We went over to the ring where the first competition, the Leading Rein Derby, was. Lucy was too proud to be led, even though I was allowed to and she wasn't very experienced. Spinet was excited and after doing the practice jump she bucked.

Michele said I should sell Spinet and get another pony without consulting Lucy. She said she had had a pony that was too strong for her as a child. She had been determined not to give in, but hadn't enjoyed it.

When Lucy was in the ring she fell off, but landed on her feet holding on to the reins. She completed the course, however. Several other children also fell off.

Meanwhile Michele, who's having her baby in a few weeks, offered me a stool to sit on. I was beginning to feel cold and shaky, though I didn't say anything. It was a typical chilly May morning.

After a while Spinet calmed down; she behaved much better in the second competition, but still got thirteen faults. This time Lucy seemed to be controlling her.

At about one we set off home. Again I stopped my bike outside the house where R had lived when I first met him. I remembered everything very clearly, yet it was now nearly four years ago. I remembered how in December, on a dark day, I'd carried in some photographs I'd collected for him in London, when all three of us, myself, my ex-husband and he, had had flu. The family he lived with were out, his clothes were drying on a clothes-horse in the kitchen and he had brought me a cup of coffee, putting a small

table in front of me because, he said, it was 'cosy'. On that day he
had seemed sweet and vulnerable.

As I bicycled on again in front of Lucy, cow parsley each side of
us, I imagined that the Downs ahead of me were mountains in
South America, where perhaps R was now. I felt peace and hope.
Although he would probably one day mean nothing to me, I
realized I did not want to give up the feelings that he had inspired
in me. These were more important to me than R himself.

Lucy said last night, before she went back to London, 'Just take
everything in your stride. Like people do when they have
Simplicity tampons.'

Her common sense reminded me of my grandmother, who'd
once told me, 'Let the future take care of itself. Don't let your
imagination run away with you.'

I thought how, because she wasn't as 'difficult' as Joseph, I took
my daughter for granted. I recalled how sweet she'd been as a
little blonde baby, waving and smiling at everyone, and how once,
when she was eighteen months, a big wave had knocked her
down on a volcanic beach in Martinique. Even so, four hours later,
hot, salty and tired, with nowhere to stay, she'd woken up on my
knee as we'd arrived in the town in the middle of the carnival and
immediately beat time to the music. My darling daughter.

I stayed on my own in Sussex. I was about to watch *The Dead* on
TV (the John Huston film, based on a rather morbid story by
Joyce, a favourite of R's), but I was too exhausted. I asked Mrs
Douthwaite to record it instead. As soon as I switched off my
bedroom light I heard a rustling. The mouse had appeared again. I
saw it by the radiator. Again it did not run away, but stared at me
for a few seconds. I said, 'Go away! Just go away!' It went behind
the chest.

12 May

This morning I woke with a feeling of awful vulnerability. I
couldn't escape the terrible pain. Yesterday evening I watched

Praise Be with Thora Hird. She talked about grief. She said it felt as though you were carrying a brick. This brick was there to remind you of the person who had died; eventually, she said, the brick disappeared and you were left with fond memories.

Today I drove to the farm shop and bought two cakes to put in the freezer for the coming summer. I then parked the car and set off for a walk along the field near Nicholas Mosley's cottage. I felt very weak and could not complete the fifteen-minute walk I had planned. Instead I went into his garden and peered in at a window. I saw he was not at his typwriter, so I banged on the front door. I shouted something and then waited for him to open it. He invited me in for a drink. His stutter was very bad and his limp seemed worse than before. He asked if I'd been away.

I said, 'You've been in Africa.'

He had been there for Christmas with his wife, her son and their fifteen-year-old son.

I told him I had had breast cancer. His face took on an expression of concern. I said some of the time it had been rather exciting, how I imagined being in a war must be like. He said yes, in a situation like that, important issues, Life and Death, are called into question.

I asked about one of the paintings on the wall and commented how attractive he'd made the kitchen since I'd last been there. He said the paintings were all by his first wife, who had died rather suddenly the other day.

I exclaimed, 'But she's quite young!'

She had been sixty-two, and the painting I was looking at was of him as a young man, leaning against a jetty on a beach. He pointed out her other, more recent paintings, of New Mexico.

I said I had loved it there, though I had only stayed for three days with my son, last summer, in the middle of my house-swap. I explained I had just got divorced and wondered if I had made a terrible mistake.

He said he and his first wife had simply drifted apart. She wanted to paint in more and more far away places, whereas he was working in London on films at that time. They had not divorced until his second wife Verity had appeared. In his opinion there was no need to get remarried until the other partner wanted it. He asked, 'You're not lonely, are you?'

We decided to go for a drink at a local pub. First we sat under the trees, then it began to pour with rain so we went inside. He asked me about my health. He said he had had a hip operation several years before on the NHS. These operations only lasted ten years, however, and he was due for another. Sometimes he had dreams about a loose bit of plastic moving about inside his body.

When he'd been ill he'd vowed to become a hospital visitor when he recovered. But when he was well again he'd soon given up his vows. He talked about Graham Greene's novel *The End of the Affair*, set during the last war. The narrator is having an affair with a married woman and after a bomb explosion she finds her lover half buried by rubble. As she's leaning over his body she swears that if he's still alive, she'll give him up. She keeps her vow. But then, Nicholas pointed out, they're both very unhappy.

This reminded me of R's guilty behaviour towards me – unlike the couple in the novel, we hadn't even *had* the affair – and I felt rather sad.

We then discussed psychotherapy and its benefits. Nicholas said he thought it was good because it could make people aware of their patterns of behaviour so they could change them if necessary.

15 May

I dream that Jill is dying. But first she comes to England to die. She's going to live with her husband again. She talks to me very seriously about the steps she'll take to make the rest of her life more enjoyable. We're then all swimming about together in a pool.

This dream is also to do with travelling. We're flying somewhere, perhaps to the Caribbean. I feel compassion for Jill as she tells me she's going to die. She makes it very plain, as she didn't in real life.

Later, or earlier, in the dream I lose a dog. Is the dog Toby or

Buzzy, the one I had as a child? We're driving somewhere that ends up being a men's club. I have to make a phone call in my dressing-gown about the dog. I'm distressed that we've driven away leaving the dog. At the same time I'm aware that the man driving the car, a man I've seen earlier in the club, may think my preoccupation with the dog is childish.

27 *May*

Katherine, who worked for my grandmother for fifty years, is staying with me this week. (She came to work for my grandmother on my mother's eleventh birthday when she was twenty-one.) I drop her at my mother's for lunch, then drive on to see Fee (Polish Sophie's daughter) with Lucy and Joseph. I enjoy the picnic in the garden – quiche and salad. Fee's very calm with her three girls. The older two are in identical yellow striped shorts.

When we return to my mother's, she and Katherine are in a dark room, the sitting-room, with the fan on.

We get out a toy dog, which moves and barks when you clap your hands or make a loud noise. (Lucy discovered this a few weeks ago; it is one of the 'toys' my mother orders regularly for herself from catalogues. She doesn't want the children to play with it in case they break it.)

My mother starts talking about the hymn 'O love that will not let me go'. Katherine sings the tune, to remind her of it, rather well. As a young woman Katherine was in the local choral society in my grandmother's village and they used to rehearse with Malcolm Sargent.

My mother points to a photograph of herself on the wall and says that in it she looks like *her* mother. I don't think she does.

My mother has a surprise for me and the children. Mr Mainwaring, who works for her, has carefully put together some of her old movies on video. We sit in armchairs to watch. The first films are of processions in Spain in 1950, in honour of Franco. My mother loved Spain. There are a lot of mounted soldiers in Arab dress. My mother says they're the Moorish guard. They look like something out of the Crusades.

Soon after this some shots of myself in a pram appear. I am wearing light blue. The screen's a bit blurred and Mr Mainwaring says the camera must have been out of focus. Nevertheless, I think I recognize my pink teddy bear Jimmy and the *Old Book of Nursery Rhymes*, which I remember tearing; I had been given it when I was too young. My friendliness reminds me of Lucy as a baby.

There's my father, throwing me up and down, looking delighted. More of my father, sitting on a wall with some other men, mountains behind them, the mountains outside Madrid.

Now there I am again, on a beach in a red sunhat and bathing-suit, playing with a little blond boy and also with Victoria, the woman I saw recently in Majorca, looking very skinny. My grandmother's briefly in these pictures, in a beautiful red bathing-dress with a skirt, showing mainly her legs, not her face.

Behind me the waves roll, the waves of the Atlantic. There are cliffs behind. How beautiful it is!

Then a little boy with light-brown hair in a light-blue bathing-suit crawls over the sand, backwards and forwards several times in front of the camera.

Joseph asks, 'Who's that?'

I reply that it's Raymond. Joseph asks if he's still alive. I say no. When he asks, 'How did he die?' I say, 'I'll tell you later.'

It was fascinating and very disturbing to see Raymond on the beach. On the way back in the car the children asked again about his death. When we reached the level-crossing on the way out of my mother's village, Joseph asked, 'Did Granny cry when Raymond died?'

I said, 'Probably.'

Joseph shouted, 'Horrible Granny! I hate to see an adult cry.'

Later I stopped to pick some primroses. The children asked again about Raymond. Lucy said, 'Maybe he wandered off on your birthday because he was jealous you were getting all the attention, so it's really your fault.'

I said, 'For heaven's sake, Lucy.'

Lucy then said she was very sorry for me, and how sweet I looked as a child in my mother's films.

Joseph had an odd reaction to seeing me as a child. He was very jealous, because I as a child looked younger than he does now. He asked, 'What would have happened if I'd hit that child on the nose?'

That evening in bed he said, 'When I see God, when I die, when I'm a skeleton or an angel, I want him to take me back to the past. Can he do that?'

I replied that I didn't know. He pointed out that the other people involved might not want to go back to the past. He said he wanted to be five again, 'when you and Daddy were married'.

I told him I thought that the only way to get back the past was to write about it.

Epilogue: May 1994

3 May

Twelve o'clock. I'm in the hairdresser's having my hair coloured.
The colour lasts six months. My hospital check-ups are now also
every six months. At first they were every three months. I have
one today at the hospital, with the professor of oncology, at a
quarter to two.

I go to Marks & Spencer and buy a white T-shirt for the summer.
Then I get into the underground at High Street Kensington. I can't
remember which stop to get out of for the hospital. After going
past it every day for six weeks during the winter that I had
radiotherapy, I remember exactly what the underground entrance
looks like, with its flower-stall outside, but still can't remember if it
was Barons Court or West Kensington.

When I get out, at West Kensington, I realize I've made a
mistake. I ask a thin, ill-looking man if he can direct me. He's so
thin and worn, yet so young, that I imagine he might have AIDS.
At first he looks suspicious and unfriendly, but when I say I want
Charing Cross Hospital, his tone of voice changes and becomes
kind. I hear from his accent that he's from the north of England.
He gives me directions, ending up, 'Walk through the graveyard
and you'll see the hospital ahead of you.'

When I get to the graveyard after a ten-minute walk I see that,
apart from the graves, it's like a little park with trees and flowers
and benches to sit on.

I turn in. Maybe I'm a bit nervous because of my check-up, so
I'm more wary than I usually am, because this first section of the
graveyard, under the trees, is deserted. I find myself walking
behind a teenager in a track suit and trainers. He's going rather
slowly. All about us are graves, many accompanied by statues and

large crosses and headstones. Wallflowers are growing in some of the plots. I slow down in case the boy's hoping to grab the purse of an unsuspecting solitary woman.

Then I too begin loitering, and look at some of the graves. 'Margaret Jones, who fell asleep'. A stone cross, with a line on it of a hymn. I try to memorize this, but can't. A few of the graves have very foreign names. One man had been a judge in the West Indies.

Ahead of me is the enormous modern tower of the hospital. I walk up the straight gravel path towards it, between the lines of graves. By now other people have appeared, some with food. It seems more and more like any small park in the lunch-hour. It's one of the first fine days of the London summer.

As I'm about to exit I hear a girl's voice behind me say excitedly, 'She told me to send Dad's ashes home to the Ganges.'

I look back and see three Indian girls sitting on a bench eating sandwiches. They look very cheerful. Perhaps they're medical students attached to the hospital.

A few minutes later I enter the hospital through the Radiotherapy Department. You're not meant to use this entrance to the hospital, unless you're a patient doing radiotherapy, but I'm curious to see the place again.

Apart from the garish oil-painting of the racing driver in bright-red clothes, the whole department has been changed and opened up, and there seem to be many more rooms now. I hardly recognize the place where I used to come regularly two and a half years ago.

I don't even recognize the area where I used to sit waiting for treatment with the man with heavy eyelids. I march straight through, in case someone tries to stop me, past Accident and Emergency, through the main lobby with the pharmacy and the shop and up the escalator to the clinic where I was first told that I had cancer.

After I've given my name to the receptionist, who's also called Tracy, like the receptionist that September over two years ago, I sit down next to a pale, thin-faced woman.

Suddenly I see it's Pam from the ward, Pam with rosy cheeks who was so cheerful, who looked as if she'd spent her whole life in a garden. She's with an older man; I think it's the one she had the secret love affair with for years. I assume she's come to have a routine check-up like me, but, when I say how surprised I was to find the Radiotherapy Department had changed, she says she knows; she's been having treatment there. She adds quietly that she has cancer on her hip and on the base of her spine.

I don't want her to see how shocked I am, and scared. I can't help myself thinking, if that can happen to her, it can also happen to me. I had liked Pam best of all the women in the ward, apart from Jenny.

As usual, she doesn't talk about herself. She asks about my children; I tell her my son was sent home from school yesterday for hitting another boy.

Then her sister, who's plumper than she is and looks more robust, arrives in the waiting-room and sits between Pam and the man, who says very little. They begin looking at a brochure of the Languedoc, where Pam and her companion are about to go on holiday. They're going by ferry. Pam says she'll never go into the Channel tunnel when it opens because of her fear of terrorists.

I ask after her daughter, and Pam claims she spends all her money on 'dogs and horses'. (I thought at first she meant betting, but then realized she meant pets.)

Pam says ruefully that the professor, with whom she has an appointment now, as I do, doesn't seem to know which treatment to give her; he keeps changing it. The Tamoxifen, which she'd been given originally, obviously didn't work. He's explained that this might be because, even before her breast cancer had been diagnosed, part of it had already spread and dispersed into other areas of her body.

I ask her tentatively what the first sign of it had been. She says she had a recurrent pain in her hip. She mentioned the pain to the doctors several times, but nothing was diagnosed. Finally she had a bone X-ray that showed it.

As the three of them sit there, leafing through the brochure on the Languedoc, with its pictures of cornfields, poppies and blue flowers – or is it lavender? – I feel incredibly sad.

I'm called to wait outside the doctors' rooms. I hear the professor ask to see me. I'm about to dart into where I saw his head through a glass door when an Irish nurse stops me. He's with the surgeon, she says, and is now about to go back into his own room. She seems very friendly, this tall blonde woman. I take off my top and wait for the professor.

He's very cheerful as he examines me; he admits I've put on weight, but says this is a good thing in the circumstances. When I've dressed, he says everything is hopeful as my tumour was very small. I remind him that three out of twenty-two lymph glands were infected and he keeps a positive attitude about this as well. We talk briefly about our unexpected meeting at a friend's party in a garden last summer – the cocktails that night were very strong. He says, 'See you again in six months.'

I go and say goodbye to Pam and her sister, who are still waiting. Then I remember that I have to have a blood test and go into a room next door. The blood test is taken by a friendly New Zealand nurse who remembers me, and we discuss how we've both put on weight since we last met. She's just ordered a tape by a hypnotist to help her take it off.

Then I make my way back to the graveyard, towards the underground station. I look again at the inscription on the cross, to check the line of the hymn that I couldn't remember: 'Nothing in my hand I bring. Simply to thy cross I cling.'

It sounds rather desperate.

I go on walking through the Park, past the picnickers, the wallflowers and the dead, leaving the hospital behind me.